RUTH'S JOURNEY

Ruth's Journey

UNIVERSITY PRESS OF FLORIDA

Gainesville
Tallahassee
Tampa
Boca Raton
Pensacola
Orlando
Miami
Jacksonville

A SURVIVOR'S MEMOIR

Ruth Glasberg Gold

00 99 98 97 96 95 6 5 4 3 2 1

Library of Congress Cataloging-in-Publication Data
Gold, Ruth Glasberg, 1930–
Ruth's journey: a survivor's memoir / Ruth Glasberg Gold.
p. cm.
Includes bibliographical references (p.) and index.
ISBN 0-8130-1400-x (cloth: alk. paper)
1. Gold, Ruth Glasberg, 1930–. 2. Jews—Romania—
Biography. 3. Holocaust, Jewish (1939–1945)—Romania—
Personal narratives. 4. Holocaust survivors—Biography.
I. Title.
DS135.R73G654 1996 95-6771
949.8'004924'0092—dc20

The University Press of Florida is the scholarly publishing agency for
the State University System of Florida, comprised of Florida A & M
University, Florida Atlantic University, Florida International University, Florida State University, University of Central Florida, University
of Florida, University of North Florida, University of South Florida,
and University of West Florida.

University Press of Florida
15 Northwest 15th Street
Gainesville, FL 32611

To my children, Liana and Michael,
and my grandson, Alexander, in the hope
that they will never know the pain and
agony I have experienced.

In loving memory of my father, Mendel,
my mother, Leah, and brother, Bubi and all
the victims who perished in the Romanian
concentration camps of Transnistria

CONTENTS

List of Maps   viii

List of Illustrations   ix

Preface   xi

Acknowledgments   xv

1   My Paradise   1

2   Facing Romanian Anti-Semitism   27

3   Deportation   46

4   Hell   62

5   The Orphanages   87

6   The Forgotten Cemetery   103

7   Many Loyalties—Many Homelands   118

8   Home Again?   138

9   From Communism to Zionism   154

10   Shipwrecked   162

11   Cyprus   177

12   The Promised Land   197

13   Kibbutz L'hagshamah   202

14   Conflicts   220

15   Culture Shock   241

16   Back to My Roots   259

   Epilogue Bershad Revisited   283

   Sources   289

   Geographic Index   291

MAPS

Ruth's routes of deportation, repatriation, and escape, 1941–46. xviii
Location of Romania and the province of Bukovina. 2
The Jewish population of Bukovina on the eve of World War II. 5
Romania before and after World War II. 31
Transnistrian camps under Romanian administration, 1941–44. 64

ILLUSTRATIONS

Me as a baby and at age seven. 3

Grandfather Littman Katz. 4

Grandfather Littman Katz with Aunt Anna and Lucie. 9

Me at age three with children of Milie, cousin Lucie,
   and brother Bubi. 10

The only family photo. 13

My father, Mendel, and my mother, Leah. 17

Bubi at age four and at age eighteen. 24

The Bershad cemetery. 107

At school in 1945 with my best friend, Litty. 148

Litty, Jenny, and me in Buzau, 1946. 156

The Cyprus internment camp. 178

Me on Cyprus, age sixteen. 179

Carrying the flag for L'hagshamah. 183

With the British officer we called "The Old Man." 187

With Elise on Cyprus. 195

Giving the valedictory speech at graduation from nursing school. 221

With a patient at Hadassah Hospital. 222

At my wedding to Salomon Gold, 1958. 239

My family in Colombia. 247

Liana and Michael as adults. 256

In our old apartment in Czernowitz. 267

With Ghiorge Ostashek, a witness to the Milie massacre. 270

The old double-log bridge behind Grandfather's farm, 1988. 273

A new house where Grandfather's stood. 275

Revisiting the Bershad cemetery in 1988. 285

On March 6, 1944, about two thousand orphans were rescued from Romanian concentration camps in Transnistria-Ukraine. I was one of them.

I left behind a place of horror, but not the memory of it. A young teacher at the orphanage urged me to write down what happened at the camp. I did, and she submitted my twelve pages of handwritten notes to *Romania Libera*, a Bucharest newspaper, which published them.

When I saw my account in print, I decided that some day I would write a book telling the whole story. My resolve was strengthened by learning that my story in the newspaper later became part of the evidence used to convict Romanian war criminals.

Forty years later I finally mustered the courage to write that book. As I struggled to recall the events of those war years and write them down, the tears I had been unable to shed as a child were finally released.

Yet, while writing, I realized that there were many situations that I could not describe, no matter how hard I tried. I consoled myself with the words of the poet Abba Kovner, testifying at the Eichmann trial: "I swear to tell the Truth, but not the whole Truth—because that is impossible to tell."

But writing this book was not a catharsis. It was instead a painful effort—the payment of a debt owed by a survivor to those who perished and a testimony to the atrocities committed by the Romanian army and the local police. The word *Holocaust* is commonly associated with images of ghettos like Warsaw and Vilna and extermination camps like Auschwitz and Treblinka, appearing as they do in countless books, films, and plays. They have penetrated our consciousness and our collective memories. But who has heard of Transnistria?

The story begins with a description of blissful summers on my grandfather's farm in the countryside. Its pastoral serenity is in sharp contrast with the Nazi horror that was about to engulf us.

When I was eleven years old, I became a helpless witness to the agonizing deaths of my family: first my father, then my only brother, and finally my mother. All this happened in three short weeks.

I became a nomad, moving from makeshift orphanages to foster homes to refugee camps. Around me, totalitarianism of the extreme right and that of the far left influenced my daily life. All the while I longed for something more hopeful.

Later, attracted by the Zionist vision of a Jewish homeland in Palestine, I escaped clandestinely from communist Romania on a freighter. I was shipwrecked in the Aegean Sea en route to Palestine and imprisoned in Cyprus by my British rescuers. One year later, I was finally freed to go to Palestine.

In 1948 the State of Israel was born, and I joined in the building of a new kibbutz in the Judean Hills near Jerusalem. There, in the nourishing soil of my new homeland, I planted my severed roots and the healing began.

Compassion for people led me to serve as the kibbutz medic which launched me on a determined goal to become a registered nurse, even though my formal education had been disrupted by the war.

In the years that followed, I married, moved with my husband to Colombia, South America, raised two children there, and finally settled in Miami. Eight years later, at age fifty, I returned to nursing. Two years after that my husband died of a heart attack, awakening a new grieving in me.

My story ends where it began. In 1988, I traveled back to the scenes of my childhood and to the scarred setting of the concentration camp where my family died.

Ruth's Journey: A Survivor's Memoir is not only a story of personal tragedy and hope; it is also an account of how Romanian fascists vilified, isolated, and ultimately tried to exterminate the Jews among them.

I am keenly aware that discussing highly charged topics like religion, patriotism, justice, loyalty, and treason can evoke a range of responses from sympathy to hostility. I myself harbor no rancor, nor do I wish to generalize. Any comments that seem accusatory are based on my recollection bolstered by the historical record of those who carried out the orders of the regime — reluctantly or willingly.

The purpose of this book is not to condemn but to illuminate. I wanted to show that spiritual and intellectual freedom can survive seemingly unbearable psychological and physical trauma — and that they can insulate a shattered child as she moves from despair to hope.

Incidentally, I have used real names throughout the book except for those of Marius and Amos.

ACKNOWLEDGMENTS

Since its inception, this book has undergone many linguistic permutations. I thought about it in my native German, wrote a part of it in Romanian, and tape-recorded parts of it in Spanish, and finally completed it in English. This project could have never been brought to life without the generous help of many wonderful people, to whom I offer my eternal gratitude.

My boundless appreciation goes to Walda Metcalf, editor in chief, who was first to realize the manuscript's potential. With great sensitivity and professionalism, she guided me gently but firmly through the process of cutting and editing. Her enthusiasm, her praise, and her constructive criticism were crucial in bringing this book to its final form.

Many thanks to Judy Goffman, production editor, who demonstrated great critical observation in the final copyediting. It was a privilege to have my book revised by such a highly competent person.

I am indebted to Rita Katz Farrell, for reading the first draft and advising me of areas that needed further work. With her encouragement, I began the hard work necessary to make the manuscript acceptable for publication.

My heartfelt thanks to Dan Porat for his steady moral support, devotion, and gentle criticism, and wise suggestions, all of which have sustained me from the beginning to the end of this venture.

A special feeling of gratitude goes to Arnold Geier for the dedication he demonstrated during our many telephone and fax consultations. His sincere interest, his tireless efforts and generosity, have contributed invaluably to the finalization of this work.

I am eternally thankful to Aharon Appelfeld, the Israeli writer, for believing in the importance of my book and for his suggestions which helped me in the subsequent revisions.

My warm thanks to Judith Kestenberg, M.D., an expert on child survivors, for her genuine interest, her positive feedback, and for her wonderful recommendations.

There are not enough words to thank Trevor Sessing, my friend and English teacher extraordinaire, who for almost two years lived most intimately with my manuscript, guiding me through the nuances of the English language and teaching me how skilled editing can contribute to organization. With saintly patience and humor he cheered me on when I wanted to give up.

For her spirit of generosity, I am forever grateful to Professor Betty Owen, who after hearing a speech I gave at Broward Community College, volunteered to critique and help me condense the manuscript.

I also wish to acknowledge some other wonderful people for their invaluable suggestions, practical advice and support: Michael Davidson, Kim Bancroft, Myriam Adler, Doris Olesky, and Professors Eugene Goodheart, Les Standiford, Peter Hargitai, Peter Tarjan, and Yehuda Shamir.

Helping me in overcoming my computer phobia and teaching me this new skill was a group of selfless young people at the Computer Center at Florida International University. To the entire staff, particularly to Ruth Pacheco, I give my tribute. My sincere thanks to Eytan Laor for rushing to my rescue every time I got trapped in both computer and printing glitches.

I also wish to thank Madeleine Wong from the Geography Information and Analysis Laboratory of Florida Atlantic University in Boca Raton, Florida, for designing the maps.

Finally, from the bottom of my heart I thank the two people I love most in the world — my son, Michael, a neurologist, who nagged me to take on the challenge of writing this book, and my daughter, Liana, a registered nurse, who insisted that I pursue its publication.

No foreign sky protected me,
No stranger's wing shielded my face,
I stand as witness to the common lot,
Survivor of that time, that place.
—Anna Akhmatova

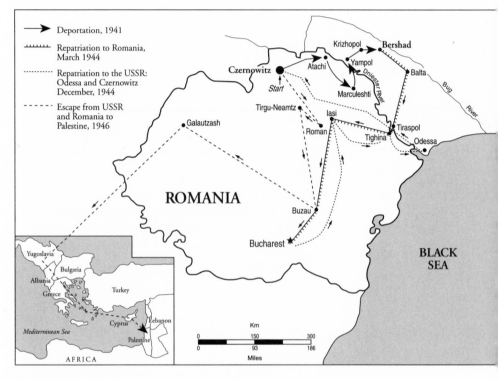

Ruth's routes of deportation, repatriation, and escape, 1941–46.

My Paradise

CHAPTER 1   The sound of galloping horses sent rhythmic percussions down our otherwise quiet street. Horseshoes meeting cobblestones created reverberations that were sweet music to me. A stately carriage moved majestically with a slight tilt along the street. Neighbors craned from windows and balconies, curious to see who the fortunate travelers would be. I quivered with excitement because I knew where it would stop, who would emerge. Papa had arranged for this princely chariot to take us to the railway station.

As soon as it stopped in front of our building, I ran from the balcony into our apartment shouting, "The carriage is here! The carriage is here!" With my tiny suitcase in hand, I quickly dashed down the four flights to be the first to marvel at the horses and the elegant, plush interior of the coach. After the driver brought down the heavy luggage, my family emerged from the doorway and we all settled into our seats.

Taking his place on the buckboard, the coachman pulled the reins, lashed the whip, and with a loud "Diioo!" gave the horses the command to start their regal trot out of the neighborhood.

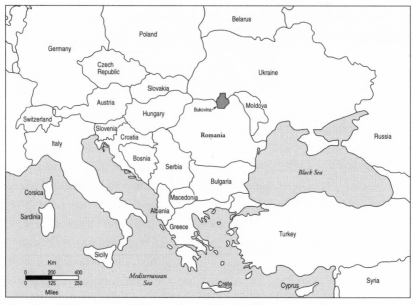

Location of Romania and the province of Bukovina

This was always the happiest day of my early childhood years, one I looked forward to and daydreamed about for months in advance.

Every year from June to September, my mother, my brother, and I would travel from the city of Czernowitz, Romania, to spend the summer on my grandfather's farm in the village of Milie. There we would join my mother's older sister, Anna, and her daughter Lucie. Unfortunately, Papa had to stay at home because of his job, but he would come later to visit for a few days.

I had been taken to this fairyland of Milie since infancy, but I remember it most vividly since age five. I was then a spindly, blue-eyed girl with freckles and two golden braids. How I protested those long braids! I longed to wear my hair loose to flow with the wind or to drape it over my shoulders like a cape. Mama, of course, would not hear of it. "You should think more about your health than such silliness," she would say. You're so skinny one can count all your ribs. If you won't eat, you'll get sick!"

Mama was forever obsessed with the idea that I would die from some dreadful illness, but on the trip to Milie her immediate concern was my motion sickness. As soon as we entered our compartment, Mama would make sure that I sat facing front, toward the engine, and sucked on lemons, which was the only remedy for motion sickness in the 1930s. With the first jolt of the departing train, I felt ill.

Notwithstanding the intermittent vomiting, I would enjoy the rhythmic clatter of the wheels and make up my own lyrics to accompany it. Gazing out the window, I would think about how fast the trees were sprinting by and how the clouds chased after them. For many years I was convinced that it was the beautiful scenery that ran alongside the train and not the other way around. These train rides evoked an air of mystery and adventure that carried with them a sense of magic I feel to this day.

The conductor shouted a welcome arrival. At last! The train stopped at the small train station, barely long enough for us to descend with the luggage.

"O Lord, thank you," I said in silent prayer climbing down the steps, drained from the two-hour ordeal. As soon as I felt solid ground under my feet and saw my grandfather, all my troubles were forgotten.

My grandfather Littman Katz resembled Tevye, the pious Jew portrayed by the great Yiddish novelist Shalom Aleichem. Although he was only in his sixties, he seemed ancient to me. He had a long gray beard,

Me as a baby and at age seven.

Grandfather Littman Katz.

and the corners of his mustache were tinged with yellow from sniffing tobacco. His short hair was always covered with a black skullcap, and his long dark coat hung loosely on his slightly forward-slumped frame. With hands clasped behind his back, he walked with a slow and gentle gait.

"Dziadziu!" I greeted him, using his Slavic nickname. "How are you? How are the cats? The cow? The calf? The chickens?"

"All of them are fine and waiting for you," he responded. "You will soon see for yourself."

A primitive, wooden-wheeled, one-horse cart attended by a coach-man in folk costume awaited our group. We boarded it, and, as we rode by, the peasants in the fields waved and greeted us with their customary *"Dobreydzien,"* which in Ruthenian, a regional dialect of Ukrainian, means "Good day!" We summer guests were a welcome change in their routine. Then there was the smell in the air! Fresh mountain air. Freshly cut grain. Camomile. Lilacs. (Ah! I inhaled deeply, feeling their magic effect.)

Milie squats on the banks of the Cheremosh River, its natural border with Poland in the northwest of what was then Romania. Its five hundred families were mostly Ruthenian peasants (Subcarpathian Ukrainians) and forty to fifty Jewish families of Polish and Russian descent. Most of these Jews, including my grandfather, belonged to the Katz family tree.

The bumpy ride on the unpaved main road lasted a short few minutes before the coachman would turn into a narrow dirt lane and pull the horses to a halt. There, in the most picturesque spot of the entire village, on the bank of the Teplitza Creek, stood my grandfather's farm.

The grass swayed in the wind—soft, wild grass sprinkled with blue cornflowers, bright poppies, daisies, and dandelions. On this colorful meadow, amidst a menagerie of ducks, baby chicks, and honking geese, our cow, Ruzena, and her calf grazed peacefully. This pastoral panorama, with the melodic flow of the creek in the background and the occasional songs of birds soaring overhead, created a feeling of being in paradise.

Grandpa Littman's farmhouse, with its wood-shingled roof, stood a few yards away from the gate. The creek in which we washed, swam, and fished was just a few steps away. Bordering the creek was a spring

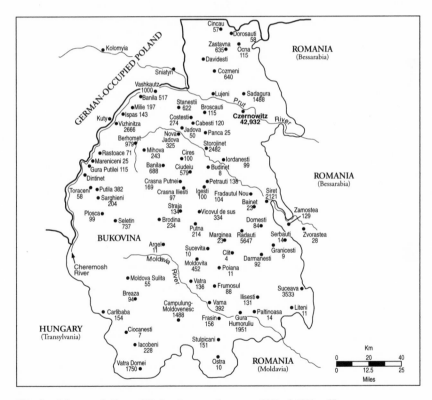

The Jewish population of Bukovina on the eve of World War II.

well, providing us with ice cold drinking water of a heavenly taste. Behind the house a plum tree orchard and a colorful garden extended for acres, brimming over with vegetables of every variety. About forty yards away, facing the house, were a barn, a cowshed, a chicken coop, and a granary.

A day on the farm started with the first rooster's crow. That was when Grandpa, oil lantern and bucket in hand, went out to milk the cow. After this chore, he washed and put on his phylacteries and prayer shawl for the morning prayers. Meanwhile, the rest of the family slowly awakened and walked down to the creek to wash. Then we began preparations for our outdoor breakfast. I picked cucumbers, tomatoes, and radishes from the garden, while someone else brought up dairy products from the cellar. Then we sat down on the wooden benches on either side of the long, rough plank table in front of the house and helped ourselves to a hearty breakfast of home-baked bread, farmer cheese, buttermilk, and a garden salad called *Schweinerei* washed down with coffee or tea.

The farm gave full play to my childish curiosity. Sometimes I would venture alone on an excursion to the mill. Carefully crossing the narrow, two-log bridge to the other side of the creek, I would follow a narrow fairylike path, dense with vegetation that sent its roots into the water.

After a few minutes I reached the mill, my grandfather's most recent invention, the first and only one in the village. Now the peasants could grind their grain locally rather than taking it to neighboring villages.

Watching the hustle and bustle outside and inside the mill was my greatest delight. In a way it resembled a small fair with carts, wheelbarrows, and even human backs loaded with sacks of grain. Inside, the shouting above the noise of the grinding stones was deafening. The peasants, all covered with flour, moving busily about filling the sacks, looked like ghosts. Amidst all the fray, I was poking my nose everywhere. My favorite fun was holding my hands under the spout that spewed out the warm, finely ground flour that tickled my skin.

Next, I skipped over to the adjoining sunflower press, another of Grandfather's inventions. It produced a delicious dark green oil, leaving a waste product of the hulls and residue of the pressed sunflower seeds, which we called *makuch*. These round, stony cakes made great feed for pigs. Little did I know that later they would play an important role in my life.

My last stop was a visit to the artificial lake, where Grandpa bred carp and trout, one more of his original ideas. With a good supply of bread crumbs, I would lure the fish toward me. So many came to be fed that I could have reached down and snatched them with my bare hands. Satisfied, I returned home.

With the dam closed on Sundays, we children had the opportunity to swim in the calm waters of the reservoir. But best of all I liked joining my brother on his expeditions in search of rare plants and flowers for his herbarium. Each discovery brought its own special kind of enchantment. I also helped him chase down the brilliantly colored butterflies that fluttered in the air like bright flowers which he preserved in his collection. He was tolerant of my whims and never directed a harsh word at me. Even as a child I felt very privileged.

The most exciting summer event was when the Gypsy caravan made its appearance and camped out on the village's main meadow. We were thrilled at the sight of these strange, colorful nomads who came every summer for a few weeks to sell their wares from canvas-covered wagons and to carry on their main business, horse-trading. They spoke an unintelligible language that sounded like Romanian but was actually Romany, the Indic language of the Gypsies. Their clothes were as colorful as their customs. The women carried their babies in immense slings made of shawls wrapped around their necks, keeping their hands free for other tasks. I was somewhat leery of them, especially after my mother threatened to sell me to them when I misbehaved.

They pitched their tents and tied the horses to the surrounding trees. Some of the women would read our palms for a small donation, while others gathered around a large bonfire to dance and sing to the passionate tunes rendered by their violinists.

Our own neighboring peasants were no less entertaining.

On Sundays these hard-working people, bedecked in all their finery, went out to enjoy themselves. The women wore heavily embroidered home-spun linen blouses with skirts of multicolored wool. Unmarried girls wore flower wreaths with long, colorful ribbons dangling down their necks, while the married ones cloaked themselves in flowery print scarves (*babushkas*). The men dressed in tight, white linen pants, and long tunics with embroidered collars and sleeves, set off by colorful sashes around their waists.

After church, they gathered on the main square to dance the *hora*, a Romanian round dance, and sing to the music of an accordion or a pan-pipe.

The Jewish population greeted the Sabbath with a festive Friday dinner. Its preparations turned our household into a hive of exciting activity. Yet all the pleasurable anticipation had also a dark side—at least for me.

Every Friday morning, Mama would enter the coop and pick two hens destined for the traditional chicken soup. The birds, clacking noisily in terror and leaping for escape, created a loud whirlwind of feathers in the coop. The victims, feet tied together, were then taken to the *shokhed*, the Jewish ritual slaughterer. For some inexplicable reason, every so often, Mama would take me along on this errand.

The shokhed, all dressed in black, would slash the chickens' throats with a razor-like knife, twist their necks, and hang their feet on a hook, heads dangling with blood squirting onto the walls and the dirt floor. The poor birds quivered, despondently flopping their wings in mortal spasms until the last drop of blood ran out of their lifeless bodies. Finally, the shokhed would hand the dead but kosher fowl to Mama.

Nobody forced me to watch. It was only morbid curiosity that made me stand there and witness this barbaric procedure. I wanted to know what was being done to the chickens I so lovingly fed every day. It was grotesquely fascinating, but at the same time it inspired enough terror and disgust to cause me nightmares and an aversion to both the soup and its contents.

Once we returned with the dead fowls everybody got busy preparing the Sabbath meal. My mother and her sister kneaded dough with an expertise that bewildered me. They never used recipes or measured ingredients, yet they produced the most intriguing baked goods out of an

Grandfather Littman Katz with Aunt Anna and Lucie.

old-fashioned, brick oven. To keep me out of their way, they would give me a piece of dough for my own little braided *challah.*

Without running water or electricity, we had to bring buckets of water from the creek, heat it on the wood stove, and every Friday afternoon take turns bathing by sitting in wooden tubs filled with warm sudsy water. That was followed by the Sabbath dinner, presided over by Grandfather. I watched with fascination as my mother and her sister lit the candles, covered their eyes with both hands, moved their heads back and forth, and murmured some sort of prayers. I always wondered what my mother prayed for but never dared to ask.

On Saturdays we all went to the synagogue. Upon our return, a gentile hired to perform minor duties on the Sabbath came to light the cooking fire to heat our lunch. After the meal everybody took a nap. Then I would go with the adults to visit our relatives.

The first stop on our tour was the Nagel family, the wealthiest of our relatives. Theirs was the largest house on the main street, with a huge mystical garden into which I would go on expeditions in the hope of discovering an unfamiliar fruit, flower, or plant.

Best of all I liked to visit Aunt Kutzy and Uncle Favel Katz. Their house, like ours, was splendidly located across from the mill on the banks of the same Teplitza Creek, surrounded by wild bushes of lilac, jasmine, and a variety of berries. The greatest attraction for me, though, were their cats because I was not allowed to have one at home. My father never permitted me to touch animals and would warn me about the dangers involved, saying, "Cats catch mice, which are carriers of bacteria." As much as I adored him and tried to follow his guidance, I betrayed him every time I secretly played with one.

The only cat on my grandfather's farm was a spotted gray and white tomcat called Ninini. He belonged to my cousin Lucie, who, being seven year older than I, could be quite intimidating as well as possessive. I could not touch or play with Ninini without creating a ruckus, for which *I* would usually be reprimanded.

It was not until one of our Sabbath excursions to Aunt Kutzy's that I got my wish to have a kitten of my own. One of her cats had just had a litter, and Aunt Kutzy's niece Suzi, who happened to be visiting, seemed to understand my yearning and gave me one newborn kitten. I naturally named it Suzi.

Me at age three (center, front) with children of Milie, cousin Lucie (rear left), and brother Bubi (rear right).

What a heavenly gift for a little girl so fond of cats! My Suzi had short, black-and-white hair with one black ear on her otherwise all-white head. As soon as she grew a bit, she would appear every morning in my room, jump on my bed, curl up at my feet, and purr happily. For a while everything seemed settled, and I thought my quarrels with Lucie were over now that I had a cat of my own. But as it turned out she developed a great affection for my Suzi, so our fights continued as before.

Besides our conflicts over cats, Lucie and I fought over the right to be the first in the morning to pick the boysenberries or the first to sit in the *Czetiner* apple tree and read.

This tree with its low, thick branches was ideal for climbing, and I loved to perch myself there, lean back on one of its branches, and snuggle up with Suzi and a book. But Lucie claimed even this place for herself. Although she made my life difficult at times, she compensated by taking me along to visit her friends, something I considered a great privilege.

My attachment to the land, its waterways and trees, was as strong as that to the animals, including our cow and her calf. With her shiny brown-and-white fur and big friendly eyes, Ruzena was as devoted to Dziadziu as a dog is to his master.

Every morning after Grandpa milked and fed her, he bathed and groomed her with a metal brush. Sometimes he allowed us to take part in the process. When Ruzena was grazing and would hear Grandfather's steps approaching, she would position herself at the gate and moo until he came and patted her tenderly on the head.

Surrounded by constant excitement, I could have been unequivocally happy were it not for my chronic lack of appetite, which was the main cause of tension and conflict with my mother, who always feared for my life. Every time Mama took me to the pediatrician, he would give her the same advice: "Leave her alone to go hungry for a few days," he would say, "and you'll see how she'll beg for food." But she could not bring herself to take such a drastic step for fear that I wouldn't survive for even a few days.

In our family I was never referred to as "Ruth" but as "The Child." It was always "The child has to rest . . . to sleep . . . to eat." I used to store the food inside my cheeks for hours without swallowing. Over the years my mother's voice resonated with the words: "Chew and swallow! Chew and swallow!"

One summer, when I was seven, my health got so bad that the doctor recommended I be exposed to the morning sun's natural ultraviolet rays. At nine o'clock every morning, Mama coated a different part of my body with a special oil and left me outdoors for at least ten minutes. This was followed by forced feeding, a dreadful experience for all parties involved. When my mother would lose her patience, her sister would take over.

Aunt Anna devised a "swing-feeding" system. She would sing songs, stopping the swing after each stanza to shove a spoonful of food into my mouth. That worked. So did feeding me under the huge pear tree behind the house. Its wide and thick branches were laden with hundreds of tiny sugar pears, which, depending on their ripeness, would fall to the ground at irregular intervals.

"Ruthale," she said, "I will tell you a story, but every time a pear falls to the ground, you take a mouthful and swallow."

"Yes, Tante Anna," I readily agreed, convinced she would give up after a while. But she was as patient as a saint and sat for hours until I finished eating.

With so many healthy recreational activities, the farm was much like a resort so other relatives and friends would send their children there during the summer vacation. The larger the crowd, the happier I was. At times our noisy bunch was too much for Dziadziu, but he tolerated us. He had lived alone after his wife died in 1929, and perhaps the very loneliness caused him to be quiet and reserved. Still, I loved him very much.

Grandfather was highly respected by the villagers because of his tireless quest for truth and justice. But among the Jews he was socially ostracized for choosing to be a farmer. Because of his inventiveness and expertise, however, he was the one everybody would consult before initiating a project. He could always be seen in his fields sowing seeds, cutting grain with a scythe, tending to his beehives, or doing some handiwork. He lived for the land he loved.

My brother, Manasse, nicknamed "Bubi," was his favorite grandchild.

The only family photo.

For him he built a fishing rod, a wooden stand for sheet music, a self-standing wooden swing, and a canoe with two paddles. When Bubi played the violin, Grandpa would silence the household so he could listen undisturbed.

Mostly Bubi would play the violin on rainy days. We welcomed such days for the different activities that were as entertaining as those outdoors: listening to Bubi's music, reading, whipping butter from cream, and collecting soft rainwater for shampooing, to name a few. After the rain we splashed in puddles and collected earthworms for fishing bait.

I would wake up every morning full of optimism and anticipation of the day's offering. Every aspect of life on the farm fascinated me. We had no electricity, running water, or shower and only a distant outhouse. Yet we adapted to the inconveniences and even found them to be exhilarating. For me it created an air of romance. And what a rich experience it was for a little girl to be in total harmony with Mother Nature!

But Milie was not the only place I experienced as a child. Papa told me that before my birth they lived for a short time in Vashkautz, where he managed a sawmill and where Bubi was born. Six years later, Papa was transferred by his employer to Vizhnitza, another neighboring mountain town where on June 21, 1930, I was born. When I was a year old, he was transferred to Kishinev, the capital of Bessarabia, presently Moldova.

The first threads in the web of my memory were spun in that place. To my astonishment I vividly remember many occurrences and a few places from as early as age two. My earliest recollection is the nightly routine by which Papa put me to sleep. He rocked my crib, read me stories in German, and showed me the colored illustrations that accompanied them. As soon as Papa turned off the lights, Little Red Riding Hood became a reality. I actually started hearing and even seeing the big brown wolf.

Tap, tap, tap went the wolf's steps. Through the rails of my crib, I watched him as he approached. Frozen with fear I held my breath until he gave up sniffing around my body and strolled toward my brother's room. I never mentioned the wolf phenomenon to anyone. His indisputable, nightly appearance remained my secret and mystery. Years later as a teenager, I realized that the sound which had triggered my spirited imagination was actually the rhythmic beating of my heart, which became audible when I rested my head on my left arm.

Another early memory stems from the time I was a toddler and had the measles. Everybody and everything in the room was red and looked strange and funny. As if by magic the color disappeared as soon as I recovered. I was told later, the red bulbs were supposed to protect my eyes. This spell of illness undoubtedly aroused excessive maternal instincts in my mother. After I recovered, she still treated me as if I were extremely fragile. At that tender age, I already sensed her overpowering obsession about my health. I never understood how I could be sick when I felt fine.

Since my earliest images were of my mother scolding me about my rickets, skinny physique, and the fact that I would not eat, it was only natural for me to gravitate toward my father, whose calm, soothing, and unconditional love I thoroughly enjoyed.

Papa spoiled me terribly. As a consequence I missed him intensely when he went to work. One morning, at about age four I was playing in the yard with the neighbors' children and caught a glimpse of my father about to exit the big iron gate without his customary farewell hugs and kisses.

I yelled, "Papa! Papa!" and ran after him. He strode on without turning around and the gate closed behind him.

With tears streaming down my cheeks, I burst into the apartment and, between sobs, pointed toward the gate exclaiming, "Papa! Papa!" My mother understood my dilemma and, with a smile, tried to console me.

"Papa is home," she said, but I would not believe her until he came in to see what all the crying was about. As usual he hugged and kissed me and repeated reassuring words. All the while I nestled against his chest stupefied, unable to differentiate between reality and imagination. I was confused and ashamed but happy: it was not *my* Papa who had left without kissing me good-bye but someone resembling him.

Because my brother was a gifted child, especially with the violin, Papa apparently wanted to mold me into another Bubi. I was barely three years old when he decided to teach me to read. One day he brought home a big box of colored letter-cubes, spread them on the floor of our enclosed glass veranda, and introduced me to the German alphabet. Pretending it was a game, we would sprawl on the floor where he would name letters, put them together into a short word, and I would attempt to read it. My enthusiasm and receptiveness were nourished by his constant praise and obvious pride. As a result, I was able to read at the young age of three, when enrollment age in first grade was seven. Next papa persuaded Bubi's violin teacher to accept me as his student. He gave up after that first hour. "She is still too small," he said. "Let's try it again later." Unfortunately, "later" never came.

As if to make up for the failed attempt, Papa, who had a pleasant voice, taught me songs in many languages so that I could produce some music and give him the pleasure of bragging about his daughter's talent. Nothing was too much for him when it concerned his "Muttika," as he nicknamed me. His gifts consisted of love, affection, caring, and praise, enriching my childhood with his lavish, unselfish giving.

Thanks to my dear father's efforts, I was able to read fairy tales that embellished my own pixie world and created in my imagination visions of princes, princesses, and kingdoms.

Then one day I got to see real royalty when the Romanian King Carol II and Prince Michael, his son and heir, made a visit to Kishinev. Perched on my father's shoulders, I watched the royal carriage making its way down the main street which was bursting with people waving Romanian flags and cheering the military bands, the marching soldiers, and the cavalry. Smiling and waving, the king and prince alternated their greetings to the left and to the right. I waved back fervently and could have sworn that they returned my greeting. This experience fed my childish imagination. In some of my dreams, I even found myself to be a member of the royal family.

In reality I was a member of a middle-class family. My mother, Leah, was a slender, petite, serious, and energetic woman with sad, brown eyes. Somehow I had the perception that my lack of appetite and her relentless worry about my health contributed to her sadness. She kept her straight brown hair combed back and twisted into a bun. Her beautiful, facial features appeared prematurely aged. She never used makeup or wore pretty clothes, and she maintained a martyr-like existence that revolved around her family and domestic chores. A devoted, loving mother and an impeccable housewife, a hard worker and excellent cook, she possessed extraordinary common sense and sharpness of mind. I loved her dearly.

Mama was born in 1896, when Milie, Bukovina, was a part of the Austro-Hungarian Empire. She was one of four children of Littman and Reizl Katz. David, the eldest, was followed by Anna, Leah, and Moishe. As the battlefront of World War I neared Bukovina, the family fled to Vienna, where my mother completed her training in a business school and worked for an insurance company, an unusual endeavor for a woman then. After the war, the family returned to Milie, then part of Greater Romania. A matchmaker introduced her to her future husband.

My father, Mendel, was a short man of medium frame, whose eternally warm smile graced his otherwise regular features. Behind his spectacles, sparkled a pair of sky-blue eyes. His attire was immaculate, and whenever he went out he covered his crew-cut salt and pepper hair with an elegant hat. Although he worked as a bookkeeper, he was an intellec-

My father, Mendel, *and mother, Leah.*

tual and an ardent Zionist. Books were an indispensable element in his life, and they soon began to play a similar role in mine.

Papa was born in 1886 in Kuty, a small town in the Polish province of Galicia, also part of the Austro-Hungarian Empire until the end of World War I. He was one of six children of Menashe and Ethel Drimmer Glasberg, who died long before Papa got married. They had four daughters and two sons: Samuel (Sammy), Maryem, Mendel, Cilli, Toni, and Pepi.

Grandpa Menashe, a very orthodox Jew, was, so the story goes, a descendant of the *Baal Shem Tov,* the holy leader of the Chasiddic movement, a Jewish mystical sect. Except for my father, who was drafted into the Austrian army, the Glasberg family also fled to Vienna. (I know all this thanks to my father's bedside stories.)

Two of his sisters remained in Vienna, while my father and the other siblings returned to Bukovina. Samuel, the eldest brother, married a woman from a well-to-do family, owners of a large timber business. That, in turn, enabled him to employ my father and his brothers-in-law.

Much to my mother's despair, Papa was not very successful in business. While the brothers-in-law later established themselves independently, Papa was frequently relocated to a number of little towns to run sawmills or lumberyards. When Sammy had enough of Papa's failures as an administrator, he offered him a job as bookkeeper in his main lumber import-export office "Engler & Glass" in Czernowitz. I was five when we moved into this beautiful town where I spent the most impressionable years of my life.

At the folds of the Carpathian Mountains, stretching along the bank of the Prut River, surrounded by ancient forests of beech, oak, linden and firs, rises Czernowitz, the capital of Bukovina province. This region of breathtaking beauty in northeastern Romania, glorified in poems and songs, was truly my native land.

Over the centuries, its earth has been stained with the blood of conquering Tatar and Ottoman Turks. It endured the Austro-Hungarian Empire, became part of Greater Romania, was annexed to the Soviet Union in 1940, recaptured by the Romanian Fascist army in 1941, and retaken by the Soviet Union in 1944. Presently North Bukovina is part of independent Ukraine.

Chestnut and white acacia trees lined the streets of Czernowitz. Its parks and squares brimmed with kaleidoscopic flowerbeds. The architecture, elegance, culture, and language evoked a feeling of *Gemütlichkeit,* of coziness. It was a little replica of classical Austrian culture—a sort of small Vienna.

The soil of Czernowitz bred many prominent Jewish, intellectuals, poets, and writers, making it a vital center of Jewish and German culture. The large yet closely knit Jewish community of about fifty thousand represented half of the city's population.

Although the area had been part of Greater Romania and Romanian was the official tongue, German was the predominant language of the general population. The Romanian government was so frustrated that it posted signs in stores and other public places demanding that everyone "Speak Romanian!"

Ironically, I never learned the language until I entered elementary school, and Mama never mastered it at all. In addition to German, Mama spoke Ruthenian and Yiddish, and Papa spoke Yiddish, Hebrew, Polish, and Romanian. Perhaps my facility with languages came from being exposed to such a wide variety from an early age, although we spoke only German with our parents.

Sometime after we came to Czernowitz, we rented a beautiful two-and-a-half-room apartment on the fourth floor of a new building. It was bright, cozy, and elegant with crystal French doors, wall-to-wall windows facing the street, and shiny parquet floors—a dream come true for my mother who had a preference for good living quarters even at the cost of great personal sacrifices.

Soon I was introduced to several girls in our neighborhood. One of them was Litty Lipson. We played well together, mostly at her place because she had many toys and games and I had none. Our favorite game was a set of paper dolls, the outfits of which we changed for hours.

One day Litty's mother was going to take the two of us to a soccer match. My mother insisted on dressing me, despite all my protest, in an ugly striped sun-dress. Mrs. Lippson threw a disapproving glance and exclaimed, "You can't go out in that dress!" And then she handed me one of Litty's. Embarrassed, I fought back tears of humiliation. I was furious at my mother. The minute I came home, I made a tearful scene, which soon resulted in our having a few new dresses made for me.

Besides Litty, I had a German friend next door, Ilse Ulrich, two years younger than myself. We became constant playmates. Her *Kinderfräulein* (nanny) taught us many songs, dances, and games. She taught us one particular ballet, or should I say a *pas de deux,* executed to the music of a Johann Strauss waltz. We decided to perform that dance for our friends and families on my upcoming eighth birthday. We feverishly rehearsed and prepared our costumes, cutting out tutus and matching capes from crepe paper, blue for Ilse and pink for me. We made our debut to an audience sitting in my family's anteroom, which doubled as a stage. Ilse came "onstage" through the bedroom door and I from the living room. It was a memorable day in that it kindled my love for dancing in general and for classical ballet in particular.

Once a year, at Christmastime, Papa would take me to the commercial center of town to window-shop, where I was mesmerized by the decorations and dolls, even though we never bought anything, but my ultimate Christmas excitement was when Ilse's parents would invite me to help decorate the tall pine tree they put up in their living room. Aside from the multicolored glass balls and silver paper garlands, all the decorations we tied to the branches were real: real candles, real candies and chocolates. On Christmas Eve, when we were lighting each candle and singing "*O Tannenbaum*," I envied Ilse and would have gladly traded Hanukkah for Christmas.

Across the street lived another good friend, Reli Rosenzweig, a Jewish girl my age. In her building also lived an eighteen-year old boy worthy of mention—Friedl the dwarf. Whenever our neighborhood group of girls played in their courtyard, he would join us, though he would not participate in our childish games. His gigantic head and odd features contrasted grotesquely with his small body. Because of his short stature, we perceived him as just another child.

Word about Friedl's "special" knowledge and his willingness to share it with us spread rapidly. But it was not until one day that he decided to let us kids onto exactly how much he knew.

"Where do babies come from?" he asked, with an edge of challenge in his voice. Then he proceeded to tell us in graphic detail how babies were conceived. And that was how, among other things, Friedl became my first sex educator.

At the late age of six, I was finally put into a private kindergarten, since there were no public ones. For me, it was heaven on earth. I flourished in that environment, where I learned to draw and paint, to sing, and to play group games with other children. Finally I was in my element.

Soon I was chosen to participate in a play "The Seasons" at a real theater. I would represent "Spring," a role for which I needed a costume, but I was unable to convince my mother of its importance. She shrugged off my request as one would a nuisance. So I appealed to Ilse's nanny, who managed to create a costume suggestive of a daffodil. Judging by the audience's applause, I must have personified spring well. Proud of myself, I expected some praise from my mother. But as usual, aside from giving me a hug and a kiss, she said almost nothing.

Nevertheless, that performance aroused my creative spark for drama.

Soon after, I started to stage my own plays with my friends, a group of five or six girls, aged five to seven. Being the only one able to read and write before entering school, I would pick a tale from *The Brothers Grimm*, write a part for each girl, then coach them until they knew their parts by heart and acted convincingly. Naturally, I took the leading roles, did the narration, and even supervised the wardrobe coordination. We would sneak the "costumes" secretly from our mothers' closets and perform everything from "Snow White" to "Cinderella."

Some of my other childhood diversions were to go with my mother on family visits, to the grocery store, and to the market, which was the most amusing of them all. Besides the variety of produce displayed, the bargaining dialogues intrigued me and held me spellbound. Most amusing, though, was the ritual of buying a hen. With childish curiosity I watched her pointing toward one specific bird in the cage for the peasant to pull out for a more rigorous inspection. Mama would appraise the weight by slightly bouncing the live hen in her palm. Next she would blow into the feathers to see the color of the skin, which if yellow, was proof of a fat hen. The thought that they would be ultimately killed the way I witnessed it done in Milie filled me with horror.

Mama had frequent dentist appointments so she took me along but, thank God, left me waiting for her return in a friend's nearby kiosk, called a *tutungerie* in Romanian. It was stocked with cigars, cigarettes, tobacco, newspapers, magazines, and, most important, for my personal pleasure, children's cartoon magazines. The sweet aroma—a fusion of tobacco and fresh newsprint—never failed to stir in me some pleasurable sensation. With a large supply of cartoons, I was left to read to my heart's content in a corner behind the counter until Mama came to pick me up.

Why my parents never bought me such inexpensive magazines, I cannot understand even to this day. Nor do I understand what their problem was with a doll. I had no toys except for my brother's hand-me-down teddy bear, which I kept in an equally handed-down doll carriage. One thing I did have was books—The Brothers Grimm, Hans Christian Andersen, and Max Nordau, who besides his serious books, also wrote a children's book for his daughter, to name a few—but not a single comic book.

Perhaps the very lack of toys stimulated my imagination and my inventiveness at group games. I was blessed with many good friends from different religions and social classes, right in my neighborhood. I am forever grateful to my parents for their unprejudiced attitudes, which helped enrich my childhood and lay the groundwork for my own views.

The affection missing in my parents' relationship was supplanted by devotion to their children. Sometimes it seemed my mother only tolerated me while my father showered me with exaggerated doting. Oh, how I responded to his love! It was mutual adoration. In my eyes, Papa was a god, if not more. He was all that God was supposed to be, only he was real and present and, at least for me, an absolute idol, a fountain of inspiration, goodness, love, intellectual stimulation, humor, and kindness. When the door opened upon his return from work, it was as if sunshine had suddenly come into the apartment.

It was Papa who took me to the children's theater, the circus, the park, the ice cream parlor, the pastry shop, and to visit with his family. His inexhaustible capacity for storytelling filled my young mind with information about his past and about faraway places, making it fun to be with him.

Yet for all that was wonderful about Papa, he had one idiosyncrasy that affected us all. Not only was he meticulous in his personal appearance, but he was preoccupied with cleanliness to the point of obsession. He never opened a doorknob with his hand, only with his elbow, never wiped his hands on a towel other than his own, and never used a toilet outside of our family home. At one point he became a vegetarian, which really drove my mother crazy, especially in the winter when there were no fruits or vegetables to be had at any price.

His list of *nevers* was endless. We were told to never touch door handles, never sit on toilet seats outside of home, never eat ice cream cones from kiosks or vendors, and so on, and so on. All these restrictions made me feel different from other children who, during recess and after school, were free to buy ice cream cones and other delightful goodies, and soon I became envious.

"Never touch money or cards," he cautioned, "because you never know what dirty hands handled them before you." To make a point, he would show me a beggar with open wounds and say, "You see, he touches his wounds and with the same hands touches the money. That's the way infections are transmitted."

It was easy to detect my mother's disapproval of Papa's whims, and often her patience was pushed to the extreme.

In addition, she also had to take a lot of abuse from his siblings, who, because they were well off, treated my mother as if they were royalty and she a plebeian.

Once I witnessed an ugly incident. Apparently my father's sister Cilli secretly took her husband's old clothes and shoes and gave them to us for Bubi. One day Uncle Max, who almost never visited our home, knocked furiously on the door. When Mama opened it, he demanded the return of everything his wife had given us. When Mama replied that we did not have anything of his, he declared, "Then I will search the apartment" and proceeded straight to my parents' bedroom, despite my mother's protests.

He flung open all the armoires and nightstands until he found a pair of his old hiking boots. He grabbed them, turned, pointed to his rear end, and made a vulgar suggestion. I was so scared that I hid in a corner. As he left, triumphantly holding aloft his old shoes and showing no concern about my mother's humiliation, she stood pale and trembling.

Though I never liked Uncle Max after that, I did enjoy visiting with his wife Cilli in their spacious, two-story house. Aunt Cilli played with me and pampered me with bubble baths and her home-baked pastries.

I was also pampered by Aunt Tony, my father's other sister, and her husband, Simon, who were also well off. Both aunts had only sons, so to them it was a thrill to have a little girl to play with; they spoiled me terribly whenever I visited.

Oddly enough, we had no social contact with Uncle Sammy's family, even though we lived only a block away from his house.

The richest of all my relatives, Samuel Glasberg was an imposing figure with his goatee and expensive clothes. He was a religious man whom our town's Jewish community held in high esteem. Neither he nor his family ever visited us or vice versa.

By contrast, my mother's sister Anna, who was my favorite, had been widowed and left with a two-year old daughter. She lived in a small one-bedroom apartment, and to make ends meet she had to rent out the living room. Fortunately for my poor mother, they moved from Milie to Czernowitz one year after our arrival.

When not visiting relatives or my friends, especially in winter, I would settle myself cozily beside the warm tile stove and read. Often Mama sat close by, knitting and listening to Bubi play the violin.

Being seven years older than I, my brother was more like a parent to me, making our relationship a twofold one. I looked up to him and so did everyone who knew him. Contrary to the notion that a person can be gifted in only one field, my brother proved the exception. He spoke seven languages and was a musical child prodigy and an outstanding student, especially in both graphic design and physics. Inventive as he was, he showcased many of his self-designed devices at school expositions and won many prizes. My parents were sure of his future contribution to both music and engineering.

Bubi at age four and at age eighteen.

Whenever I think of him, the same scenario presents itself—a handsome boy with classic facial features, crowned by an uncontrolled, upturned mane of frizzy brown hair, which he tried unsuccessfully to control by wearing a special hair net at night. I see him either practicing the violin for hours, filling the house with sounds of Bach, Vivaldi, or Mozart, or sitting at the dining room table, forehead resting on his upturned palm, deeply immersed in reading.

To watch him play the violin was like watching a magician's performance. His face seemed transfixed, while his skilled fingers performed quick, intriguing movements that resulted in divine melodies. With his eyes half-closed and nostrils flared, he seemed drawn into a world of his own. Often he did not even notice my dancing improvisations to the tune of his music. And when he did, he tolerated my audacity without complaining.

He was much too serious for his age and had few friends. Neither sports nor girls particularly interested him. Instead, his life was filled with books, music, crafts, science, and research. He was the recipient of the lyceum's scholastic award, and for his outstanding achievements at a national level he once received a prize from the royal house of King Carol II. It consisted of several cartons of books, each book stamped with the royal seal. My parents were proud of his achievement, but he was nonchalant about it, not at all arrogant, showing more interest in the quality of the books than in their origin.

He was Mama's favorite, her dream, her hope, and her reason for living. Despite his genuine interest in the sciences, she secretly harbored visions of his becoming a famous violinist. He practiced for hours without being told to, but Mama always felt it was her duty to remind him. Her daily nagging voice still rings in my ears: "Nashku"—a diminutive of Manasse—"Go and practice!" And without a word, my brother would do just that.

Bubi played in many local chamber orchestras and accompanied visiting singers. He was so advanced that his violin teacher, Samuel Flor, recommended that he be sent to either Paris or Vienna to pursue his career as he had exhausted all resources in our town. Unfortunately, my parents could not afford it.

But as shy and studious as he was during the school year, he would undergo a drastic change during the summers at Milie. He seemed to turn into a butterfly that had just completed the last stage of metamorphosis. There, the quiet loner would become more outgoing, participating with other children in swimming, canoeing, fishing, and hiking, all noncompetitive sports. He loved noncompetitive activities probably because he only knew how to compete against one person—himself.

Even in Milie he still spent most of the time either alone or with me tagging along. Paddling our canoe down Teplitza Creek, we would quietly share the excitement of exploring the beautiful scenery around each bend and make believe we had discovered a new continent. Bubi would let me paddle by placing his bigger palms on top of my tiny ones, and I would believe I was doing the hard work. At a wide embankment, he would pull the canoe onto the land and jump into the creek to swim, while I would imitate him by crawling on all fours in the shallow part, kicking my feet as hard as I could and making the same splashing noises as Bubi. Later we would stretch out in the sun. Lying back on the fragrant grass, my brother would cup his hand to his mouth and entertain me with a panoply of simulated bird songs.

Facing Romanian
Anti-Semitism

CHAPTER 2

1937. I was seven years old when dark, foreboding clouds of change threw a shadow over our pleasant lives. For the first time in my life, I heard the word *anti-Semitism*. And although Papa explained to me that it meant hating Jews, I had difficulty understanding its implication. But day by day, the word began to sound more and more ominous.

Romania is a country with deep-rooted anti-Semitic traditions. Inflammatory slogans such as "the Jews are bleeding our country" and "the Jews are drinking the people's blood" were aimed to divert popular attention from the true discontent caused by economic hardships and territorial losses throughout its history. If there were times of more leniency, it was only because of diplomatic pressure on the Romanians, to improve their treatment of the Jews. Only during the late 1930s did the fascist movements reach their height of popularity. There was the Iron Guard, also called the Legionary Movement, a Nazi-type party in Romania which the Gestapo furnished with money and weapons and taught the Nazi methods of genocide. And then there was the Goga-Cuza government, with an anti-Semitic platform, which laid the foundation for the persecution of the Romanian Jews.

As a child I overheard adults whispering the name *Cuza-Goga*, as if by merely forming the words some evil was about to happen. In reality it was the first avowedly anti-Semitic government installed by King Carol II and headed by the poet Octavian Goga and the veteran anti-Semite A.C. Cuza. Although it lasted only a few months, the seeds of hatred soon sprouted with lightning speed, intoxicating the minds of the masses. Their followers continued in the same systematic oppression of the Jews, aiming at the eventual destruction of the third largest Jewish population in Europe.

The pictures of Cuza-Goga were prominently displayed in shop windows and public places in our town, where Jews at that time represented half of Czernowitz's population.

Each day new decrees were issued, limiting Jewish activities and prohibiting access to certain areas and buildings. For instance, one of the movie theaters located in the *German House* was made off limits to Jews. But my friend Ilse's mother, angered by the new laws, set out to challenge them and took me along to see a Shirley Temple film. My mother was apprehensive, of course, but Mrs. Ulrich calmed her down.

"Ruthi does not look Jewish," she said. "She looks just like any Aryan girl." In my innocence I thought that it was something to be proud of. We did, indeed, go to see the film, enjoyed it, and nobody ever suspected that I was Jewish.

But in school everybody knew who was and who was not a Jew, not based on physiognomy but on names and such revealing clues as not kneeling and crossing oneself during morning prayers or whether one attended the Jewish religion class. Personally, I did not experience any insults, but my brother did.

He went to a predominantly Gentile high school and was often humiliated by students and teachers alike. I remember Bubi sharing with us one such incident. As an outstanding student he often came up with the correct answers. But because he was Jewish, the teacher, instead of praising him for his knowledge, said with contempt to the whole class, "You see, even though Glasberg is a *zhidan* [kike] he knows the right answers."

Gradually the government began stripping Jews of their citizenship, seizing their businesses, and barring them from jobs and education. Since our town had not yet been fully affected by the decrees, our lives continued as normal as before. Papa still worked, we still spent the summers in Milie, and, come September, Bubi and I returned to school.

In 1939, there was talk of war for many weeks. It was much too remote a concept for me, so I continued to go about my business as usual. I spent a lot of time at Ilse's, not only because of the fun I derived from our games but also because they had a radio. It gave me immeasurable pleasure to hear music, regardless of its genre. But that year much of the music was replaced by the barking speeches of Adolph Hitler, speeches that sounded angry and aggressive, and even though I did not understand their implications, they scared me.

Often programs would be interrupted by a shouting voice repeating the word: *Uwaga! Uwaga!* which made no sense to me, but Papa told me it meant *Attention!* in Polish, and that it was warning the population of an oncoming air raid in Poland.

Ilse's German parents listened with grave misgivings to all that was said, yet we children genuinely enjoyed singing the patriotic German marches, many of which we already knew by heart. Our favorites were *"Deutschland, Deutschland Uber Alles"* and *"Wir gehen gegen Engeland."* Little did we know that these songs were the very tunes that accompanied inhuman atrocities.

That same year bad news kept coming from all over. I will never forget my father's face as he read the last letter he received from his sisters in Vienna. It must have contained some dreadful information. He turned aside my inquiries, though, and they remained unanswered, because it was Papa's hope to forever shield me from any anguish.

Much later I learned that in that year, Aunt Maryem and her husband, Gedalia, succeeded in sending their daughter and son to Palestine. But in 1941 they, as well as Aunt Pepi, were deported and later murdered in an extermination camp.

I could feel the uneasiness in the air, and, watching Papa and Bubi anxiously pore over the newspapers, I grew increasingly frightened. As usual I sought solace in my father, who always repeated the calming, reassuring words, "Don't worry, everything is going to be fine."

But as time went by, I was no longer so sure. The adults spoke of war but did not want to share the details with me. I sensed an imminent danger lurking around the corner, threatening my happy childhood.

August 1939. Some bizarre political developments took place. The German foreign minister, Joachim von Ribbentrop, and the Russian foreign minister, V.M. Molotov, signed a pact that contained a secret proviso to return Bessarabia to Soviet sovereignty. But a year later when the Soviets occupied these territories, they also claimed North Bukovina, which included our town, Czernowitz, its capital.

At first, this German-Russian pact brought hope to some, and mixed feelings to others. The rich were fearful of deportation to Siberia, the poor welcomed it in the hope of a better life, and the middle class was undecided. One positive thing to look forward to was that as Jews we would not be discriminated against anymore.

The new order, which was called *communism,* forced many capitalists to flee to Old Romania, Palestine, and other countries. Others remained in the hope that nothing would change. But things did, and they changed rapidly.

Amidst all this political turmoil, luckily Uncle Sammy and Aunt Fanny were out of the country. If they had not been visiting their two daughters in Palestine, the Soviets would surely have deported them to Siberia.

Having had to finalize a large timber shipment from Romania, Uncle Sammy came back alone a few months before the Soviets marched in. He packed most of the household and entrusted the shipping of it to Palestine to a Romanian colonel who lived in their apartment. He placed three huge Persian carpets with us. Other items he gave to his siblings to safeguard until better times came again. After giving a set of apartment keys to Aunt Cilli, he left for Bucharest, just before the Red Army marched into our town.

During all that confusion, a ray of light penetrated our home when Bubi's violin teacher brought us some good news. Bubi was invited by Romanian Radio Kishinev to play the "Violin Concerto Number One

Romania before and after World War II. Northern Transylvania was annexed by Hungary in 1940. In 1944 the Hungarians deported the province's Jews to Auschwitz. Romania took back the province in 1945.

in A Minor" by Johann Sebastian Bach. We were ecstatic! Bubi was only seventeen at the time but was already well known and in demand. The surprising part was that, for the sake of his talent, even in the last weeks of the anti-Semitic Romanian rule, the bureaucrats were ready to turn a blind eye to the fact that he was a Jew.

But my parents' towering happiness was overshadowed by a lack of money for the many things Bubi needed: a new suit, a train ticket, and a hotel room. Somehow they managed to scrape up some money but not enough for us to go with him. So Bubi had to travel alone.

And there was another problem: Where to listen to the concert? Though our relatives the Zloczowers had a radio, and so did the Ulrichs, we ended up listening to the concert at Uncle Sammy's vacant apartment. We got the keys from Aunt Cilli and, accompanied by Aunt Anna and Lucie, went upstairs. Hesitantly, Papa turned the key in the lock and let us into the dim, stately, but deserted quarters. To me it felt spooky being in this uninhabited, luxurious home, sitting down in the plush arm-chairs, and listening to the radio.

May 10, 1940. With eager anticipation I waited for the broadcaster's voice. As soon as he announced the concert to be played by violinist Manasse Glasberg, and the first chords of the concerto filled the air, a memorable shiver ran through my whole body. From Bubi's frequent practicing, I knew the piece by heart. Accompanied only by a piano, he played it so beautifully, that we all exchanged glances of sublime approval. I was bursting with excitement at the thought that the whole world might be listening to my talented brother.

"He is famous," I thought. "My brother is famous!"

Bubi returned home jubilantly, and our pride in him extended to that of our beleaguered people. The local *Morgenblatt* newspaper wrote the following review: (*Morgenblatt*, May 10, 1940)

"Radioconcert M. Glasberg. The violinist Manasse Glasberg is a Czerno-witzer whose artistic genius and fame have spread throughout our town. Barely seventeen years old, steadfast and serene, he follows his artistic path. He was invited by Radio Kishiniev to play the Bach Violin concerto in A major. His tone appeared to be especially appropriate for the microphone, often of blooming fullness. His interpretation was clear, faultless and of genuine classicism. If his teacher, Professor S. Flor, helps him to pave his road and to overcome his first obstacles to a public appearance, this talent certainly has a predictable future that will surpass the average." *(translated by the author)*

June 1940. Romanians, ethnic Germans, as well as some Jews living in the disputed territories, prudently decided to leave the area before the arrival of the Soviets. It was sad to see the exodus of people amidst an atmosphere of uncertainty and fear. I experienced the first pains of part-ing when Ilse and her family said good-bye to us in a way that implied finality.

Once the Romanian Army had left, the Red Army marched in. They rolled in on trucks, on rumbling tanks, and on foot, under red banners and slogans. Some of the cheering bystanders tossed flowers at the sing-ing soldiers. The streets were crowded with curious adults and playful children like myself, who, like any ten-year-old, thought of a parade as a joyous spectacle, an expression of happiness. The grinning, good-natured, singing soldiers impressed me. It was a reassuring feeling after a year of anxiety.

But the change from a capitalist to a communist system had its disadvantages, as it automatically eliminated all private enterprise, causing unemployment and austerity. Depression and disillusionment quickly followed. Intellectuals and executives had to be content with any kind of job just to survive.

My father, who had never done any manual labor, had to accept the night shift in a bakery. It was demeaning to him and did not provide enough to feed us. He would come home in the morning, exhausted and depressed, with only one consolation: he at least brought us warm Danish pastries, a luxury at that time and a welcome breakfast before leaving for school.

Soon thousands of Soviet government employees filled our town, radically changing its ambience.

For us children, conversion to the Soviet system was a welcome change. Gone were the private and segregated schools. Boys and girls mixed for the first time. There were no more separate religion classes for Jewish and Christian children and no more morning prayers in class. In Romanian public schools, Christian children knelt during those prayers facing an Orthodox Christian icon. The Jewish children, although excused from kneeling, had to stand facing the icon with palms clasped. Now we were relieved of that humiliation.

In its place came a daily dose of communist ideology. The new curriculum taught the basic ideas of fraternity, equality, and liberty, regardless of religion or race. To me, a government that promised justice for all seemed to be a fulfillment of all my childish optimism. Still, I couldn't erase my patriotism for Romania and my love for the king and the prince.

One significant drawback of the Soviet occupation was the loss of one year of schooling as we were forced to repeat our previous grade in order to learn the Russian language. The Soviet school structure consists of ten grades, *dyesyatilyetka,* housed under one roof. At this point I was assigned to a new, larger, and nicer school, slightly farther from my home.

The novelty of mingling with children of all ages and of being under the same roof with my cousins, acquaintances, and some of my friends who had gone to private schools before was especially exciting.

We were encouraged to study hard in order to become Pioneers, future members of the Communist Party, a privilege given only to top achievers. The school also provided an array of social activities, quite unlike the Romanian schools.

I had no problem mastering Russian in a short time and, in a pompous ceremony during which a red triangular necktie with its special ring was placed on our white blouses, I soon joined the ranks of Pioneers.

Just a few months earlier, I had worn a grey necktie on a similar uniform representing the Romanian youth order, the *Strajer*. My loyalty to the Romanian monarchy, once expressed in patriotic songs and poems, was switched to Stalin and the Soviet regime. I belonged to the elite of the school, something I was proud of, though I did have a problem with one aspect of Soviet education: atheism, which our teacher constantly preached. Having come from a religious home and believing strongly in God, I could not easily accept such a radical theory. Nor was I alone in that predicament.

One day our Russian teacher became exasperated with the class and exclaimed, "*Bozhe moy!*" ("My God!") That was when I immediately seized the opportunity to confront her.

"Comrade Teacher, excuse me!" I said sheepishly. "How come you just called on God, but you insist on teaching us that He does not exist?" Before she could answer, there was a collective murmur of approval from my classmates.

"Well, children, you have to understand that it is a habit, a matter of speech," she answered, in an unconvincing manner.

While we as children rejoiced in the novelty of the Communist regime, our parents were worried, particularly since the economic situation was worsening. There was no money and little food, and, to make things worse, the Communists started to limit the living quarters of each family to a set number of square feet, thus crowding several families into the one apartment. Total strangers had to share kitchens and toilets, a possibility deemed inconceivable by my mother. Unfortunately, one day we came face to face with this reality.

We were all at home when the doorbell rang several times. Papa went to answer it, only to find himself confronting several Russian-speaking officials who said they were bringing new tenants to share our apartment. Papa apparently did not understand what they meant but let them in anyway. Mama, on the other hand, who spoke Ruthenian, similar to Russian, did understand—and went literally berserk.

She started screaming in German, "*R-a-a-a-us! R-a-a-a-us! R-a-a-a-us!*" ("O-o-o-ut! O-o-o-ut! O-o-o-ut!"), which they ignored, and proceeded to enter the living room.

When Mama saw their defiance, she did something very strange. She planted herself on the sofa, teeth and fists clenched, eyelids shut, and screamed with a prolonged high pitch "R-a-a-a-us, r-a-a-a-us!" I had never imagined my mother being capable of such an outburst. We could not reason with her. She just kept on repeating the same scream, "R-a-a-a-us! R-a-a-a-us!" I pleaded, crying, "Mama, please. I'm scared! Stop it!"

But to no avail. Nor could my brother or father succeed in pulling her out of that state, which scared not only us but also the commissars; after a few more minutes of high drama, they left, threatening to return.

It took several hours for Mama to calm down. It was a shocking incident, after which we came to understand how strongly she felt about our home and to what extremes she would go to protect her family's territory. She was a fighter, my mother, but destiny spared her from one perpetual and difficult battle she had to fight: the battle to get me to eat.

The sudden austerity mainly resulted in a deficiency of food. This in turn eliminated mother's nagging me to eat. Miraculously it resulted in a reversal of my past eating problems. For the first time in my life, ironically, I actually felt hunger, and intense hunger at that. Now I *begged* for food, but there was not enough for all of us.

Things got so bad that Mama, who always worried about my health, now was really petrified. Frustrated and anxious, she searched and found a temporary solution. Through the intervention of Reli's mother I was invited to eat lunch at the home of a rich neighbor. It was humiliating, but it was the only way to pacify my hunger—a new and unpleasant sensation. My visits lasted only a short time, as these neighbors were soon able to leave for Romania and from there they went to America.

They were among the lucky ones, because at that time deportations to Siberia were in full swing. Over 3,800 Czernowitzians—80 percent Jewish—were banished there. Even at age ten I understood that Siberia was a godforsaken place from which not many would ever return. For once I was grateful for not being rich.

My grandfather was spared from all the upheaval of those chaotic times, only to die of pneumonia in 1940. That was my first brush with death in our family, although it was not quite clear to me what it really meant. Yet somehow I worried about returning to his farm when he was no longer there. I did not comprehend the finality of death, and that prompted me to ask many, many questions. From my mother's evasive answers I feared that with his death and the new political developments my "paradise" was endangered.

To relieve my suffering, Papa suggested that the two of us visit an aunt of his in a nearby village. We traveled by train and were met by the elderly couple. The Greifs had a farm much smaller than my grandfather's. Still it was beautiful and serene there, and for a few days I enjoyed the country life.

About the third night of our visit, we were awakened by a loud knock on the door. When our relatives opened it, a peasant entered in a very agitated state, warning them to leave and hide somewhere because they were on the list to be sent to Siberia. Chaos reigned in the household. It hit my relatives so unexpectedly that at first they did not know what to do—except to see that my father and I were out of danger. Finally the same peasant promised to hide us for the night.

All three of us walked inconspicuously in that foreboding darkness toward our hiding place. I was so frightened that my knees buckled. When we finally reached the little house, the kind peasants offered us the floor to sleep on. Even then, trembling with fear, I would not let go of Papa's hand. I worried about ever seeing Mama and Bubi again.

Luck was with us, and in the morning we were able to return home by train, unharmed but shaken. It was my first encounter with real danger. Worst of all was not knowing anything about the fate of the Greif family.

Later came more shocking news: Uncle Sammy had been murdered in Bucharest during a pogrom led by the Iron Guard. Had he stayed in Palestine and not been concerned about material things, he might have been spared.

June 1941. One year after the arrival of the Soviets, the German Army suddenly and without warning attacked the Soviet Union, in spite of the nonaggression pact signed by the two countries.

General Ion Antonescu, the Romanian fascist dictator, promised Hitler total allegiance. As our region was now part of the Soviet Union, we found ourselves right in the path of the secret invasion plan, code name *Barbarossa.* Among the first targets were Bessarabia, Bukovina (us), and Ukraine. Antonescu ordered his army to cross the Prut River on June 21, 1941, a date that coincided with my eleventh birthday. Instead of celebrating, I spent the day in a bomb shelter.

The Axis started bombing our town. We had to cover windows so no light would filter out, and because of rumors that poison gas bombs would be dropped, some people, my family included, bought gas masks.

Words like *camouflage, blackout, air raid,* and *all clear* began to enrich my vocabulary. I did not even know our apartment building had a bomb shelter until we were forced to share it with neighbors from older structures that had none. As soon as we heard the piercing sirens announcing imminent bombardment, we put on the masks, ran to the poorly lit shelter, and sat on crowded benches along the walls. At first, I resisted putting on the mask—mainly because of the fear of suffocating, a sensation I couldn't tolerate—but I had to.

In that ghostly attire people resembled my vision of the boogeyman. I couldn't accept the feeling that now my parents, into whose bed I would run for refuge from nightmares, had taken on the ghoulish appearance of the very creatures I feared.

At each thunderous explosion a shudder ran down my spine. I covered my ears, closed my eyes, and visualized the destruction of my beloved Czernowitz. I clung to my father, who still kept saying, "Everything is going to be fine."

Meanwhile the Romanian army advanced toward our town, leaving behind a trail of blood throughout the small towns and villages where they massacred Jews in the most barbarous ways.

July 5, 1941. Two weeks after the initial attack, the Romanian vanguards entered our city, attacking, plundering, and murdering thousands of Jews. The next morning the mobile killing units (*Einsatztruppen*) arrived and did the rest of the job. These Nazi savages executed every Jew they encountered. At the end of twenty-four hours, over two thousand of our townspeople had been killed.

Panic invaded every fiber of our bodies. Fearing sporadic executions, people stayed hidden in their homes.

When the initial savagery had subsided somewhat, a barrage of decrees was issued, all aimed at Jews. First the obligatory wearing of the yellow Star of David, followed by prohibitions on employment, schooling, group gatherings in the streets, and being outside after dark. These humiliations were difficult to deal with, but not being allowed to go to school was the worst one for me. Next they started to round up thousands of Jews and select the young men for forced labor. The older ones were taken to local police stations, or *gendarmeries*, where they were beaten, tortured, and kept for days without food or water.

Besides the military and police, a horde of money-hungry Romanians swarmed into these territories to enrich themselves by looting Jewish properties. They were properly nicknamed the "gold-rushers."

Then came the most grisly account: word that the entire Jewish population of Milie had been massacred! The bearer of that latest tragedy was my mother's cousin, Yona Itzhak. Miraculously he escaped from Milie, and somehow made it to Czernowitz, where he was apprehended by Romanian gendarmes and escorted through the streets past Aunt Anna's building, to prison. In a desperate, breathless voice, he managed to shout to her fourth floor window, "Anna! Anna!" "All murdered! All murdered!" before the soldiers hustled him away. And that was how Aunt Anna and Lucie heard of the tragedy.

Later, we were even more horrified to learn that all our friends and relatives had died not at the hands of soldiers but at the hands of their fellow villagers with whom they had once lived in perfect harmony. Dr, Emma Lustig, a surviving member of the Nagel family, gave this account of what happened:

Two weeks after the beginning of the war, in July 1941, after the last Soviet soldier left the village, we felt a radical change in the attitude of the peasants. The Ukrainians, who had always been very friendly, stopped greeting their Jewish neighbors, did not purchase the bread and groceries from their stores, and avoided them by just walking away.

My father, who was on good terms with the secretary of the town hall, went over to inquire about the significance of this recent change. The secretary told him to stay home and assured him that nothing would happen. Nevertheless, a heavy atmosphere was felt in the streets of the village. Nobody walked outside, no voices were heard, there were no meetings in the streets. Here and there, a peasant would walk down the street, averting his eyes from the Jewish homes.

Most of the Jewish homes were located on Main Street. These were the ones most exposed to danger, so the people decided to hide at nighttime in the other Jewish homes near the Cheremosh River, and return only during the day. This procedure was repeated on several nights. On Friday the housewives prepared for the traditional Sabbath dinner, while the men decided not to go to the synagogue for the usual prayer. Instead they would stay home and wait till morning to see what would happen.

A neighbor peasant came to our house to warn us of the ongoing events but was afraid to hide us in his home. "Who knows what will happen?" he shrugged.

Indeed, that same Friday night, groups of villagers in gendarme uniforms adorned with blue and yellow ribbons on the sleeves went to the Jewish homes and assured everybody to go on as usual with our prayers, to eat our challah and fish, and nothing would happen as long as we stayed inside. Later that same night, another peasant came to our house and offered to hide us in his home for the night. It was Shweike Michaele, who saved our lives. We accepted the offer.

In the morning, father went out to the center to find out what was going on and to see the house, but as he walked for a few minutes, his brother-in-law (Yona Itzhak) came running down the street horrified, bleeding from his face. He related the horrible news: His wife had just been murdered.

Father ran back to our hiding place and begged the peasant to go out and see what was happening. He left, and when he returned after a few hours, he asked us to leave his house because "I could not bear to see your blood shed in my yard."

"Something horrible is happening! *Hospode pomoze* (God help us)!" he cried.

We left his house for lack of choice and crawled on our hands and feet through the grass until we reached a dense meadow in which we hid the whole night. We heard them searching for us, groups of our "friendly" peasants who so often had frequented our home. Luckily they did not discover us. The next day we fled to a neighboring town, Viznitza. We walked along the Cheremosh River, hiding all the time until we reached the town. From there we were deported by the Romanians to Transnistria in Ukraine.

The peasants, armed only with primitive, agricultural tools like rakes and saws, murdered the whole Jewish population of Milie in a systematic way. They went from house to house and killed everybody in sight.

My uncle Yona Itzhak saw with his own eyes how they murdered his family. After beating him unconscious and assuming him dead, they threw him into the cellar. He later regained consciousness, crawled out of the cellar into the garden, and from there made his unbelievable escape into Poland by crossing the Cheremosh River. In Poland it was still peaceful, thus enabling him to travel to Czernowitz, where his children lived.

Yona Itzhak also told about the murder of a prominent Zionist figure, Mr. Keller from Czernowitz, who happened to be visiting his parents in Milie. They forced him to watch the murder of his thirteen-year-old daughter whom they cut to pieces with a saw on top of a pile of wood. Then they killed him the same way.

Hiding in the bushes, Yona Itzhak also saw what happened to my mother's sister and her husband. They had been hiding for a few days, only to be discovered later. They were undressed and dragged naked through the whole village, forced to dig their own grave, dance around it, and finally were shot. They were the only ones to be executed by a firearm. Later they found some more hidden Jews. They took them to the Christian cemetery, made them dig their own graves, and then killed them.

I refused to believe that all the Jews I knew were murdered in Milie, my "paradise," which had now vanished forever.

We had been sitting on a series of time bombs all along, only they didn't go all off at once. With every passing day one of them would explode—some tragedy or another, usually close by, but not directly in our midst—until one day we experienced the devastation of zero impact.

For our own security, we stayed secluded in the apartment. One morning Papa decided to venture out for an hour or so in search of some news. The hours ticked away slowly, and soon it was afternoon but no sign of Papa. We began to worry. When by evening he failed to return, we became jittery. We refused to believe he might have ended up in one of the round-ups, but suspicion plagued us, and we were inconsolable. Fearing the worst, I cried for hours despite Mama's attempts to comfort me.

When we found out the next day that Papa was among the thousands of Jews who had been caught in a police round-up (*razzia*) and thrown into the dungeons, we were devastated. The women were searched for valuables and sent home, but the men were detained. After a few dismal days, we were allowed to visit him and bring him food and water. There he was, behind bars, thrown together with hundreds of other Jewish men. The face of my poor Papa, unshaven and dirty, with deep-sunken eyes, expressed desperate fear. To see him this way broke my heart. He could hardly eat the bread we brought for him.

"What crime had he committed?" I asked myself. "Why him? Why did they punish my honest, gentle, father?"

I wanted to scream for justice, to plead for his innocence, but I had been warned not to open my mouth, for fear that we might all be punished. "Why? Why?" I demanded of my mother.

"Because he is a Jew," was her only reply. I looked at her in amazement, trying to understand, but in the end I simply couldn't.

Five days later, to our relief, we were told that all the men would be released, provided that a collective ransom of forty or fifty dollars per person was paid. Our community leaders quickly collected the needed money or the equivalent of such in jewelry to pay the Romanians. Indeed soon after the deal was completed, they released the prisoners. And so gold, dollars and jewelry eventually bought people's freedom.

But our joy over Papa's release was short lived. The next morning, the police took my brother for forced labor. Miraculously, he was released a few days later, but from that moment on we hid him in the vacant apartment of our landlady, who had left the keys with my mother before going to America.

Keeping Bubi hidden was exasperating. We secretly supplied him with food and water as if he were a jailed criminal. The intense fear for his life and the precarious circumstances under which we now lived made me wish we had never been born Jews.

I overheard snatches of conversation about more murders in the streets, about labor camps for young men, and about a possible relocation to Ukraine for the entire Jewish population of Bukovina and Bessarabia. One positive rumor was that, once relocated, Jews would be given a piece of land to cultivate. That was the one I liked. Another rumor, which I tried to turn a deaf ear to, was that we would all be deported and killed.

October 11, 1941. The governor of Bukovina decreed the formation of a ghetto just a few blocks away from our street. Within twenty-four hours, fifty thousand people were sent to the ghetto, evicted from their homes with only what they could carry in their hands and on their backs. The entire area was surrounded by barbed wire, and armed soldiers guarded the gates day and night. One would have to visualize a perimeter that could hold ten thousand people now housing fifty thousand in addition to the Christian population that lived there.

It was my parents' formidable task to find a place to settle in the overcrowded dwellings where up to fifty persons shared one room. Those who couldn't find accommodations had to sleep in attics, cellars, and, in extreme cases, in open courtyards.

After an exhaustive search, we found a place in a dwelling without proper hygienic conditions. We had to share a room with three other families. Access to food was almost impossible. The ghetto was not just to be a place we were forced to live in inhumane and desperate conditions; it also served as a transfer camp from which thousands were banished daily to Ukraine.

Miraculously, sometime later, the authorities either enlarged or dismantled the ghetto, enabling us to return to our apartment into which we now took in other families. For a while we enjoyed an almost normal life.

In the interim thirty thousand Jews from Czernowitz were deported before an order to stop the transports was issued. I learned many years later how things actually developed.

The most important role in the enormous effort to change the tragic course of events, was played by the mayor of Czernowitz, Dr. Traian Popovici, one of the few righteous Romanians who had the courage to speak out against evil.

Popovici, in a desperate appeal, begged Corneliu Calotescu, governor of Bukovina, to dissolve the ghetto and stop the deportations, warning him about the paralysis the city would experience if professionals and those dedicated to culture and the arts were deported. After his intervention, and that of many Jewish and Romanian personalities, as well as clergy of various denominations on a national level, Ion Antonescu, Romania's dictator, exempted about twenty thousand Czernowitz Jews from deportation. Upon this order, the governor authorized the mayor, the German consul, and General Ionescu to proceed with the screening of who would stay and who would be deported, but reserved for himself the right to sign whatever authorizations would be made.

Popovici personally signed four thousand of those authorizations for highly skilled Jews to remain in the city; thus they were called "The Traian Jews." Upon receiving the good news, Dr. Popovici came personally to the ghetto to bring a ray of hope to the despondent people.

The screening committee called upon the leaders of the Jewish congregation to prepare the lists. The desperate efforts to be included bred bribery and corruption; thus money became a more decisive factor than justice.

It was the privilege of the rich to buy themselves freedom. Thousands of people, including our close relatives, bribed corrupt Romanian officials. At least the Romanian *baksheesh* or bribery system offered a lifesaving alternative, something that was inconceivable in Germany. Aunt Anna, and others like her who were widows of government employees were exempt by law.

Now the hunt for Jews without authorizations began. Every day Romanian soldiers raided another street, herded the Jews into columns, and chased them toward the railroad station, looting all they could from the abandoned homes.

Although I had lost the sense of childhood security, I still saw a glimmer of good in all this upheaval. Considering any sort of trip as an adventure, I kept telling myself that it would be just another train ride to the country in the company of my friends. I tried and, sometimes, succeeded in completely blocking out all the adult preoccupations with hiding, escaping, and bribing to avoid deportation.

Unfortunately, we did not make Traian's List. My father was not deemed indispensable, nor did we have money to bribe, and that prompted fierce debates with our relatives. I remember my mother's ever-defiant words: "They're playing tricks in order to take our money, but in the end they won't deport anybody."

She did not believe that they would actually do anything so atrocious. Our relatives tried to convince her to sell the Persian rugs Uncle Sammy had left with us and buy a certificate of exemption, but Mama categorically refused. "These carpets were entrusted to us and we have an obligation to keep them until they return," was her reply. No argument could convince her that our lives were in danger and that, should Sammy ever return, he would understand why we did what we did.

The other argument was about asking Uncle Max for help. The Zloczowers were wealthy and could easily afford to buy us a certificate. I remember how Mama pressured Papa to go and ask for the money, but he was reluctant; he was too proud. However, when the first deportations started, the danger became real, despair crushed his pride, and he did indeed ask. We anxiously waited for him to return with the good news. Some time later Papa walked in with an expression on his face that said it all. We were stunned. My parents never forgave Max. The bitterness and resentment at being let down in a matter of life or death was the subject of conversation for days afterward.

In view of the imminent deportation, we began to transfer all our household goods to the Zloczowers who lived a block away from us. Ironically the Persian carpets ended up in their house, instead of saving us. We remained in our apartment with everything packed into knapsacks and bundles: one per person in accordance with the orders. Because I was small, mine was also a smaller knapsack Mama had sewn from an old brown dress of hers. When it became obvious that we could be deported any moment, the Zloczowers started to feel pangs of conscience and came running to our place with a plan to hide us in a cellar apartment once occupied by their housekeeper. We obliged and stayed there for a few anxious minutes, but Bubi and I, afraid of being discovered, pressured my parents into returning to our apartment to await our fate.

The total chaos and the panic surrounding me, as well as the fear of the unknown, threatened to destroy the last brick of my childhood fortress. From then on, like an avalanche, my family's misfortunes started downhill.

Deportation

CHAPTER 3

November 1941. Zero hour struck!

That morning it was *our* door the soldiers pounded on, cursing and shouting obscenities. They ordered us out of the apartment onto the street. With knapsacks hoisted on our backs and some luggage in our hands, we left our home forever.

Terror-stricken, I silently watched the pandemonium in the once peaceful, familiar streets of my childhood. There was merciless shoving, people swarming, panicking and shouting, as horses neighed and reared.

Before we knew it, we were engulfed in this chaotic exilement: humans of all ages and walks of life, women carrying wailing babies in their arms, sick people aided by children, the elderly crouched low, their backs bent by the weight of knapsacks. Others struggled with heavy bundles. Some even pushed wheelbarrows with valuables and trinkets stuffed inside bedding weighted down by bundles of clothes hastily bound with crude ropes. For a fee, a few horse-driven carts would ferry luggage and passengers through that sea of anguished souls.

My parents placed me atop such a cart full of luggage. From there I could look onto the immense caravan, which, I would later learn, contained some two thousand people. And as I heard the cries of women and babies and loud shouts of *Shemah Israel* (Hear, O Israel), a Jewish prayer chanted in the most dire circumstances, I suddenly began to realize what was happening. To me it looked like a grotesque funeral cortege . . . our own. There were heartbreaking scenes of parting families, cries that reached a tormenting pitch, and a wailing moan like that of a captured animal.

Amid this anguish and confusion, a thought crossed my mind: How could either of our Romanian or German friends and neighbors turn their backs on us? Some were even collaborating with the Fascists! (I did not know at that age that many had not supported the system, did not collaborate, and that some actually endangered their lives and positions by helping Jews to hide or to escape.)

The soldiers led the caravan to a railroad, different from the familiar main station. On the tracks a long train of about thirty cattle cars with open doors stood ready. The surrounding area overflowed with bayonet-wielding police and soldiers shouting derisively, "A year ago you welcomed the Russians! For this treachery, Transnistria will be your reward!"

At first I could not believe that these cars were intended for us. But there was no time to think as the soldiers incessantly screamed orders at us to get aboard.

So *this* was my dream train ride, turned into a nightmare.

We climbed aboard, and filled one car: ten, twenty, thirty . . . and more and more until there was no more room. It was so crowded we felt as though we would suffocate. There must have been close to eighty people packed like animals in a cage. I held on to Papa's hand in complete silence. I wanted to cry and say something, but fear devoured my speech.

As the doors were about to close, everybody pushed and shoved toward the opening, hoping for the last opportunity to wave good-bye to a loved one. Many people with permits to stay, or those whose streets had not yet been raided, came to the station to see the departure of their loved ones. Soldiers kept them at a distance from the train.

I took a last glance at what used to be my cherished Czernowitz, and in doing so I suddenly spotted a familiar face among the waving, grieving crowd. It was Uncle Max! How amazing! He stood alone, waving to us. We were dumbfounded, but Mama immediately offered this explanation: "He's remorseful for not having helped us to buy a certificate, so he came to show us his concern."

After a few shrill whistles, the soldiers struggled to slide the heavy, wooden door shut and bolt it from the outside. We were trapped like animals. I thought it was our end.

Too late, Uncle Max.

We tried to accommodate ourselves the best we could in the overcrowded space. Most sat on the floor leaning against their bundles, while others remained standing, glued to the locked doors, perhaps hoping to escape should they open again. But it did not happen. Instead there was a familiar whistle, the smell of engine smoke, and the screech of metal against metal as the train lurched ahead toward the unknown.

With the first jolt, all hell broke loose. People prayed, cursed, cried, moaned, and clung to each other for support. Worst of all were the cries of the children.

I asked God, "Why the children? Why us? Why me?" I believed in God and had been brought up in a home steeped in religion. I believed in the goodness of men, in beauty, in friends, in freedom. What could possibly have caused such a change that turned my childhood world of simple joys and sorrows irrevocably upside down?

The car had a small vent for air, adequate for a few cows but not for eighty human beings. That we didn't suffocate was a miracle. It was dark inside during the day and pitch black at night; as the train rolled on, we lost track of time. Day and night blurred into one bleak endless ride.

We tried to sleep sitting up and leaning on each other, but I could not find a comfortable position to sleep and the longer I stayed awake, the fiercer my stomach churned from hunger. We still had a tiny reserve of dry food and a small quantity of water for a few days, barely enough to keep us alive. But eating and drinking even this minimal amount created another problem; being able to go to the toilet became really critical. After a while, even my personal necessities became a matter of urgency. We held back as much as was humanly possible. But children and old people soon began to succumb. Under this duress, people became very inventive. Some had brought potties, while others used regular pots or cups to collect their waste. The rest used a common pail. To provide privacy, family members held up blankets and sheets as screens. Unable to dispose of the overflowing receptacles, we had, for the duration of the trip, to contend with our own excrement and its unbearable stench.

After about two days, the train stopped. We heard the soldiers unbolting the door and finally opening it. It was a fearsome night, somewhere in the fields of Bessarabia, yet a glorious moment of respite from suffocation and stench.

When the escorts allowed us to get out, everybody rushed to inhale some fresh, cold air, to take care of bodily functions, and to empty the accumulated waste of the previous day. What a relief it was to be allowed to do that in the fields or behind bushes! Notwithstanding the total lack of privacy, people opened undergarments in front of one another, dropped trousers, and pulled up dresses.

From then on the concept of privacy was a luxury none of us—rich or poor—could afford. We were like animals doing whatever was necessary for survival.

Soon, the soldiers ordered us back into our human cages and bolted the door again. Leaning against one another, hungry, dirty, and tired, we were to endure this torment for two more days and two more nights.

I desperately tried to get some sleep, to dream of some salvation at the end of this unimaginable journey, but the anguish, the extreme discomfort, the paralyzing hunger, and the stench of human excrement was just unbearable. So throughout the journey, sleep eluded me.

On the fourth day, the train stopped. The soldiers unbolted the doors, shouting, "Out, out, you dirty kikes!"

Starving, exhausted, and filthy, we could barely stand on our feet. They ordered us to form a column and marched us through deep mud into the Bessarabian town of Marculeshti, about 150 miles southeast of Czernowitz. We found out later that on the night they had let us out, they separated the train into two sections. The other fifteen cars, with more than a thousand people, were taken to Ataki, then to Moghilev, a town on the Dniester River and north from our location. We also heard that some of the elderly and babies who died during the trip were thrown out into the fields like discarded rags.

There were now only about a thousand of us left.

The soldiers mercilessly marched us on in a cold and pitiless rain, through ankle-deep mud that made it difficult to walk burdened as we were with bundles. Approaching the edge of town, we heard a sudden chorus of screams coming from the head of the column. We could not see what it was all about. Not until we entered the camp of Marculeshti did we hear the gruesome explanation.

Some people stumbled upon a ditch full of bodies: men, women, and children stacked on top of each other. According to rumors, these were the massacred Jewish residents of that little town. More than one thousand were shot and partially buried in mass ditches.

We noticed freshly dug mass graves near some of the homes. There wasn't a living soul within reach or sight. I was overcome with an eerie, foreboding feeling. We were herded into a camp of tiny, primitive houses that the local Jews used to inhabit. The windows and doors were missing, probably taken for firewood in the general looting by villagers who wanted to keep their stoves burning. The Marculeshti camp served as a clearing center from whence Jews were sent to various "points of transfer" to Transnistria.

We were mystified by the white crosses painted on every second or third home. Someone explained it was a warning that there had been typhus in these houses. More than likely, it was a sign indicating the execution of its inhabitants. But whatever the reason, spending the night outdoors in the icy rain was not an inviting alternative. We preferred at least to have a roof and walls to protect us. Along with our neighbors, the Korns, we dared to enter one of the marked houses, and in the numbing cold we spent our first night in exile.

The next morning we heard that we would be sent farther away and would have to go through a checkpoint.

I remember how Freddy, the eldest of the two Korn sons, came back one day to tell us how, hiding in a tree, he was able to see what was going on at the checkpoint. The soldiers were routinely confiscating everything of value as the column came through.

In the first few months before the deportations, people found ways to hide jewelry, gold coins, and money by sewing them into the hems of clothes or into the bottoms of knapsacks. That was fine for small items, but larger ones like silverware were just packed normally in suitcases or bundles of bedding. A few days later as we were driven toward the checkpoint, we saw many proud people throw their valuables into the mud rather than give them to the greedy Romanians who took away not only our few remaining valuables but also destroyed our documents of identity. Perhaps that was their way of wiping out all trace of us forever. Up to this point, my brother had clutched his violin case in ardent hopes of eventually playing his music again, somehow, somewhere. As we passed the checkpoint, the inspectors overlooked it, or thought nothing of the violin, to our great relief. A few minutes into the march, however, one of the escorting soldiers noticed the violin and kicked it out of Bubi's hand with his filthy boots.

"Dirty kike, your yearning to play the violin will soon disappear!" he shouted.

Bubi recoiled in fear as he helplessly watched his cherished instrument defiled by ugly mud. The expression of humiliation on his face cut me deeply. I was choking with tears and I felt like screaming, but I had already learned to keep quiet and to hold back my tears for fear of being beaten or shot. Instead I looked at my parents, and all I saw was deep pain etched into their faces. I guessed their thoughts: Here was their gifted son who would have contributed to the culture of the world, forced to watch as his violin was brutally wrenched out of his life.

Papa was only fifty-five, but he was suffering from a double hernia and could not walk far. From the small reserves of money my parents had hidden, they paid for the privilege of having my father and me mount one of the luggage carts, on which only small children, the old, and the infirm were allowed. To our escorting soldier Papa looked too young for such pampered treatment, so a short way into our journey he stopped our cart, hurling insults at Papa and ordering him to get off.

"What's the matter? You too lazy to walk? Get off, you dirty kike or I'll kill you!" Papa begged for understanding. "Please, Mr. Gendarme, I am old and sick, I can't walk much."

That infuriated the Romanian Nazi even more. That he did not shoot him was a miracle; instead he swung the bayonet of his rifle and hit Papa viciously over the head. The blow sent Papa tumbling down from the cart, screaming in pain and bleeding from his temple. Everything happened very quickly. His spectacles were whisked off his face, and as people trudged across the area his glasses were soon buried in the mud. Without them Papa was almost blind.

The pain and degradation inflicted on my father had me trembling with rage. In tears I climbed down from the cart and rushed to Papa's side. I looked wild-eyed at my fallen hero twisting in agony and humiliation—my pillar of strength destroyed before my eyes. Mama and Bubi appeared, and the three of us helped him to his feet.

Without thinking of the consequences, and still hoping for a human streak of kindness in this hardened soldier, I supplicated in tears, "Please, please, let my sick father ride on the cart, and I will walk instead."

"Shut up, you dirty seed of kikes. Get back on the cart or I'll kill you," he said, and drove the barrel of his rifle into my shoulder.

Defenseless, and in severe pain, I succumbed to watching Papa gather his last ounce of strength and join the rest of the column in line with Mama and Bubi.

Crying silently I climbed up on the cart and kept turning my head continuously to see my family. Through tears and anger, I kept a watchful eye on them as they tried desperately to keep pace with the convoy. How Papa did it I will never know. I prayed that none of them would remain behind, convinced that I possessed a power to shield my loved ones as long as I kept my eyes fixed on them.

At the same time I felt guilty for riding while they had to walk under severe duress. The primitive dirt roads were extremely muddy following a catastrophic flood of the Dniester in the summer of 1941. To make things worse, the heavy fall rains and the unusually early winter had made the mud so deep and sticky that walking tested everyone's endurance.

Originally there were supposed to be enough carts for everybody, but in reality only a few were provided. In these conditions, many elderly, the sick, and the young fell behind to be either killed or abandoned forever. Heartbroken family members had to tear themselves away from loved ones, to abandon them helplessly.

Under a barrage of humiliations and insults, this human caravan of all ages braved the mud, the hunger, the thirst and the fear. The people trudged like shadows, with bowed heads and pain-distorted faces, behind the overloaded carts under the gray, unfriendly skies of that November day.

Leading and surrounding us were strong, well-fed, and well-armed Romanian Fascist soldiers and commanders. Driving the carts were insensitive Ukrainian or Romanian peasants in their native attire of sheep-fleece jackets and hats, totally oblivious to the tragedy, behaving as if they were doing a regular job transporting cattle or other products to market. Rain pelted us for hours and hours on end, making an already impossible task even more difficult. Still believing in God's power to control nature, I was convinced that he had completely abandoned us, his "chosen" people.

Toward evening, battling that terrible downpour, we finally approached a forest in the vicinity of the town of Cosautzi. "Stop! Stop! Stop the horses! Everybody down from the carts!" the soldiers barked.

The coachmen pulled back the reins and immediately took care of their horses, feeding and watering them. I could not understand why beasts were taken care of while no one offered us even a sip of water.

Before I could give this much further thought, a voice boomed at us, "Everybody enter the forest! Don't attempt to escape or you will be shot!" As soon as I descended from the cart, my family came to look for me so that we could spend the night together in the forest.

We were so tired, hungry, thirsty, and demoralized that even the dark, wet forest seemed like a promising comfort. All the people who had walked the whole day yearned for rest and for something to drink.

"Water! Water! Water!" was a ubiquitous, hoarse plea whispered or shouted from everyone's lips. "Water!"

That precious, vital liquid, which we had always taken so much for granted, now became our primary focus of attention. Survival depended on it more than on food, so it was only natural that many people ventured out to find it, especially for their children or for the sick.

At night in an unfamiliar forest, they did not know exactly when they were off limits and ran into guards who shot them without warning, taking them for escapees. There were a few courageous or desperate people who indeed tried to escape, only to be shot as well.

Making that night even more uneasy were the rumors that we would be abandoned in that forest or even executed that very night. The constant sounds of gunshots convinced us that some executions were already taking place. Regardless, we uneasily prepared for our long-awaited and needed rest.

Ingeniously, people pulled out sheets, coats, and other large items and tied them between trees like tents, transforming the forest for one night into an overcrowded, bizarre gypsy camp. But the makeshift roofs barely kept out the rain. Many, including us, had neither the physical strength nor the items to create such roofs. We huddled together for the night under a huge tree with a thick and wide crown.

We did hear shooting, but from our location we couldn't see what went on. The natural rustling of the forest was drowned out by screams, shots, snores, moans, and cries that turned the night into one of ghostly horror. Who could sleep? I was paralyzed with fear, unable to comprehend the chaos around me. I suspected that people were really killed that night, but my parents wanted to shield me from the truth.

It was dawn when we heard the voices of the commanders. "Up! Up! Get out on the road!"

As we took up our positions in the column and started the march, new rumors began to circulate regarding our fate: we would be shot near the Dniester River toward which we were being driven and our bodies thrown into its waters, or they might throw us alive into the water and let us drown.

These rumors were by no means a product of the imaginations of terror-stricken people. They were based on firsthand information by some in our midst who had managed to escape previous transports but had been caught and re-deported. Having witnessed all kinds of atrocities, they were a great source of information. Someone even saw the execution of Mama's brother Moishe and told her about it in detail.

Moishe Katz was a charming, handsome man, a natural leader, who easily befriended the Romanian commanders of his transport. When the deportees from Bessarabia had reached the Dniester River, an order to shoot them and let them drown was issued. At the last minute, one of the commanders approached Uncle Moishe with a generous offer: In return for a huge sum of money he would be willing to let the Jews cross the river alive.

Hastily Uncle Moishe collected the requested amount and handed it to the commander. This sadist commanded the column to start crossing the bridge, two by two, and as soon as the procession began, he ordered the soldiers to start shooting with machine guns. The first bullet was fired at my uncle, who like the rest of the victims fell into the river and drowned. This monstrous information left us all stunned, but it absolutely devastated my poor mother.

Our convoy continued on its route for many hours, since the leaders enjoyed taking us on detours to exhaust and further demoralize us. Those in charge were given complete jurisdiction over us and our lives, and they took every opportunity to act out their most sadistic fantasies.

They enjoyed cursing and bombarding us with sarcastic remarks like "So, you received the Russians last year with flowers, eh? Our people will really roll out the red carpet for you on the other side of the Dniester." "Do you miss Stalin very much? You'll meet him soon on the other side of the river, but as corpses, with your heads cut off," the commander said, his voice dripping vitriol.

We started speculating and asking each other, "Will they shoot us? Will they allow us to cross alive?"

It must have been late afternoon when from a distance we spotted the river, the natural border between Romania and Ukraine. Now it was our turn.

As we reached the dreaded Dniester, the march came to a halt. We were made to descend from the carts and form a column of two to a line. Ahead was a venerable old bridge, which creaked and swayed whenever a cart crossed over. All of us had to hand-carry our luggage to ease the load on the old bridge. But that was a silver lining for us: What a relief to discover that at least we would be allowed to cross over alive!

The carts crossed first and behind them a column of people dragging their bundles. I joined my family on foot and we put the luggage back on the cart with me on top. We were now in Nazi-occupied Ukraine.

The road was muddy and partially covered with snow. I continued to keep my eyes fixed on my family with such intense fear of being separated that little by little I felt swept away, as if into another body and another mind.

After we reloaded the carts, the convoy advanced slowly, passing through vast, endless sugar beet fields. As far as the eye could see there was snow and sugar beets, nothing else. We had never before seen such an enormous extension of land with only one crop growing on it; it was the Communists' system of collective farming, called a *kolkhoz*.

At the sight of the beets, we broke ranks and rushed into the fields to gather them. We were so ecstatic to be able to wet our lips and fill our empty stomachs with the sweet, raw beets that we did not think of the consequences. For the next few days, we survived on those beets, our only source of nourishment, which soon became the source of stomach-aches and diarrhea.

As we advanced, a strange phenomenon caught my attention: At irregular distances, snow-covered fallen tree trunks resembling human figures lined both sides of the road. Perplexed, I tried to figure out their origin and purpose, but the view from the cart was not good. While I could clearly see that they all had human heads, the trunks certainly were not those of human bodies; they were huge in proportion. My imagination told me that they might be some road markers specific to that region, or perhaps some tree logs ready for transport. I asked the old people sitting on my cart for an explanation, which they at first hesitated to give. My insistence finally forced them to offer the shocking truth: They were bloated human bodies, frozen stiff, corpses from previous transports, people who had been unable to keep up with the strenuous march and remained on the road forever.

The sight of these corpses did more than shock me. It petrified me, because I had always had a dreadful fear of death and dying. The mere thought of cadavers used to send shivers through my body. I had always averted my eyes from funeral processions and shunned all that dealt with dying. Now there was no way I could avoid this macabre scene.

Finally, we reached the outskirts of the first Ukrainian town, called Yampol. There in an abandoned kolkhoz with its few houses and barns, our persecutors allowed us to rest for a few days. The crowd dispersed quickly, and by the time we reached the first barn it was already full of new arrivals in addition to leftover corpses from previous transports.

We somehow succeeded in finding a crowded room to bed down, and quickly claimed a vacant crib. Although we had to share the room with several families, we were grateful to have a roof over our heads again, and to give our exhausted bodies a break. We slept on the crib in a sitting position, appreciative of that minimal comfort. Our major outcry continued to be for food and water.

Having seen the corpses on the road from a distance was bad enough, but coming face to face with piles of them was unbearable. They were everywhere: in the barns, in the cellars, and inside the houses. Inevitably the dead became an integral part of our environment. There was nowhere I could avert my eyes from them. They were abandoned like animals, without the minimal benefit of someone's closing their glassy eyes, eyes that seemed to beg for eternal peace.

Though we were living intimately with the dead, we were still alive and desperately needed food and water. Out of dire necessity, we devised all kinds of schemes, including a unique barter system by which we offered our belongings to the peasants in exchange for food. A shirt might be swapped for an onion, a coat for a loaf of bread, and so on. Naturally the people with more and better goods, more jewelry, or other possessions made better deals. That in turn gave them a better chance for survival. Those were harsh lessons in the facts of life.

This barter system became standard practice, and in the following years my perception of value was entirely fixated on the amount of food one could get for a piece of clothing. I soon learned how useful it was to have gold coins or jewelry to carry on one's person in case of emergency. These had saved many lives. That experience left me with the conviction that I should never acquire anything of value I could not put in my pocket and run with in case of emergency.

Another lesson had to do with common hygiene. It was just another event that made me ponder on the question of how quickly we had been reduced to the level of animals.

I had heard of but had previously never seen lice. But here I had been scratching myself for days before I discovered what these live, six-legged, bloodsucking creatures were. My mother became hysterical when she made the discovery. She showed me the tiny bubbles adhering to the seams of her dress, explaining the metamorphosis of the parasite. "These nits develop into live lice that suck blood from our bodies and infest us with disease," she explained, while squashing them between her thumbnails. Disgusting!

We had gone many days without washing or changing clothes, so everybody was scratching itchy scalps and bodies, busily delousing themselves. It was a tragi-comic scenario which resembled grooming monkeys at a zoo. By the time we reached Yampol, there was already a full-fledged infestation.

To prevent an epidemic, someone advised cutting the women's hair short. Ironically, this newest adversity would at last free me of my long braids and fulfill my everlasting dream of short hair. A child is a child even under duress, and so I derived joy from a small thing like wearing my blond curly hair in a style I had always yearned for.

Snip, snip, snip went the scissors and down fell my detested braids. This time Mama did not object; she had no more rules to enforce. Sadly, I couldn't admire myself as there were no mirrors, nor could I be admired by my friends because they were not there either.

My happiness lasted exactly two days. Then more bad news arrived: We would have to shave our heads completely in order to stop the lice infestation. A barber who shared the room with us carried out the procedure with a little machine. I watched in dismay as my lovely hair cascaded to the dirt floor, leaving me with a feeling of nakedness and shame.

It was not only the vanished dream of looking pretty and feminine that hit me, but the fact that I no longer looked like a girl. I was robbed of my identity and humiliated. My only consolation was that even bigger girls had to suffer the same indignity, and whether man or woman, once our heads were shaved, we all looked alike in a strange, grotesque way.

This humiliation reduced me to just another face in the crowd. The lack of hair imprinted on me a terrible self-image, so I covered my bald head with a woolen hat.

Despite the shaved heads, the lice did not vanish. On the contrary, they laid eggs in our filthy clothes and continued to multiply. They thrived by sucking the blood from our dirty, emaciated bodies. As a result, many people started to fall victim to typhus.

Worst of all were the unbearable hunger and the thirst. Their intensity often dulled our minds. To fetch water from a well was a dangerous venture. Only the fit and courageous dared to slip behind the fences. The lucky ones came back; the others were caught and killed on the spot.

After a few days we were ordered to resume our march toward another unknown destination. The only change was the addition of Ukrainian Fascist collaborators, who did their best not only to supervise but to humiliate us even further, a task they relished with sinister efficiency. Robbing, torturing, killing, and even selling some people to peasants was their greatest pleasure. The peasants who bought the unfortunate victims executed them just to get their clothes.

And so, with new escorts, the same configuration of carts loaded with luggage and people, the same walking column of human beings tramping in the muddy roads, the march continued. Again, we were exposed to the same landscape of bloated corpses, adorning both sides of the road.

The heartless guards made us walk approximately eighteen miles a day without food or water. All they allowed us was one three-hour rest stop. Only at night would they let us have an extended break, usually in another abandoned barn which we had to share with corpses. A small concession was made, though: whoever wanted and could afford to bribe the escorts was allowed to stay overnight at a peasant's house in the village. Appalled by the prospect of sleeping on dirty hay in another stinking barn, Mama opted for the former.

This concession was made only under the condition that one member of the family stay in the barn under surveillance to ensure the return of the rest. Papa volunteered to stay with the luggage so that the three of us could find lodging for the night. My mother was the brave and daring leader—she was a fighter. Papa, on the other hand, had completely given up.

On that freezing November night, we set out into the tiny village eager to find warm accommodations. We knocked on the doors of every lighted house begging the owners to let us in. Some already had lodgers, others did not respond. We finally found one kind family who would put us up for the night in their only room in exchange for some clothes.

My eyes filled with tears at the familiar sight of a humble peasant home and at the scent of wood burning in the whitewashed mud stove, on the warm extension of which we were allowed to sleep. Their seeming normalcy of life amidst our wrecked and dangerous one was like an oasis in the middle of a desert. They gave us a hot meal which we devoured like hungry dogs. Slowly I felt the warmth penetrating my frozen body, and the coziness made me soon fall into the sleep of a saint. For one night I forgot the enormity of our sufferings.

Early the next morning we went back to the barn, where we found Papa shaking and pale as a ghost. He told us how a Ukrainian militiamen had walked about for hours, looking around, observing every movement of those who were sleeping. He was probably searching for a victim who did not present a challenge; hence he chose my father, shoving his loaded rifle toward his chest, saying, "I have a strong desire to shoot someone tonight!" Papa begged him for mercy and offered him one of our knapsacks full of clothes as a bribe. "That's not enough! Give me some money too!" the man countered. In despair Papa gave him some money he had hidden, and only then did the militiaman leave him alone. We were so shaken and felt such pity for poor Papa that we totally ignored the material loss which would have helped us buy more food or shelter. We were just happy that Papa's life had been spared.

The next morning our trudge continued. Leaving behind us the village of Kachikovka, we wondered how far the next night stop would be. Except for the first and last village, we stayed in stinking, freezing, dark, and overcrowded barns with no food or water and witnessed the ongoing drama of separating families. A wheezing grandparent had to be torn from his bawling grandchild; couples, parents, siblings, and children had to leave behind loved ones who were too sick and weak to continue the march, destined to die in the stables or on the road.

We arrived at a barn in Balanovka where, amid the corpses left behind from the previous transport, we found many withered, old Jews still alive. Their eyes were expressionless and glossy. I thought they were dead until I heard them whisper, "Water! Water!" But we could do nothing for them.

Words of wisdom continued spreading through our ranks. The latest was watching out for anyone sleeping too long. It was feared that most people would freeze to death in their sleep. Therefore, it became a habit not to let anyone sleep for more than two or three hours. For whatever reason, I decided one night to test my mother's alertness by pretending to be asleep. But she was watching me and after a few hours shook me to make sure I was not dead. That was reassuring.

Worn out by hunger, thirst, and the constant forced marches, we still managed to reach the last abandoned Soviet kolkhoz, Balanovka, where we again found shelter for the night at a peasant's home. Only this time it was my brother's turn to stay with the luggage as a warrant of our return. When we came back in the morning, we found him in a state of panic. Tearful and with a tremulous voice, he related an almost identical incident to my father's in which a Ukrainian militiaman had ripped his knapsack from his shoulders and run away.

We passed through as many as ten villages in total, all offering us the same scenario of misery. I would not have remembered their names were it not for my brother's notes. I am still mystified by the fact that he had carried in his pocket a photo depicting him as a baby lying on some furry blanket. Nobody thought of taking along any photos or safeguarding the family album. Probably for lack of paper, Bubi scribbled the names of all the villages we passed through on the back of that photo: Yampol, Kachikovka, Olashanka, Romanovka, Krizhopol, Zhabokritch, Tsibulovka, Obodovka, Lobodovka, and Balanovka.

Little by little our assets dwindled and so did our caravan. Approximately two weeks from the time we left Czernowitz, we approached a town by the name of—Bershad.

Hell

CHAPTER 4

*No fear can stand up to
  hunger,
no patience can wear it out,
disgust simply does not exist
where hunger is;
and as to superstition, beliefs,
  and
what you may call principles,
they are less than chaff in a
  breeze.*
JOSEPH CONRAD

Our noticeably thinning column barely dragged itself along toward Bershad, where we hoped to find some relief from our continuous wanderings. But Bershad was not to be our last stop. We would have to walk for another forty kilometers, then cross the Bug River to be delivered to the German S.S. By that time everybody knew that the other side of the Bug was synonymous with death. However, we heard that a bribe to the Romanian commander would make it possible for us to stay. Apparently, the requested bribe, in the form of jewelry and cash, was collected from within our group, so that we were allowed to stay.

On successful completion of the transaction, the exhausted, emaciated people were herded into a perimeter surrounded by barbed wire. This was the Bershad ghetto-camp. A primitive place partially in ruins, yet it had some normalcy to it compared to all the other places we had passed through.

To describe Bershad in detail is difficult. My recollection of the place is vague, as hunger had dulled my senses. I was too sick to roam around and see for myself, but I was told that it was a small area where the local Jews had lived before the war. The camp consisted of approximately twelve narrow, unpaved streets, two wider main streets, and a few hundred tiny, low, clay houses. Within this perimeter some twenty thousand people had to find room—often just enough space to sit on the floor.

I began to think: "Was this the 'promised land'? Was that what the Fascists had in mind for us when they told us there would be land for us to resettle and colonize?"

Bershad was the largest and the most infamous of the hundred-plus Transnistrian camps. It soon became notorious for the worst conditions, for the greatest number of victims, and for having had, in the beginning, the most sadistic administrator, Florin Ghineraru. The Romanian Fascist government had also earmarked it as a site for mass murders.

Many thousands had already been executed when, in the fall, a change of heart had taken place and the mass executions had been halted. What we learned later was that after this change of policy, no new scheme had been devised to provide housing or other accommodations for the tens of thousands who would later arrive. These new deportees were instead to be abandoned without any means of sustenance, so that they would perish on their own. Some of the local Jews had fled with the Soviets before the town fell to the Nazis, but of those who stayed a great number were murdered, leaving only a few families who would escape the massacre. These Jews were allowed to stay in their homes inside the ghetto. But the majority of the Jewish homes were abandoned and in ruins as a result of bombing and shelling.

Normally a ghetto is a part of a town in which members of a minority group live but have free access to the outside. But the ghettos created by the Nazis in Transnistria, Poland, and Lithuania became concentration camps. The only difference was that instead of barracks people were forced to stay in overcrowded existing dwellings. We were imprisoned, surrounded, and watched over without even the minimal provision of food and water. It was hoped that we deportees would expire slowly and quietly, but nonetheless that did not prevent our jailers/persecutors from going on sporadic killing sprees, depending on who was in command at the time.

By the time we arrived, a bitter, oppressive winter had succeeded the

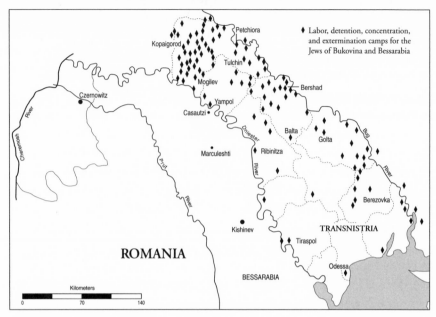

Transnistrian camps under Romanian administration, 1941–1944, with a list of camps in Transnistria. Adapted from Dora Litani, Transnistria *(Tel Aviv, 1981).*

Concentration Camps in Transnistria for the Jews of Bukovina and Bessarabia, 1941–44

Akmitchetka
Alexandrovka
Ananiev
Arva
Balanovka
Balki
Balta
Bar
Bershad
Birzula
Bogdanovka
Bondarovka
Brailov
Britovka
Bucov
Budi
Capusterna
Capustiani
Cariera de Piatra
Cariskov
Carlovka
Cazachiovka

Chernevtz
Chetvartinovka
Chianovka
Chichelnik
Chiorna
Chirnasovka
Clocotma
Codima
Conotcautzi
Crasnoye
Crivoie-Ozero
Crizhopol
Cucavka
Cuzmintz
Derebcin
Dimidovka
Djurin
Domanovka
Dubasari
Frunza
Golta
Gorai
Grabivtz
Grosolovo
Haltchintzi
Hrinovka
Israilovka
Ivashkauta
Kopaigorod
Ladizhin

Lohova
Lozova
Lutchinetz
Lutchinik
Malo-Kiriuka
Manikovka
Marinovka
Mishkovka
Moghilev
Moloknia
Mostovoi
Murafa
Nesterovka
Nikolayevka
Nimratz
Obodovka
Odessa
Olgopol
Olianitza
Ostia
Ozarinetz
Pankovka
Pasiuka
Pavlovka
Pechiora
Popivitz
Raschstadt
Ribnitza
Savrani
Shargorod

Skazhinetz
Slidi
Slivina
Stanislovtschek
Stefanka
Suha-Balka
Sumilova
Tatarovka
Tiraspol
Tivrin
Tridubi
Trihat
Tropava
Trostinetz
Tulchin
Tzibulovka
Vapniarka
Varvarovka
Vaslinovo
Vazdovka
Vendiceni
Verkhovka
Vigoda
Vindueni
Vinozi
Vitovka
Vladislavka
Yampol
Yarishev
Yaroga

Zabokritch
Zatisia
Zemrinka

Concentration Camps beyond the Bug River under German Administration

Berezovka
Bogokov
Bratslav
Corievka
Gaisin
Ivangorod
Mateyevka
Mikhailovka
Narayevka
Nicolayev
Nimierov
Ordovka
Seminka
Talalayevka
Taplik
Tschiukov
Zarodnitza

rainy, muddy, cheerless fall. Snow was piled high, covering everything in sight. The biting cold froze one's breath. It must have been the end of November or the beginning of December. I don't really remember.

As our caravan entered the narrow, snow-covered streets, everybody tried to find shelter in the homes of the few local Jews. Masses of weary, haggard people knocked on the doors of the local Jews in search of shelter. Naturally the first, the fastest, the fittest, and the richest occupied the best accommodations. We too knocked on many doors. Curiously enough I do not remember ever seeing a human face; all I recall hearing is the word "*Tief!*" meaning "Typhus," shouted at us from behind locked doors. We soon got the impression that the local Jews were using this excuse to scare us away. That left my family no choice but to settle down in the rear room of a partially demolished house. Just like in Yampol, in one corner of the room stood a vacant crib. My mother immediately claimed it. We already knew how to squeeze ourselves into it, two or sometimes three at a time. That way at least some of us were protected from the ice-cold dirt floor on which the others slept sitting on a blanket or some garment.

The house consisted of three rooms in a row with a front and rear entrance. The front and middle rooms were still intact but occupied. Our rear room was in shambles. Its back door and only window were missing, frames and all. But at least we were under a roof and protected by four walls even if we had to share that space with twenty other people.

By the farthest stretch of human imagination, it would be impossible to visualize the inhumane conditions we lived under. Twenty of us were packed into a small room of a half-destroyed house with a leaking roof and without doors or windows, not to mention electricity, running water, and toilets, all luxuries unknown to the local population. They did not even have outhouses; the back alleys were used instead.

The only luxury we enjoyed in our new "home" was a makeshift stove called a *trinitchka*. It consisted of two bricks set on the dirt floor about a foot apart. In the space between the bricks a fire was lit. On top, some discarded metal served as a grill to support a pot. To keep the fire burning, people would painfully search for any little piece of wood they could find among the ruins. That stove not only provided us with some warmth but also allowed us to melt snow for water to drink. Lack of food continued to be the most pressing problem.

The intolerable fatigue from the two-week march, in addition to the freezing cold, was cause enough for despair, but worst of all was the ferocious hunger. Papa, already reduced to a human skeleton with a short, gray beard and deep sunken eyes, had become totally apathetic. It was left to Mama to venture out in search for food. She took several personal garments, and the two of us walked to one border of the camp where the peasants were allowed to sell their produce in a kind of a "market." There the odd business of exchanging valuables for food began anew.

It was the first and last time I went with Mama to the "market." After that I was too weak, so I stayed in the room. My brother was in no better shape, yet the occupants of the room expected him to go out and gather wooden pieces from the decrepit houses to feed our little stove.

I felt profound pity for him, my idol, the virtuoso and genius, reduced to a wood-collecting skeleton. But he continued doing this errand for days without complaint, even though it was obvious he was already being consumed by typhus.

One day Mama returned from one of her bartering expeditions with her shopping net full, having successfully exchanged some shirts and shoes for a few onions, potatoes, and a loaf of round bread. That day we feasted on a boiled potato and a slice of onion sprinkled with a few drops of oil, washed down with a cup of *kipiatok* (Russian for boiling water). The bread, though, we did not touch, as we needed to ration it. Before going to sleep, Mama put the bread and the rest of her purchases back into the net and hung it on the side pole of the crib.

We took turns sitting in the crib. That particular night it was my turn to bed down with Papa. He managed to fall asleep—but I couldn't. The room was still. My senses were consumed by the loaf of bread dangling from the side of the crib.

Bread! Whole, dark, round, heavenly scented bread.

The small voice of my conscience kept warning me against doing something impulsive. The forces of right and wrong were locked in a fierce battle. It was neither greed nor selfishness that corrupted me, but that ferocious hunger which I had endured for so many weeks, a tormenting hunger I will never be able to describe in words.

Just one tiny corner of the bread for now, I told myself. My skinny fingers broke off a small piece. God! The taste was divine! Driven by some unknown force, I reached for another piece, then another, and in the end it was gone.

Next morning as Mama intended to feed us, she reached for the now empty net, and in sheer disbelief asked, "Where is the bread I bought yesterday?"

"I don't know," I lied.

I shall never know if my mother believed me or not since she did not say a word. Nor did Papa or Bubi. But I knew the truth; that *I* was responsible for depriving my family of that precious nourishment for the next few days. It was a primal sin, the repercussions of which still haunt me to this day.

We were rooming with total strangers, except for the Sattinger family, acquaintances from Czernowitz. Thrown together by fate, the twenty of us learned to adapt to a situation where privacy and human dignity were forgotten notions. In the beginning, people slept sitting, semi-reclining on their bundles or on each other. To stretch out was a luxury allotted by turn, available as soon as a corpse was taken out. The more corpses removed, the more space to stretch out.

We learned to adapt to such a grotesque situation by developing some kind of emotional paralysis. Otherwise we would have lost our minds. It got so that I could not distinguish between a corpse and a sleeping, motionless person—except that corpses would eventually be picked up. Only *then* did I realize who the dead person was.

Silently, without commotion, without a cry, one by one, those around us died. The poor souls were too feeble to moan or complain. It was deafening, that silence, "the loud silence" in which they slipped into death.

For days, those bodies would stay in the same room with us until they were picked up by the undertakers. Every so often I would hear the clanking sound of a metal bell. At first it reminded me of better days when such sounds were associated with the joy of sleigh bells. Closing my eyes I could even daydream and see myself riding on sleighs that glided in Czernowitz during the winter, the horses' bells chiming melodically and cheerfully, inviting children to play.

It was nearly Christmas. But the clanging here was neither a call to play nor a sound of joy. It was followed by a man's loud voice repeatedly shouting the same words: *"A meth?"* (A corpse?).

Someone would go out and indicate where the corpse was. Soon two men would come in, grab the dead person by the feet and arms, and drag the body out. I still did not comprehend what was happening until one day I glanced out of the windowless window. I froze in horror.

In a wooden sleigh, with two high poles at each side to increase capacity, lay the naked skeletal corpses of men, women, and children, their limbs dangling through the spaces between the poles. This macabre scene was a daily occurrence.

There was no escape from death. It no longer lurked around the corner. It was everywhere, permeating every pore. We inhaled, smelled, and watched it all the time. In the beginning these undertakers used to make their rounds daily, filling their sleigh. But as more people died, they stuck in the poles in order to be able to load more corpses and to avoid multiple trips to the cemetery located on the outskirts of town. Later, they came only every few days due to growing demands and to the intense frost which froze the soil, preventing the digging of graves. So they just piled up the corpses on the frozen soil without burying them at all.

Despite the undertakers' gruesome presence, the surviving family members were eager to have their loved ones buried as soon as possible; according to Jewish law, there should be no more than twenty-four hours between death and burial. Not until the early spring did we learn the truth about the unburied corpses.

The inhuman conditions in which we lived provided fertile soil for infestation and disease. Weeks passed without a bath or a change of clothing. The temperature outside was below zero and froze every drop of liquid; inside our shelter it was not much warmer. Water was brought in from faraway places which only the few healthy and fit could reach. And that seldom happened, leaving the majority without it. When there was no other water available, we melted the snow and drank it.

The lifesaving liquid was so scarce that we preferred to boil and drink it rather than use it for washing. All we did was scrub our hands and faces with the snow instead. The rest of the body remained dirty, so lice continued to feast on us. As a result, typhus invaded our haggard bodies at a frightening rate, and became the number one killer, followed by starvation, dysentery, freezing, and sporadic executions.

My father was an easy target. He probably had no immune defenses because of his obsession with cleanliness and sterility. I never realized how sick he really was, until one day I tried to shake him out of his silence and make him talk to me. "Papa, tell me everything is going to be fine," I begged. Through great effort, and not wanting to let me down, he managed to whisper, "Yes, my Muttika, don't worry. All is going to be all right." Little did I know that these would be his last words.

A few days later Mama called in Dr. Menschel, our neighbor from the front room to take a look at Papa. I can recall the scene as if it were taking place now. The doctor came in, stood behind my father's head, glanced at his withered figure in the crib, and without even touching him, announced his verdict.

"Mrs. Glasberg," he said, "what your husband needs is medicine, food, a warm bath and a comfortable bed, none of which I can offer; there's nothing I can do."

I looked at him in disbelief, ready to scream and hit him. I felt the pain and fear my poor father must have felt at hearing such a verdict—if he could still hear. How could a doctor be so cruel and tactless?

The crib was now occupied by Papa and Bubi, who were very sick by then, while Mama and I, the relatively healthy ones, slept on the floor.

One morning in December, my brother called out from the crib in a frightened voice: "Mama! Mama! I think—"

I did not understand what his unfinished sentence meant. Only after Mama got up to look at Papa and turned her horror-stricken face to us did the truth hit me like thunder. My heart stopped beating for a moment and a choking sensation followed. Stiffened inside, I approached the crib and found myself looking into my father's open, expressionless, blue eyes.

I got hysterical, and screamed, "Papa, Papa, answer me please!" all the time hoping for my imaginary power to have an effect. His serene face and slightly open mouth, as if smiling, gave me the impression that he was pretending not to hear my screams. I touched his face—it was cold as ice. My screaming was all in vain.

He was dead. My god was dead. He died silently, unnoticed, extinguished like the flame of a candle with the expression of goodness frozen forever on his face.

Without a word, Mama and Bubi pulled me away from the crib. Nobody stirred or showed any compassion, nobody offered a word of consolation or a hug, as if death was expected and was just a matter of one's turn.

I continued screaming for some time, until a numbness of emotion took over. An icy sensation crept into my whole being, and I could not cry.

Somebody closed Papa's eyelids without covering his body and put him on the floor with the other corpses. I stared at the lifeless body of my beloved father. The rebellion, the anger, the pain, the fear—all were slowly suppressed. My feelings split off from the appalling world around me where he would no longer live. At that moment I became emotionally numb; all of a sudden I was watching all the madness as if it did not concern me at all, as if it were a projection of a film from some other world, one I had no connection with. I could survive only by pretending it was but an awful nightmare, all the while disassociating myself from reality.

As I learned not to speak, that very numbness protected me. Then as now, no words could do justice to the horror of what we witnessed.

Suddenly the undertaker's bell took on yet another meaning for me; it was going to be *my* father who would be dragged out like a log. Three days later, it happened. Papa was gone forever, and along with him went a part of me.

As the mortality increased, fewer dead people were picked up. Now it was every few days, and after that it would be weeks. One wall of the room became a makeshift morgue with corpses piled up from the entire house. The wait for the undertakers became almost an obsession for the living who had to share the room with the dead. Nobody accompanied the bodies; nobody knew what happened to them once they were taken away. Few had the physical strength to follow the sleigh on foot to the outskirts of town. The undertakers had been left with a free hand to claw inside mouths, pull out gold caps, rip off clothes, and simply drop the corpses on the grounds of the Jewish cemetery without digging graves in the frozen soil.

A few weeks later our overcrowded room of twenty held only six: the two Sattingers with their two-year-old girl and the three of us. While the Sattingers crouched in one corner of the room on the floor, we occupied the baby crib in a sitting position, knees bent, in the other corner. Although I do not recall all the conversations among the adults, I certainly recall the exact dialogue between my mother and Mrs. Sattinger that started right after my father's death.

"Frau Sattinger, remember what I am telling you," my mother would say. "Everybody in this room will die except Ruthi and the two of you." She articulated this premonition with an air of authority. She knew. But how?

Did my devouring the bread indicate to her that I was a fighter and would do whatever was necessary for my survival? Or did she believe in the saying that the slender tree withstands the hurricane?

Mrs. Sattinger reprimanded my mother: "How dare you say such a thing, Frau Glasberg! It's a sin." She tried to change the subject by engaging my sick brother in a conversation about the future.

"Herr Glasberg, what do you want to become after you get out of here?"

"An engineer," my brother replied without hesitation. I could see a look of disappointment with his answer flash across my mother's face.

My brother had shown the Sattingers the notations on the back of his baby picture listing the names of the villages we had passed on our way to Bershad. "Why did you write them down, Herr Glasberg?" Mrs. Sattinger asked. "If we survive this hell, I would like to remember everything in order to tell the world about it," he answered.

My mother, though, kept to her predictions and insisted *I* was to be the only survivor in our family. She wanted to die in peace assured that I would be looked after by somebody, and that "somebody" was to be Mrs. Sattinger.

"Frau Sattinger, please promise to take care of Ruthi when she will be left alone," she implored.

"I am not going to promise anything because you are not a clairvoyant. And stop scaring your children," Mrs. Sattinger said. But Mama would not give up.

I sat there listening, not believing, hoping for her to be wrong. Deep down I was petrified. That anguish intensified in my starving, freezing, gaunt being. How could I survive? I could barely stand on my feet.

Now that Mama and Bubi were so desperately ill and I was unable to walk, we were totally dependent on the mercy of the Sattingers and the Menschels. Dr. Menschel's family lived in the front room, and, being a physician, he was given permission to go outside the ghetto and treat Ukrainian peasants, who paid him with groceries. We survived on the fringe benefits of his fees in the form of a once-a-day meal of salty water in which their potatoes had been boiled. To us this was a delicacy we looked forward to with great anticipation. It was a lucky person who accidentally fished out a fragment of a real potato.

This kind of nourishment did not keep the Sattingers' toddler alive for too long. Soon the little girl died. Sick as she was, Mama, sharp and as resourceful as ever, seized that tragic moment to get assurances from the grieving mother.

"On the corpse of your dead child, you must swear to me that you will take care of Ruthi so that I may die in peace," she insisted.

There was no answer. All night long Mrs. Sattinger clung to the dead child, and only in the morning before she finally placed it on the floor did she comply with my mother's request. Repeating Mama's words, she said in a solemn voice:

"On the corpse of my dead child, I promise to take care of Ruthi."

Suddenly I was caught up in a drama with increasingly bizarre twists.

The house that sheltered us had three rooms: a well-preserved front one that held the Menschel family, a small, middle room teeming with people, and ours—the most derelict. Because of its back entrance, our room also served as a morgue. Thus, the hideous corpses from the other rooms were brought into ours and piled up against the wall next to the door opening.

By now Bubi had ceased to talk. He sat with hunched shoulders and head, his chin on his chest, his eyes partially covered by the fur hat that had fit him before, but now was too large and slipped over his forehead and eyes. I thought that he did it on purpose to avoid seeing all the suffering.

Mama sat motionless opposite Bubi but said that she could not see anything; she also claimed to be unable to move. She was fully alert and coherent but refused to take the potato liquid. She refused everything, including water. It was beyond my comprehension how she could so suddenly become blind and paralyzed at the same time.

"Ruthi, check on Bubi!" Mama asked me.

"Why don't you look for yourself?" I replied.

"I can't see anything and I can't move," she said.

Bubi was directly in her field of vision, yet she said she could not see him. That really intrigued me, but I obeyed and checked. Lifting the fur hat slightly, I could only see a pair of glazed eyes.

"Ruthi, how is he doing? Is he breathing?" Mama inquired.

"Yes, Mama, he's breathing. But he doesn't answer me," I reported.

"Give him the hot water with a spoon," she instructed me.

"You do it, Mama, please," I begged her.

"I can't. Don't you understand?" she answered feebly.

No, I did not really understand. I obediently did what she told me, but every time I tried to put a spoon of water into Bubi's mouth, it came back out with froth. That infuriated me. I thought he was playing games with me. I was also angry at my mother for not doing things herself. I sat at the side of my brother watching his slow agony, not knowing at that time that he was in a coma.

Child that I was, I only reacted with irritation, suspecting that everybody was playing games with me. I was trapped in the middle between my silent, nonresponsive brother, and my "unseeing" paralyzed mother, while I myself could barely stand on my feet. Weeks of starvation had sapped my body, and the events of the last weeks must have also done something to my mind. I do not know what kind of chemical or electrical changes take place in the brain when a child is faced with such unspeakable traumas and losses, but changes surely do take place.

Nearly two weeks after my father's death, my brother, who had been motionless and silent for many days suddenly screamed, *"Ruzena-a-a-a!!!"* This was his last word.

I was shattered at the notion that of all the things he could have been dreaming about, he chose the name of our cow in Milie. Many years later, I came to understand that in his tortured moments, and in a obviously comatose state, he had chosen to return to Milie and relive the joys of his earlier life. I hope he was transported in spirit and died with happy memories.

I took off his fur hat. The lining was swarming with lice.

I was petrified at the sight of his hairless scalp covered by a thick layer of lice, resembling a crop of short hair. His eyes stared into a vacuum; his face was white. He was still sitting, but his head slumped forward on his chest. My mother asked Mrs. Sattinger in a detached and weak voice to confirm his death. She did.

My Bubi was no more.

The guilt crushed me. What did *I* do wrong? In my naive mind, I assumed that my ignorance had somehow resulted in his death. It was my fault that he died.

I was terrified to sit shoulder-to-shoulder with his dead body, but I kept silent and did not cry. Mama remained rooted to the spot. Although I was able to move, I felt numb. Both of us took his death with quiet resignation.

Some people took him down from the crib onto the dirt floor. I remained seated, both dumbfounded and enraged. My beloved, talented, handsome eighteen-year-old brother was nothing more than another stiff corpse.

We had no real shroud to wrap him in, so Mama begged the people who helped put him on the floor: "Please dress him in a clean white nightgown! We still have one in our bundles somewhere."

But they reproached her: "Don't be foolish! The undertakers will only take it off anyway and sell it."

However Mama insisted. "It doesn't matter what they do. He should leave us according to Jewish law and tradition. What those crooks do afterwards is out of my control."

I did not know then that according to the Torah, the last rite was considered the greatest act of loving-kindness. I now understand my mother's action, albeit void of logic.

After a few days the sinister clanging of the undertakers' bell echoed from outside. "*Meth?*" As usual somebody had to go out and flag them down. They came and pulled out my Bubi with the other corpses. "Who would be next?" I asked myself.

Every day the death toll rose in the camp. In our house, in particular in our room, in a matter of one month, all that remained out of twenty people were four survivors.

During that time I did not know what was going on outside. Here and there I heard fragments of information about cruelties and killings, but they did not affect me; I saw the results of the "other method" (no less lethal) and that was plenty.

My world was confined to that morbid room, and I never ventured far for lack of physical strength. I hardly had enough energy to go out and take care of my bodily functions behind the house. There, men opened their trousers to urinate into the snow, while I squatted, cowering in the freezing cold.

After a while the Sattingers moved to better lodgings with a local Jewish family. Our neighbors in the adjoining room were sick and rarely appeared, so Mama and I remained alone in the morgue-like room with the uncollected corpses.

Outside the wind howled, blowing the biting cold air through the missing window and door. The snow was piled up to the window. Inside there were just the two of us . . . and corpses. There was no food, no heat, no hope.

I clung to my mother in gloom and despair, all the while hoping to hear an encouraging word. Mama in turn started preparing me for the eventuality of a life alone.

"Ruthika," she said, "you have to understand that having lost Bubi—my only hope and purpose in life—that I can't continue living now. You are the only one who will survive." Then she began preaching sermons about life and values.

"People are kind and will take care of you. Be good, obedient, honest and well-behaved and everything will be fine. One day you will return home where your aunts and uncles will watch out for you. You will be Aunt Anna's child. And remember, all our assets are at Aunt Cilli's. That will help you to survive until you grow up."

Such talk frightened me, and I begged her to stop it. "Mama, Mama, please don't leave me alone," I repeated over and over again.

For two weeks my mother talked to me about nothing else but her imminent death and my future thereafter. I rebelled and tried to persuade her to make an effort for my sake. But she only replied that when a mother loses a son, there is no reason to live. The implication that I was not worth living for hurt me deeply. What she did not say was how desperately ill she was. But at least she talked and that was a small consolation, the only straw I clung to in order not to drown in that stormy sea of anguish and sorrow.

Each day I begged her not to die and leave me alone, but she continued talking about her death until one day she could talk no more. I realized at that point that all my efforts were in vain. Yet I decided to redouble my efforts to keep her from dying. I stayed awake day and night for two weeks, shaking her periodically and calling "Mama! Mama!" to which she responded with a faint, "Hmm, hmm." It sounded as if she were in another world, but it was the only sign that she was still alive— the last ray of hope I clung to.

Gradually, my stamina began to fade. With stubborn willpower, I suppressed my sleepiness for two whole weeks with the sole purpose of keeping my mother alive. To block out this unspeakable eventuality, I closed my eyes for short periods and imagined myself back in the tranquil surroundings of Milie.

I am planting vegetable seeds in the freshly plowed beds behind the house. I have come to check on my little babies. They are sprouting! I watch them grow day by day, green onions and radishes. I wander through the garden and pick red raspberries, popping them into my mouth.

How wet and delicious they are! I want to eat them with sweet fresh cream.

The cold, dark, and desolate room seemed to be closing in on me and my dying mother. I thought it was the end of us, when suddenly some people from the middle room took pity and moved us in with them, crib and all. They helped put Mama flat on her back with knees bent to fit her into the crib, and I continued my vigil from a sitting position near her head.

Water! Fresh water after a rain in Milie. I rush outside with the rain still coming down and place buckets under all the drains. The water makes my hair so soft, our clothes so soft and clean. The rain stops and the air smells fresh. Now I run out to the swing, and with my bare feet, I splash in the puddle under the swing. Bubi calls me to gather earthworms with him and go fishing. Then Mama will cook up a tasty trout.

"Mama! Mama!" I called out, remembering my vigil. "Hm, hm," was all she could murmur.

As Mama was now paralyzed, she had lost all control of her bodily functions. She soiled herself, and when she could not endure it any longer she whispered something to me about cleaning her. I was so weak and shriveled myself that I had no energy whatsoever. Besides, where would I find water, soap and rags to do such a thing?

Slowly, I climbed down from the crib, collected some papers and rags from old clothes, and attempted to clean my mother. I tried to lift her, but because of her paralysis, her legs felt as though they weighed a ton. I fought with all my strength not to collapse under the weight. The nauseating sight and the odor almost made me faint. I succeeded in cleaning her somewhat, but after a while I had to give up, leaving my poor mother to rot in her own waste.

The helplessness and guilt devastated me. Defeated and ashamed, I climbed up again to my spot in the crib. From there I continued the vigil in spite of my deteriorating condition. On the fourteenth sleepless night, my willpower crushed, I succumbed to sleep. But the obsession with my vigil crept even into my dreams. Startled out of my sleep, I woke up and shook her calling out: "Mama! Mama!" Silence. I shook her some more, but not even then did she respond with her usual faint "Hm, hm." She had chosen to die when I ceased for a while to call her and keep her from dying in peace. She took advantage of the silence to slip away from that crazy world.

I touched her ice-cold face and screamed with all my strength, "Help! help! Please, somebody help me!" No one answered.

Death was so common that it evoked no emotion anymore. People had grown numb, and I must have grown numb as well. But now I became like a wounded animal.

I yelled at my dead mother, rebuking her, "How could you leave me alone in this crazy place?" Then I cried out, "Dr. Menschel! Dr. Menschel!" Through the closed door, came his muffled response: "It's too late now. There's nothing I can do."

The doctor did not even bother to come and take a look. Nobody cared; people's souls were dead after all the tragedies they had witnessed. Everyone silently awaited their turn.

I sat clinging to my mother's cold body, screaming at the top of my lungs, hoping that somehow she could be revived. In doing so I had the feeling that I was still not totally left alone. I had lost all sense of reason.

Later, the people I shared the room with came to our crib, took a good look at her, and without words, just with that typical expression of resignation and helplessness in their faces, confirmed her death. As I remained clinging to my mother's body, conflicting thoughts raced through my mind: On the one hand I could not let go, yet I also wanted to flee from her cold, lifeless body.

I cannot recall who finally took Mama away into the morgue-like room we had previously occupied. As she was placed with the other corpses, my eyes shed not a tear, though inside me reigned a hideous turmoil. *Was Mama right in her predictions about my survival? Why wasn't I the one to die from hunger and cold?*

The lifeless body of my mother lay on the dirt floor like a bundle of bones held together by a layer of transparent skin. I hoped that the gravediggers would pick her up soon. I was bewildered by the senselessness of it all and amazed at my own survival against all odds. In retrospect, I must have harbored some spark of hope that kept me going. I wanted to live, to hope, in spite of that gruesome reality. When things got unbearable I retreated to my rich inner life and built a wall around it. Daydreaming about my happy days in Milie or in Czernowitz helped me to endure the most incomprehensible experiences. Some of my strength must have come from all the love I had absorbed from my family over the years, especially from my father. But it must have been equally something my mother had spiritually passed on to me. Perhaps Mama detected in me some special gift that she secretly knew would help me to survive. I thought: I have to survive since on the brink of death Mama commanded me to live. She willed my immortality—at least for the time being.

To my great surprise, Mrs. Sattinger kept her vow to my mother; three days later, she and her husband showed up. Unwillingly they had now become my guardians. Mrs. Sattinger was not a friendly woman, perhaps because of the handicap of a crippled foot. Her husband Markus, though nicer, was still quite unaffectionate. Neither was able to offer a word of comfort or a shoulder to cry on. In their matter-of-fact way, though, they did help me in my fight for survival. They told me that there was not much they could do except take me to some women from our hometown, who were willing to give me shelter and some nourishment in exchange for items stuffed in my bundle. In the frame of mind I was in at that time, I could not have cared less what they wanted.

We went out in the middle of January and walked through narrow alleys I now saw for the first time since we had arrived. They were depressingly desolate, save for a few scrawny stray dogs searching for food. Snow was piled high everywhere. The shabby little houses indicated no sign at all of human life. In this icy cold and deep snow it took a great deal of effort to reach the home of the two sisters who were to be my foster parents. The Sattingers took me inside, introduced me, and left shortly thereafter.

The two sisters received me in a friendly manner, which was a welcome, pleasant feeling. I was particularly relieved to see no corpses in the otherwise overcrowded room. They fed me a piece of potato with a drop of oil and sat me on a bench between them. I liked sitting there, helping them to rip and restring the wool threads they used for knitting. But above all, I enjoyed the warmth of their large, fat bodies, which protected me from the fierce cold of the room. The days were short at that time of the year, and the nights, especially without electricity, were unbearably long. A makeshift oil lamp or a candle was all they could afford, so most of the time was spent in the dark.

The two women chatted incessantly in a strange language that both annoyed and fascinated me. I paid a lot of attention to it, and after many days of careful listening, I found they were actually speaking in a pig-German (like pig-Latin), using a secret code. What they did was alter the words by inserting a *p* between all the syllables in order to make it sound different. To my great astonishment, I caught on to the trick very soon, but I made sure not to reveal my secret. And in doing so I was able to hear a lot of amusing adult chit-chat.

From time to time the ladies fed me a scanty portion of *mamaliga*, a cornmeal mush, a typical Romanian dish. On a very lucky day I would get to eat it flavored with a piece of onion and some oil. It was not much, not frequent enough and not very good, but it tasted heavenly compared to my previous diet which was totally devoid of solid food. The dirt floor was my bed, my bundle of possessions my pillow, and my short, blue, sailor coat was my mattress and blanket.

In spite of the improved lodgings, my thoughts were constantly with my mother's abandoned body, which I knew had not yet been taken away. I was very weak, but in spite of it, I ventured out every day to see her. The cold was so intense that I could observe the white clouds of my own breath. Alone with my grieving thoughts, I went back to the gutted house; some force drew me to my dead mother. I understood she was dead, I saw that she was dead, yet I could not let go. I still wanted to see her every time I visited. Yet I could not find peace of mind until she was taken away and, I hoped, properly buried. By that time I understood that this was what should be done with the deceased. The conflict and the pain almost totally consumed me. It now seems impossible to believe the grotesque setting: A bald, emaciated eleven-year-old girl, fighting the bitter frost, standing alone in deep snow outside that morgue-like room for hours, just staring through an opening that used to be a window at the dead body of her mother.

Then an eerie phenomenon baffled my already bewildered mind. Every day I found her body in a different part of the room. It gave me the shivers. I could not understand what was happening. If she was dead, why wasn't she in the same place all the time? In my childish fantasy I had invented a multitude of explanations—from the ridiculous to the most macabre. I then asked my "foster parents" about it. They explained to me that besides hungry people, there were plenty of hungry dogs around that helped themselves to abandoned corpses. That unraveled the mystery. Horrors of all horrors! My mother was being dragged around and perhaps even being eaten piece by piece by ravenous dogs! How could I prevent it? Why hadn't the undertakers picked her up?

From then on I became a crusader in the quest for my mother's burial. Each time I paid my daily visits to my mother's corpse, I would desperately follow the gravediggers, trying to run after the overfilled sleighs, begging the men to go to the abandoned morgue-like room and collect my mother's body. I could barely walk, yet the power of despair made me, somehow, run. I was out of my mind, obsessed by the thought that they would never get there. At that time they were making up to fifty trips a day to the cemetery with full loads, and every time I caught up with them, they either had no time or no space for her.

For two long and painful weeks I went religiously back and forth to see Mama. I looked into her lifeless face, afraid to enter the room or to get near her. Every day I stood in front of that window space for hours until I almost turned to ice. Only then did I leave with a heavy feeling in my heart, fearing that in my absence the dogs would devour her. I knew I had to persuade the diggers to pick her up, but who would listen to me, a "skeleton-child"? Perhaps they even expected a bribe to collect her corpse, but I had nothing.

On the fourteenth day, I set out to see her as usual. This time, at long last, she was gone.

A mixture of relief and sadness befell me. I felt a stab in my heart at the realization that it was final, and now I was really and truly alone. I was no one's child anymore. There was no one to love me unconditionally anymore, no one to care about me. An ice-cold sensation settled in my heart. With my head bent and with frozen tears on my cheeks, I walked back to my foster home.

January 27, 1942. At age eleven, I was left alone in the world.

I laboriously reconstructed the Hebrew and Christian calendar dates of my family's deaths with help from the Sattingers and other survivors, so that I would be able to observe the anniversaries should I survive— which did not seem likely.

Soon I was experiencing the terrible sickness of typhus, which left me floating in and out of consciousness. At times I did not understand or even recognize people. I heard murmurs but could not make out a sentence. I saw shadows and perceived the surroundings in an unreal and fragmented form.

I thought to myself: "So this is it! Mama may not have been right after all. I'm going to join them all in the other world."

From my "sick bed" on the icy dirt floor, on one of my better days, I saw a rather healthy-looking man—itself a rare occurrence. I was told later that he was a *Feldsher* (an old-time barber-surgeon). He kneeled down, listened to my heart with his naked ear, checked my burning, feverish body, said something to the sisters, and left. As usual they talked in their *p* language, which I was able to understand at that point. I picked up a single sentence: "The doctor said her heart can't last much longer."

I had heard my verdict and waited for the executioner, yet I did not want to die.

Days and nights merged into one dark cloud, preventing me from seeing anything at all as I drifted in and out of delirium. Then quite suddenly, the cloud lifted as if blown away by a strong wind. The fog dissipated and before I knew it, my eyes opened and I was wide awake—much to the great disappointment of my foster parents, who were waiting to take possession of my few miserable belongings. I saw the expression on their faces: indifference and maybe resentment. Miraculously, I had recovered: without medication, without nutrition, without a warm bed, and above all without loving care.

But nobody was happy to see me recover. Where once I had been pampered and watched over for the slightest cough and cheered by my family when I felt better, now as I recovered, all I got were scornful looks. I was a burden. Unwanted. An extra mouth to feed.

The conduct of the sisters did not go unnoticed by a young boy who shared the room with us. He, as I was told much later, ran to the Sattingers to tell on them. He said that they had sold almost all my belongings without giving me the equivalent in food. That was how I learned that they indeed were greedy and dishonest. Annoyed at this latest turn of events, Mr. Sattinger came and took me away. Without further ado, he led me to a young Bershadian Jewish couple, who were to be my next foster parents. Living with them was the woman's elderly mother. They lived in a two-room house, simple yet clean and furnished. It was the first real home I had seen since leaving ours. The agreement was that my guardians were going to pay for my bed and breakfast from the sale of my remaining goods, but for one meal a day I was to go to the Sattingers' place. I knew that they were struggling as well and doing their utmost for me. So I was grateful that at least I had guardians.

In my new home I was to share the unheated drawing room with the landlady's mother. We slept on individual sofas, a luxury I could hardly believe. But it was still cold, and I shivered all night in the fierce iciness of the room. This triggered a cluster of aches and pains, which I did not know then were a precursor to a relapse.

I was gripped by a particularly sharp, piercing pain in my right upper abdomen that had me moaning and screaming loudly all night long. "Ayayayay, it hurts! It stabs!" I screamed in German. "Stab back!" snapped the old woman at me in Yiddish, annoyed at my disrupting her sleep. This ludicrous bilingual dialogue went on all night, every night, yet nobody helped me.

Soon the idyllic situation of sleeping on a sofa came to an end, probably prompted by the old lady's complaints about my nightly moaning. The young couple took me into their tiny bedroom and put me to sleep in—surprise—a crib. I suspected it must have belonged to their deceased child, a subject they never mentioned. Seeing a fourth crib fated for me, I was convinced that a conspiracy existed, one that made cribs appear for me wherever I went. But at the same time, I was happy to be in a modestly heated room, and did not mind the crib. In fact, my skinny body and short stature fit perfectly into it; I could even stretch out without any problem.

Sleeping in the couple's room also caused me to be an inconspicuous witness to their marital intimacy. It was here that I discovered the act of lovemaking for the first time. In the dark of night I could not see anything, but I could clearly hear the moans and sighs of the woman pleading in Yiddish, *"Pameilech, pameilech, pameilech"* (Gently, gently, gently). It sounded to me as though the husband was hurting her and she chose to endure it. What I heard excited and intrigued me, while at the same time it scared me to think that she was being hurt. But I kept quiet, making believe that I was asleep so as not to make them throw me out.

At the beginning of my stay, the Bershadian couple would give me a piece of sour bread spread with oil and garlic for breakfast—a delicacy. For lunch I would walk a short distance to the Sattingers' for a similar treat, which had to keep me going until the following day. As long as there was anything in my stomach once a day, I was content.

But my health continued to deteriorate to the point where finally I could not walk anymore. Without ever having regained my full strength from the first bout of typhus, I suddenly suffered a relapse with high fever, cramps, diarrhea, and delirium.

Instead of nurturing me, my foster parents, afraid of contamination, moved my crib out onto the freezing porch. Still, they at least had the decency to notify my guardians, who came to see me a few days later.

I lay in the crib without the slightest notion of time. I lived an isolated life without human contact and without conversation except for the occasional visits from the Sattingers; I don't know how I did not lose my mind.

In the interim, fewer and fewer of my belongings were available to exchange for food. My guardians were now giving me less food each day, which did not bother me much since I had lost my appetite anyway. I felt as if I were fading away and thought that now my time had come for sure. Once more I retreated into my "guarded area," the memories of my beloved Milie:

It's July, time to harvest fruit, especially the prunes from a dozen trees. Everyone's involved. We children pit the prunes while the adults prepare the bonfires. They put the huge copper kettles over the fire and mix the fruit with sugar and spices. The jam cooks and cooks, while Mama and Tante Anna stir the boiling mixture with a long, oar-like spatula. The whole village smells of the rich aroma of the prune butter. I spread a big gob of it on a piece of bread made from wheat grown in Dziadziu's field, ground up in his mill, and baked in the hot oven. Milie!

Forgotten by God and the world, tossed from place to place, treated like a leper, I could have surrendered myself to despair were it not for my enduring optimism and the devotion of the Sattingers. They came once a day, bringing me something to eat and providing me with human contact. They even brought a doctor who diagnosed my illness as "paratyphus" yet could not offer any medical help. I cannot recall how long I drifted in and out of delirium or how I took care of my bodily functions when the outside temperature paralyzed one's movements. But, unbelievably, I recovered once more.

Waking up from a long hibernation, I looked outside and could not believe my eyes—it was springtime. I stretched my limp legs and sat up slowly, eager to walk again, only my legs had forgotten how. I was shocked at my total lack of strength and an unbearable fear overcame me. Still, I didn't give up. Instead I decided to make the enormous effort to learn how to walk again.

Attempting to take my first steps, I held on to the wall and like a baby, slowly, slowly, stumbled outdoors. Where there had been snow, a few green patches of grass were coming to life, and the air was fresh.

I took a deep breath. Everything seemed new and exciting. I had forgotten that there was some kind of life out there, that there were still some children able to play in the alleys of the camp, that there existed some other families and other houses. I felt like a stranger lost in an unfamiliar place.

Every day I took a few more steps determined to walk like a normal person. When I noticed children my age playing hopscotch, jumping, running, and laughing, I tried to join them, remembering that game as if from another life. But I failed at my initial attempt to jump into the first square. Oh my God! What had happened to me? I took a good look at my feet, and noticed that they were swollen twice their normal size. I later learned it was something called hunger edema. I was a wreck. Alive, perhaps, but a part of me was dead. *What was in store for me next?*

Mrs. Sattinger answered that question with her next visit. Diplomatically, she explained that all my belongings had been sold. There was no more money to pay these foster parents, and they, the Sattingers, did not have enough to feed themselves. The next step was to put me into an orphanage recently established by the Jewish community.

The Orphanages

CHAPTER 5

Now I had to live the very life I so much dreaded, the life of a double orphan. The only orphanage I knew was the one I had visited in Czernowitz when I was seven. My aunts were members of the Women's International Zionist Organization (WIZO), which catered to children's needs. They had taken me along one day to watch a performance staged by orphans. I was told that these were children without parents, living together in one big building, cared for by strangers. My empathy for these poor souls grew to the point of obsession. I pictured myself in such a predicament: without parents, without a home, without a hug, without kisses, and, above all, without love. The thought made me shudder, and I prayed it would *never* happen to me; I would rather be *dead* than live like that.

After that visit I began busily painting pictures of doom. Mainly they revolved around the fear of what would happen if my parents died and left me alone. To assuage the fear, I came up with a consoling solution: that by then scientists would have invented an immortality pill. And so off to sleep I would go, secure in the knowledge that these things only happened to others and would never happen to me.

But here I was, only five years later, being led by the hand to that terrible destination. I felt like I was being sentenced to spend the rest of my life in a prison. I wondered if there, too, a crib would be waiting for me.

Hand in hand with Mrs. Sattinger, I walked the few blocks to my new "home." I had no luggage, only the clothes on my body—a torn brown skirt, a blouse, a dark-blue sailor coat with gold buttons—and, in my free hand, my only heirlooms: a silver fork, a knife, and a spoon.

As I stood in front of the shabby orphanage, a three-room house that faced a small square, I couldn't avoid comparing it to the orphanage back home, which was a beautiful villa surrounded by lush gardens and trees.

Mrs. Sattinger handed me over to a volunteer lady in charge of the children. She walked me through all three rooms in search of a space to sleep. Each room was outfitted with one low, wall-to-wall platform made of rough wooden boards that served as a common bed. Children of all ages, including a few babies, were packed onto them like sardines. There was no more room, so I had to be content with a corner of the floor. Still Mrs. Sattinger thought I should consider myself lucky to have a roof over my head, because the age limit was ten and I was already eleven. It was only through the intervention of Benjamin Korn, the president of the Jewish Committee, that they had made an exception.

It so happened that the Korns had been our neighbors in Czernowitz, and Mrs. Korn was also a distant relative of my father. Their two sons, Freddy and Friedrich, were tutored by my brother. Quite coincidentally we had been in the same transport to Transnistria, often staying overnight in the same barns until Bershad, where we lost track of each other. They had some hidden money, which enabled them to rent a room in the home of a local Jewish family within the camp. Thus they were spared the typhus epidemic of that first winter. Also the death toll in Bershad decreased somewhat in the summer of 1942, mostly due to a new, less harsh commander than Florian Ghinararu and to the pressure from both the Romanian Jewish communities and international organizations.

Mr. Korn had been a wealthy owner of an estate, accustomed to dealing with the Romanian authorities and Ukrainian peasants. He was a towering figure who exuded both self-confidence and humor. With his charismatic personality and organizational talent, he pulled the community together and, in spite of the reigning chaos, created a small Jewish committee. They collected what little money they could from among the very same inmates, making the creation of an orphanage their first priority.

Orphans were picked up from the alleys, rescued from ruined houses, from barns, and from among piles of corpses. Most were sick, frozen to the bone, skinny, dirty, and silent. They did not speak about their personal tragedies, nor did they show any outward signs of mourning. Tiny people. Children with aged faces. Bundles of sorrow. Silent, scared, and deeply saddened. A stark mirror image of myself.

The kitchen was staffed by women volunteers who cooked mamaliga, but there was no one to assist in the actual physical care of the orphans. Infants and small children were assisted by the older ones. And that's how I came to take care of several smaller children. I became especially attached to a beautiful little girl, perhaps a year old, who was very sick. She could not talk, but her eyes did the talking for her. I will never forget those big, black, sad eyes. Probably out of maternal instinct, I adopted her and we developed a strong bond. I convinced myself that I would be the one to nurture her back to health and she would be my little sister.

I sang lullabies, told her the story of Cinderella, and fed her that dreadful corn mush, which was certainly unfit for a sick baby. I prayed to God for her survival, which became integral to my own. By declaring her my sister I hoped to rebuild a family, any family. This nameless baby gave me a new purpose in life.

But in spite of all the love I gave her, one day the little baby died in my arms. Once again I felt the pain of yet another loss in an accumulating chain of losses. A devastating feeling of emptiness took hold of me and I asked God, "Why do you take from me everyone I love?"

Seeing in the baby's death a warning not to become attached to anyone, I retreated into my little corner of the floor to mourn. Knees to chin, I crouched, protected against the cold only by my short sailor coat, half of which served as a mattress, the other half as a blanket. I remained lost in my thoughts until I fell asleep. But even that sleep was fitful.

Night after night I felt an intense nibbling, first on my head, then on other parts of my body. Because of the darkness, I could not see anything, so I brushed it off, thinking it was a fly. But one night it felt more like something scratching or biting. I tried to chase it away and in doing so I felt something furry. *It was a rat!*

I screamed in horror . . . but nobody even stirred. Frightened to death, I stayed up all night, anxiously waiting for the first rays of light to have a look around. To my great disgust, I discovered a hole in the floor right at the place where I lay my head. The mere thought of that appalling rodent digging around next to my face was reason enough to stay awake. But there was no place else to sleep.

After many sleepless nights spent sitting up, I could resist no more. With a piece of rag I finally stuffed the hole, hoping for the best. Remembering Papa's lectures about the danger of playing with cats which eat diseased rats, I wondered what that rat had given me.

Back home, I slept in an open crib at the foot of my parent's bed until age seven. As I loved reading on my own, particularly Grimm's fairy tales, some of which deeply disturbed me because of the injustices and suffering inflicted upon innocent people, I would often experience nightmares. Every time I woke from one of those horrifying dreams, I would climb into Papa's side of the bed. He would caress and assure me with calming words, and I would eventually fall asleep. Still, I would toss and turn, and Papa, in order not to wake me, often abandoned the bed to sleep on the floor.

Finally, at age seven, I was moved into the drawing room to sleep on the divan next to the tall ceramic stove. Another divan near the window was Bubi's bed. I am sure he was not thrilled with his new roommate, but, as usual, he did not complain.

I always put off going to bed, but on cold winter nights Papa would tempt me by heating my eiderdown on the ceramic stove, tuck me in like a mummy, and kiss me good night. This procedure made me feel loved and protected, and soon I would fall asleep.

But this was not a nighmare, it was reality, and there was nobody to caress me and say soothing words.

The summer of 1942 crept slowly along. We spent the long days waiting for the one life-saving meal, sleeping, and squashing lice. The only cheering news was a rumor of an eventual repatriation to old Romania of all double orphans (children who lost both parents) under age fifteen. To our great joy, those rumors became fact.

We did not know exactly how the arrangement came about, but we heard of an agreement between the Jewish communities of Romania and the Romanian government. In fact, the plan was to release several thousand children and ship them to Palestine. We thrived on the thought of being free again, daydreaming about food, a hot bath, and a warm bed. These fantasies gave us strength to deal with the misery and the suffering at hand.

One late summer day, that dream became a reality. The little square outside the orphanage filled with children from the whole camp. They came: little and big, sick and healthy, boys and girls, most clad in torn clothes, with shaved heads, dragging feet either bare or wrapped in rags.

Since Bershad had no railroad connection, we needed to get to another camp called Balta to board a train to Romania. Dozens of horse-drawn wagons stood ready to take us there. The organizers called out names from a list: "Appelbaum . . . Berkowitz . . . Cohen . . . Glasberg. . . ." As each name was called, that child was allowed into a cart, with Jewish delegates acting as escorts.

I have only a hazy recollection of the trip because I was sick. At first I thought it was just motion sickness, but it turned out to be more serious than that.

The convoy made its slow trip on dirt roads, through valleys and hills. At the foot of each hill the older children had to get off the carts to ease the load on the tired horses. Walking uphill, I suddenly had difficulties keeping up with the rest. My pace became slower and slower; my feet would not obey me. I ended up being the last one, falling farther and farther behind the column. I could walk no more.

Panic-stricken, I sat down at the roadside and cried bitterly, remembering in horror what happened to people who remained behind during the march to Bershad—they were either shot or froze to death. Circumstances had changed, but the memory remained.

Just as I was about to give in to despair, from out of nowhere, a cart appeared and stopped right in front of me. It carried some of the convoy leaders, who pulled me aboard, calmed me down, and let me ride with them to the next village.

I thanked God for saving me from abandonment but not for the lashing rain. Shivering and soaked to the bone, I was dropped off in front of a church, at the end of a long line the children had already formed to enter. Distressed and eager to seek shelter for the night, they did not notice me. Without help I could hardly stand up or walk. Only my will to live apparently unleashed a spiritual energy from nothingness that helped to drag me inside, and I collapsed on the already congested floor. There were no pews in the church, and the children filled every inch of the floor. From that point on, until our arrival in Balta, all I remember is that we were met by a disinfestation squad that sprayed us with a smelly powder and shaved our heads. For this we had to stand in line.

The lengthy wait made me feel very queasy, and the room started spinning around and around until it went dark. I fainted. When I opened my eyes, I was in some kind of hospital. The doctor told me that my affliction was called *malaria tertiana* which, as I later learned, meant the disease would recur three times and could be fatal if untreated. This was extremely discouraging, as no medicines were available to us.

Throughout my stay in the hospital, I was mostly unconscious, with high fever and violent shivers. It was not until later that my friends told me about the unsettling events that had taken place while I was sick.

Apparently there was supposed to be one large regional orphanage for all the children from the smaller camps of Transnistria in transit to Palestine—or so the organizers had thought. In fact there were no such accommodations, nor was there ever such a plan. When this reality became apparent, a great confusion arose. In the chaos that followed, local Romanian soldiers arrived, herding the children into a walled-in yard, keeping them under guard. A rumor of imminent execution sent hundreds of orphans into a frenzy of loud crying and screaming that could be heard miles away.

The Balta Jewish committee immediately intervened and succeeded in persuading the commander to free the children. The frightened children were calmed down and taken into a community building, where they were fed and housed for the next few days. Unable to keep us in Balta, the committee arranged for us to be returned to our respective camps. Sick as I was, they put me on a cart, and with the rest of the children, I somehow made the trip back to Bershad. We returned to square one deceived and depressed.

Meanwhile, the Bershad Jewish committee had acquired a larger house to hold more orphans. Located on the bank of a tiny river, this new structure consisted of four rooms, with the same wall-to-wall sleeping plank-platforms.

Eventually this house had to accommodate some two hundred children. Still there was not enough room for all the orphans. Many had to find shelter elsewhere but were entitled to one meal a day here. A small portion of *djir* (liquid corn porridge), or mamaliga was our main source of sustenance.

In the new building, each room was assigned a room mother, who in return for her services received her own narrow, plank-bed but the same food as the rest of us. In the beginning I was in a room with children of both sexes, all under age twelve. Girls and boys over that age were separated and assigned to other rooms. At the back of the house, accessible only via an outdoor flight of wooden stairs, was another room. This one was called the "sanatorium," for sick girls twelve and older.

The room I was placed in held twenty to thirty children packed together on one large platform-bed. It was so overcrowded that we had to sleep with our knees bent in order to allow other children to nestle horizontally at our feet. During the day, it was no problem. But at night territorial battles erupted over every inch of space. In our sleep we had no control over involuntary movements, which often resulted in a fall or injury.

I was fortunate to be allowed to sleep on the platform, because I was still convalescing from my first malaria attack. For many children there was only room on the floor to sit during the day, but to go to sleep at night they were allowed to climb up and curl at our feet. My "foot person" was a little boy to whom I tried to be especially considerate. But regardless of how much I tried to be careful and control excessive movements, involuntary ones still happened during sleep.

One night I was jerked awake by a sharp pain in my leg, as if my flesh had been cut by a knife. I screamed in agony—my screams merging with that of the poor boy who had fallen heavily to the floor. Apparently he had clawed at my ankle in a desperate attempt to prevent his fall, and in doing so tore off a piece of my flesh. I was bleeding profusely, the pain burned, and I was furious, but, realizing that it was my fault for having stretched out and pushed him off the platform, I relaxed. Unfortunately, my wound became infected and did not heal for two years.

In the fall season, I suffered my second bout with malaria. My frail, wasted body burned as if on fire with temperatures that climbed beyond the thermometer's scale. The shivers were convulsive and uncontrollable. My teeth chattered so violently they threatened to break, and without blankets to keep me warm the seizures were more than my emaciated body could endure. After each attack I passed out.

Desperately ill, I was floating in and out of consciousness for days, or perhaps weeks, probably even lapsing into a coma. I had a vague remembrance of those dreadful days. From time to time I would hear faraway voices or see shadows, but I could not recognize people. There was nothing to keep me warm during the shivers but my torn clothes. I sensed the end nearing. But it was not to be.

Once again the haziness vanished enabling me to recognize the surroundings. What puzzled me was being on the floor instead of on the plank-bed. The room mother later explained the reason: my forceful shivers disturbed the children's sleep, therefore she moved me onto the floor. Besides, she thought, it might frighten them if I died in their midst.

One day my condition was so critical that the children thought I had actually died. But before calling the undertakers, the room mother, wanting to make sure, bent down for a more rigorous assessment. That was when she detected my faint breathing, the only sign of life. Exhausted, consumed by fever and tremors, without liquid or food, I had miraculously survived, to my surprise and everybody else's. Perhaps I did have "guardian angel"—or I was immortal.

I had survived to the age of twelve, although I did not look it. Even so, because I had reached that age, I was to be moved out of the "mixed" room of boys and girls. I was transferred to the "sanatorium," to join the other sick girls. It was like a promotion.

The upstairs room was indeed less crowded—only twenty girls. It was cleaner and better organized and supervised. Most important to me was that the girls were nice. They were older than I was, except for one ten-year-old.

The room had two platform beds along the wall; we were assigned ten to a bed. By extending one blanket width-wise, it would cover us all. Our room mother, Mrs. Tierer, sitting on her plank in another corner, kept a watchful eye on us at all times. We shared not only the space, the intense hunger, and the general suffering but also the pain of having lost our families. Within that crowded orphanage, we supported each other instinctively and became close in every respect. As misery loves company, we did not feel alone. By fate we became one.

Our conversations would mostly be about the circumstances under which our loved ones had died, about what we ate, what we *wanted* to eat, about our ailments, and of course, about our dreams and hopes, all of which did not preclude an occasional quarrel.

We were a mélange of children from different social backgrounds. The majority were from Bessarabia, where Yiddish was spoken among the Jews, whereas in Bukovina the Jews spoke German. So in order to communicate properly, we had to become proficient in Yiddish. That happened through sheer osmosis.

The characters were as varied as our backgrounds: Some were astute, some naive, some industrious, others totally passive and dependent. Of course, cliques developed. We German-speaking Czernowitzians, who were a majority, tended to be somewhat discriminating, considering ourselves a better class of people because of our education, manners, and background.

The sanatorium held the sickest, most gaunt, and crippled children. About five or six girls suffered from a rare affliction which impeded their mobility. Three of these crippled girls—Henia, Mitzy, and Adela—became my best friends. Their skeletal bodies were clad with potato sacks or rags and their heads were shaved bald, making their sunken and sorrowful eyes appear all that much bigger.

They told us that even after their families died, the acute lack of space and the need to protect themselves from the cold forced them to sit and sleep in a fetal position. They continued to stay in the same position for weeks or even months, awaiting their turn to die. Their prolonged inactivity caused their joints to stiffen and the muscles to waste away. They were unable to flex their legs—at best they moved around by squatting like ducks. That was how many were found before being brought to the orphanage.

It was painfully depressing to observe the hundreds of bald, shriveled, dirty children moving about like shadows, their bodies covered with lice and oozing sores. Such cruel reality taught us to fight for our survival in any way we could. It was a hard school but one that made our senses more keen and alert. It taught us to lick our wounds and to realize that prayers were not enough.

We found strength and purpose in supporting and nurturing each other. We shared happy memories as well as painful ones. Able girls massaged the legs of those who could not walk. Healthy boys, being more daring, would go out to the river, crack the ice and bring back water for washing, a greatly appreciated luxury in winter. Altruism was the rule, not the exception. Some children risked their lives by sneaking out from the camp to beg or steal food, which they then shared with others.

Within the orphanage we formed a small community with its leaders, followers, and inevitable subgroups. Boys showed greater respect to those children whose parents had been killed rather than those who died as a result of starvation or epidemic. By contrast, girls respected those who came from well-known families and projected a more sophisticated air. Yet in the potato sacks and ragged remnants of clothes we wore, we were, ironically, all rendered rather uniform.

As for me, preserving my individuality and my identity as a human being were crucial. After having been stripped so thoroughly of both, I forced myself to grope for my existence like an animal. I also sought to safeguard my connection to my past, my sense of being Ruthi, however possible. I maintained codes of proper behavior instilled by my parents and reinforced by my mother on her deathbed. I would not, for instance, participate in the other children's daily routine of begging or stealing food. I did not criticize them for doing it; I just could not do it myself.

In addition, I held onto my only heirloom, that single set of silverware with the engraved initials "M.G." for my brother's name, Manasse Glasberg. I had used that set ever since I learned to eat with a knife and fork. It was made of genuine sterling silver adorned with dotted edges, and it was smaller than ordinary flatware, since it was made for a child.

I was always convinced that it was made for me, but one initial engraved on it was not mine. It often baffled me, until one day I confronted Papa with the logical question as to the meaning of the *M*, since my initial was *R*. He quickly made up a story that it stood for "Muttika," his nickname for me. I wanted to believe him, and I did until I grew older, when I realized that it had originally belonged to my brother Manasse, Bubi, but had been given to me.

Although I had no control over the fate of my other possessions that had been sold, I somehow managed to hold on to this set which I would not exchange for any amount of money. I preferred to go hungry. This material link to my short childhood gave me a feeling of dignity and served as a reminder of who I had been and, inevitably, who I still was. I practiced my table manners and used the silverware even with a humble piece of mamaliga, ridiculous as it may have looked. It did provoke a lot of sarcastic remarks by some of the children, who nicknamed me the *Preetze* (Baroness).

Although their taunting remarks were hurtful, they certainly sounded better than some of the nicknames that the other children had been given. At least it had a noble sound to it. And their perception of me being different made me feel special and, therefore, more alive.

Other than that, I was just as miserable as the rest of the orphans. Almost twenty of us had to share a single plank-bed and two blankets. We slept molded into each other's bodies facing the same direction in order to fit on the limited surface of that hard, bedbug-infested platform. If one girl turned in her sleep, we all turned toward the same side so as not to disrupt the formation and continue sharing the blanket.

We turned in mute military precision: *Left! Right! Left! Right!* Claims for a share of the blanket often resulted in a ludicrous tug-of-war. As soon as the person on the extreme left pulled the blanket toward her side, the girl at the extreme right would scream and pull it toward *her* side . . . and so it went. We took turns sleeping at either end of the blanket so that everybody would experience the same annoyance. Such an arrangement might seem tolerable for a few days or maybe weeks. But we had to deal with it for more than two years.

The close body contact had only one advantage: It at least kept us warm. On the other hand it spread disease and infestation. Next to debilitating hunger, the worst and most painful afflictions we had to endure were lice, scabies, and boils with their unceasing itching. We spent most of each day grooming ourselves or one another, squeezing out pus from abscesses, from scabies wounds, or squashing lice between our fingernails. Lice were everywhere. Even without hair on our heads, they found other parts of our bodies on which to thrive. They continued laying their eggs in our filthy clothes which we never changed. They were merciless.

Biting bedbugs were another nuisance. We fought them with fire by dismantling the bed planks and using a burning wick or a small fire we lit in the room. For a few short weeks we would get some relief, and then they would be back.

In despair and lacking medication, we started taking "old-wives" tales seriously and began using absurd home remedies. One in particular stands out for its absurdity. Urine cures scabies. In the one potty we possessed, we collected urine from several girls, and one by one we soaked our scabies-infected hands, expecting some miraculous cure. Instead, we only reinfected ourselves and the endless cycle continued.

One freezing winter night we stood around a small fire that was smoldering in an iron container in the center of the room warming our hands. Drifting too close, one girl's dress caught fire. Without water to extinguish the flames, another girl instinctively grabbed the only liquid available—our full urine potty—and doused her with its contents. It was gallows humor that made us burst out in laughter. Under the circumstances she did not mind the humiliation. And so the urine that failed to cure scabies at least saved a life.

But no matter what we did, we could never rid ourselves of parasites, nor could we be cured of disease. The only disease I *was* cured of was malaria, and that was because I received some quinine pills from a camp doctor who must have gotten them from a recent Red Cross relief shipment. Unfortunately, I was unable to swallow the tiny pill, and I had to crush it into a powder to avoid gagging. Three times a day I had to swallow those bitter pills, the taste of which remained in my mouth for months afterwards. I did not even have a lump of sugar with which to neutralize it.

Concurrent with malaria I suffered from dysentery, intestinal worms, and chronic diarrhea. These, combined with the plaguing hunger, caused me such fatigue that at times I felt too weak to even sit up for the daily food ration.

Our sanatorium members were privileged in not having to stand in line for food in the downstairs hallway. Considering our poor health, the volunteers cut out a small hole in the wall so that we could receive our food directly from the kitchen.

In the hallway, hundreds of children had to stand in line; they were the ones who had no room to sleep at the orphanage.

Volunteers from among the camp inmates performed a variety of chores, from cooking to teaching. The person I appreciated most was Israel Pesate, a cantor from Czernowitz, who acted as our a choirmaster. He organized a group of the best voices, after testing each child. When my turn came, he informed me that I had a perfect alto voice for solo parts. That stunned me, as I had never known I possessed such a gift.

Pesate's visits meant a lot to us. We anxiously looked forward to the few hours of singing together because they made us forget the gnawing hunger for a while. He taught us songs in many languages, including Yiddish, Hebrew, and German.

My friend Mitzy, with a soprano voice, was the only other soloist, and we both felt special; it gave us a measure of popularity that would have been important to any ordinary child, but to us it was vital. We rehearsed diligently for our performances. People from the camp would come to listen to us and pay a token contribution, the proceeds of which would go for more flour or oil. It would take more than human imagination to visualize the grotesque picture. A choir of emaciated, bald, sad child-performers, singing tear-jerking Yiddish songs that reflected their own pain. It was perhaps the only way we could express our inner turmoil. Of course we also sang happy songs, but they were few.

It was there that I learned to use my voice to conquer hearts. Too proud to go begging, I came up with an alternative: I would visit my family's acquaintances on a rotating basis, making it look like a casual visit. As soon as I came in, some kind of food would be offered to me. Sometimes a piece of bacon or a whole potato, on other occasions even a piece of bread with a slice of onion and oil. After I devoured these delicacies, I was asked to sing. After our performances, my fame as a singer spread, so I was asked to sing wherever I went. I did it gladly, knowing that it would get me something to eat.

But for every child like myself who would not beg, there were others who would. Some clever boys even found ways to steal potatoes or beets from the peasants' fields. Others dared to sneak out of the camp and to find odd jobs for which the peasants paid them with food. All this gave birth to a food-bartering enterprise within the orphanage accompanied by daily dialogues:

"Who will give an onion for a slice of bread?"

"Who will trade a piece of cold mamaliga for a potato?"

"Who wants a piece of *makuch* for a garlic?"

Makuch was the residue of pressed sunflower seeds. It was like eating nails. It tore up our stomachs, but it was our only source of calories. Ironically, this was the same makuch that my grandfather used to give the peasants to feed their pigs in Milie.

The children got these "intestinal razor blades" from either the peasants or from the sunflower oil press, where they would work from time to time. It was mainly the boys who provided the lifesaving fragments of these cakes. They would share them by cutting them into tiny pieces so that everyone could get some, or they would exchange them for other foods. Makuch kept us alive, but it ruined our digestive systems forever. It certainly ruined mine.

On days when I was too weak to go on my "singing tours," these child-merchants came in handy. I took advantage of their provisions whenever I had something to exchange. Naturally, procuring food was the most important issue on the daily agenda and the most popular topic of conversation. I would often dream of bread and butter covered with black cherry preserves or prune paste or honey from my grandfather's beehive.

Over and over again we talked about our hopes to be free, to go back to school and turn the white pages of a book, to take a hot bath with fragrant soap, to exchange our rags for clothes, and to sleep alone in a clean, soft bed.

These visions gave us strength. It seemed that we developed some ability to bear the unbearable. I have no idea how we tolerated each other's odors, each other's filth, and each other's dirt. In the summer, we could manage to wash ourselves in the nearby river, but during the harsh Ukrainian winter it was virtually out of the question. Still, even then, some brave children would scrub themselves with snow. They would also relieve themselves in the snow.

The whole camp, in fact, was one large outdoor toilet. Every alley and backyard served as such, as did the river bed. And we who lived next to the river had to deal with that stench day in and day out. On the way toward the river, it was impossible to avoid the piles of excrement that practically covered the surface of the river bed.

Our cellar and the adjacent walls of a ruined house were all used for the same purpose. Male and female alike relieved themselves, totally undisturbed by each other's company. We had been reduced to the behavior of animals; shame and modesty had no place when survival was at stake.

We bathed in a river polluted with human waste and drank its water. Only in the winter when our public toilet area froze were we spared from the stench.

At night we did not venture outside even to relieve ourselves, because that was when the Romanian and German soldiers roamed the camps, randomly raping and killing. Instead we used a single bucket until it was full. Every morning one of the healthier girls would be assigned to empty it into the river. All the while the fear of being killed was pervasive. We tried to repress it, but we always dreaded the moment when some crazy officer would give an order to raid the orphanage.

Compared to the fate of children in other parts of Transnistria, Bershad was bearable. Grisly rumors about Nazi savagery circulated widely. The worst one was about children being buried alive.

The Romanian newspaper *Scanteya,* dated October 1944, carried the following account of the village Valegotilovo:

In the path of the Nazi-Sympathizers: Children buried alive in Transnistria

The Nazi beasts have plundered all the countries they have occupied, but never has their savagery manifested itself so much as in the U.S.S.R. where hundreds of thousands of Jews have fallen to the cruelty of these beasts. The Ukraine itself became the Nazi execution field.

Let the documents speak. Here is what Constinenko from the village of Valegotilovo declared:

"The village was occupied by the Germans on Aug. 6, 1941, at mid-day. Immediately the shooting of Jews and Communists started. A lot of people hid in the fields. The special S.S. units intercepted them and started a hunt. The beautiful girls were distributed among the officers, then shot after they had been used. . . . The executions were done in trenches, 500 meters from the edge of the village. The men would form one group, women and children another. They kneeled facing the edge of the trench. The Germans passed by on horseback and shot them in the head. The screams of the women and children would make you tremble. . . . The pregnant women were shot in the abdomen. Sometimes they were slit open and the child would fall out. Children under two years of age were buried alive.

"When the last remnants of life had been extinguished, the criminals would wipe off the blood on their weapons and hands using the faces and clothes of the victims. Then they started to sing, eat and drink while the unfortunate peasants covered the dead with dirt." (translated by the author from a copy found in the Library of Congress in 1989)

The Forgotten Cemetery

CHAPTER 6

Slowly, very slowly, the winter months passed. The snow melted, and spring 1943 arrived. The awakening of nature brought about an upsurge of my foreboding thoughts about the obscure circumstances of my family's burial place.

I had imagined some sort of mass grave in a far-off and inaccessible place. But according to rumor the reality was even grimmer what with stories of unburied corpses and unmarked mass graves. Visualizing the gruesome picture, I shuddered.

To my great relief, I learned that the Jewish cemetery was in fact only about a mile away from the camp. And although it was off limits, people did go there despite the risk of being caught. Disregarding the danger and my frailty, I decided to go. After having seen so much death, one would think that the sight of a cemetery would not stir me. Paradoxically, I remained terrified of anything having to do with death. However, the burning need to find my family's graves and to be with them in spirit suppressed my fears.

One day, together with a group of older orphans, I ventured on my loneliest and most dramatic pilgrimage. It was a long and exhausting walk. When we finally arrived, everybody dispersed into different directions, leaving me alone among ancient Chassidic tombstones and newer monuments of Bershadian Jews who died before the war.

Trembling with fear, I looked around, scanning the area for a recent marker. But there wasn't a single sign to indicate the last resting place for the thousands of victims who had perished during the devastating winter of 1941–42.

Walking deeper into the cemetery, I noticed some fresh graves of various sizes but no markers. Suddenly I made a grisly discovery. Scattered throughout the whole area were entire, unburied skeletons and individual bones—human bones that covered the soil like shells on a beach.

My search for a mass grave was futile. There were only bones and more bones—a phantasmal, nightmarish vision. To be sure I was not hallucinating, I stopped to collect myself. There was no doubt—it was real. Momentarily it occurred to me that among these bones might also be those of my family. I panicked. Blood rushed to my head. Possessed, driven only by a mad impulse, I began to talk to the bones as if they had human characteristics.

First I picked up a long bone. "That could have been one of your legs, Papa," I thought. Next, I picked up another one. "Bubi, is this one of your arms?" I saw a skull and slowly touched it as I continued my inquiry. "Is it you, Mama?"

At this point the numbness of emotion that prevented me from crying dissipated. It was as if a dam had suddenly opened. Tears cascaded down my cheeks, tears I could no longer suppress. I cried loudly and hysterically. Then I felt someone touch me and shake me. When I regained my senses somewhat, I recognized that it was one of my companions. The group had to wait a while before I was able to pull myself together, and return to the orphanage.

Bitter and heartbroken, I vowed to do everything in my power to keep alive the names of my parents and brother.

With the memory of that experience, I began to understand the importance of Jewish customs and religious traditions. Death was still a daily occurrence in the camp, but because the rate had abated somewhat there was more time to treat the deceased with humanity. Now when I would heard the recitation of the *kaddish*, the prayer for the dead, it had a special meaning.

But it was another prayer, the *yizkor*, that evoked overwhelming sadness. Even though I did not understand the words, the sorrowful melody tore at my soul. I cried inside every time I heard it and felt heartbroken at not having a male relative to perform these rites, or the means to pay someone to do it, as only an adult male may recite such prayers.

Even though in smaller numbers, people continued dying daily. There seemed to be no relief in view, as if the world had forgotten us. In our isolation we could not have known that the Jewish Council in Romania was desperately trying to obtain permission to send us aid. Such an undertaking was possible only because Romania, although allied with the Nazis, was not under their occupation, and therefore could and often did act independently in defiance of the Germans.

Although under a Nazi dictatorship, many Romanians, be they intellectuals, clergy, or simply humanitarians whom I always call the "Silent Majority," were opposed to this genocide and dared to intervene on behalf of the Jews. This was possible only because many important personalities maintained their relationships and contacts with prominent Jewish leaders who tirelessly fought for the liberation of their ill-fated brethren. Rabbi Dr. Alexandru Safran, Dr. Wilhelm Filderman, and Fred Saraga were just a few of the many outstanding Jewish leaders. On the gentile side to name but a few, were the Queen Mother Elena, the metropolitan Nicolae Balan, Major Agapiescu, Charles Kolb (the representative of the International Red Cross in Romania), and Mrs. Ioan, the director of the Romanian Red Cross. Urged by the Jewish Council, the papal nuncio Andreas Cassulo visited Transnistria in 1943, sending back a report to the Vatican. As a result, the Holy See transferred more than one million Romanian *lei* to help the deportees.

Finally permission for aid was approved. Marshal Ion Antonescu, the Romanian leader, ordered the Transnistria relief not necessarily to save the Jews but rather to comply with an urgent request from German army commanders in the area who were afraid of the typhus epidemic. At any rate we were the beneficiaries. In view of the latest war developments, Marshal Antonescu loosened the noose around the Transnistria camps, probably because he feared being judged as a war criminal. That in turn allowed more help in, to alleviate hunger and disease.

All the camps received some money to help the orphanages, the hospitals, and the soup kitchens. A line of communication with the deportees' families back home was established. In my case I did not know how anyone learned about my survival or my location, but someone did. Soon the walls of our tiny community center turned into one big bulletin board with notes of all sizes and colors. Everybody ran to search eagerly for their names in the hope of establishing contact with families and friends.

One day I was told that my name was posted on the wall. I could hardly believe there was still someone who actually remembered me. Indeed there was a short letter from my dear Aunt Anna. I was ecstatic. As soon as I could find a piece of paper, I replied. After a wait of what seemed an eternity, miraculously I received an answer and a small amount of money. Money!

Deutschmarks! Or, more accurately, *RKKS. Reichskreditscheine* was the currency during the German occupation. Never had I touched more than a coin of ten *lei* in my entire life! But now that I had a few paper bills, I was hesitant to touch them because of what my father used to tell me about handling money. Then I sadly realized the irony of the circumstances and eagerly grabbed the paper bills.

With that money, I bought myself a slice of bread and a sliver of butter every day from the peasants who were now allowed to sell their products in the ghetto. Sometimes I even indulged in a dish of meatballs that, I later heard, was made of dog meat. The hot meal was cooked and sold by a shriveled old woman who lived in a hut across from the orphanage. The aroma emanating from that hut often made my mouth water, but until now I could not afford to buy any of her "delicacies". My finances got an additional boost when my Aunt Cilli also learned of my survival and sent some money and a package of used clothes. I particularly remember the dark blue ski outfit that had belonged to my cousin Guido. That suit kept me warm in the winter, replacing my only skirt, which was so torn it looked like a fishing net. The drawback of the suit was

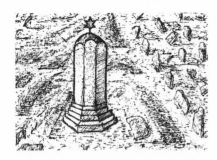

The Bershad cemetery. In the middle, the obelisk erected by the survivors in 1943, in memory of the 20,000 deported Jews who died there.

that with my bald head I looked like a boy, and to my annoyance some people addressed me as such.

Now that many inmates had received financial help from their relatives, the Jewish Committee decided to collect money for the construction of a large monument in memory of the Bershad victims. A specific amount of money had to be paid for each name that would be engraved on the monument. I paid my share, an amount that would have helped feed me for several weeks. Yet I preferred to go hungry in order to honor my loved ones—penitence for the sin of having survived.

The completion of the monument took a long time, but finally at the end of 1943 the wish of all the survivors came true. It took the form of a tall, five-sided prism, into whose marble plaques were inscribed the names of thousands. For the victims whose relatives could not afford to pay and those with no surviving kin, the fifth side bore the inscription in Hebrew by Rabbi Berl Yasser of Briczene, dedicated to all the victims:

> In eternal memory,/in commemoration of the destroyed world/of the eternal people/ in the valley of destruction:/Do not keep silent/at the sorrow of the myriads of Israel,/[forsaken] without a teacher, without a savior,/ fathers and sons, babes and elders;/inseparable, in mass graves, they never parted./ they died of hunger, frozen by cold,/exiled wanderers, those deprived of freedom,/martyrs of the land,/victims of tyrany./In their life and death they were joined together./In the year 5702 (1943) in Bershad. May those here inscribed by name/also[be remembered]amongst the thousands of the renowned./May their soul be preserved in the bundle of life. (Hugo Gold, *Geschichte der Juden in der Bukovina* [History of the Jews in Bukovina]; translated by the author)

The unveiling ceremony was a mixture of sadness and gratification. The names of my loved ones were chiseled into marble for posterity, for my children and their children. I experienced a profound satisfaction and relief from the great burden; at last they would be remembered. There would be a place where I could come and pay my respects to my family and to the thousands of victims of Bershad. In my heart, I knew that one day I would return.

After having made my contribution to the monument, I was penniless again, existing on a daily ration of mamaliga. Later, some children, including myself, continued to receive small amounts of money from relatives in Romania. That helped to increase our daily calories; it also helped increase the variety of food we could barter with one another. The hottest items were tiny slivers of butter wrapped in green leaves, pieces of bread, lumps of sugar, and an occasional egg.

The demand for the horrible makuch went down, but mamaliga continued to be the basic meal. A touch of butter made it more appealing to our palates. Except for the slight improvement in our daily nourishment, life continued in its relentless monotony, misery, and fear.

Just when I thought that I had regained my strength, another relapse of typhus gripped me. I had to be admitted to an improvised hospital on the main street. It was outfitted with about forty stripped cots, with rags as mattresses, but no linen or running water. It was dirty and stank of human waste. One doctor and a few nurses did the best they could for the most sick, some of whom had to wait a long time for an empty bed. It was only after someone died that the next in turn would be admitted.

I was kept under quarantine and given injections of strychnine, which was supposed to strengthen my failing heart. From time to time as if through an opaque curtain, I would see a figure waving to me through the window. With effort I managed to recognize Mrs. Korn's landlady. Curiously, she was serving as a courier, bringing me a daily supply of soup and applesauce sent by Mrs. Korn. It was the only nourishment I received. Such acts of kindness by fellow deportees helped keep me alive.

Besides a burning fever, I was plagued by continuous diarrhea and such severe abdominal cramps that I often lost consciousness. I really did not have any more strength to fight. For some undetermined period of time, perhaps several weeks, I was suspended between life and death. To conquer my despair and fear of death, I welcomed an eventual reunion with my family. But I must have had a "guardian angel," because, defying all medical odds, I slowly recovered . . . again.

Released from the hospital, I returned to the orphanage, and again I had to learn to walk. I was happy to be back with my friends, whom I had missed very much during my hospitalization. When I regained some of my stamina, I started singing again in the choir. I needed to: it was the strongest outlet for my sadness. Music and singing were my emotional anesthesia and my spiritual resistance. Another way of building up that resistance was learning whatever and wherever possible. Under the absurd circumstances, listening to an older friend of mine recounting stories and reciting poetry by heart was all I could do. Eliezer Sternberg (now Professor Elazar Kochba) was a handsome boy and a scholar who took it upon himself to introduce me to Yiddish literature, especially to the writers I.D.L. Peretz, Shalom Aleichem, and Itzhac Manger. He probably never knew how much he meant to me.

Later, I met a girl called Donia. She and her brother were among the children who stood in line for their daily ration of food. During a conversation, we discovered that she had known my cousin Lucie and my brother, Bubi, and a special friendship developed between us.

Donia had difficulties walking due to a painful, chronic infection in one leg, which soon became life-threatening and required hospitalization. Even though she was a few years older, somehow I became her guardian. To visit her in the hospital, became my daily mission. And I always brought her something to eat, even at the cost of missing a meal or two myself.

Suspecting my sacrifice, she would always ask me, "Have you eaten today?" and I lied by answering in the affirmative. The amount of satisfaction I derived from that small charity superseded food. Determined to help her recover, I prayed she would not have to face an amputation. After six months, her condition improved, but it took her years to recover.

One day, visiting Donia, I noticed a tumult in the square next to the hospital. Ignoring the event, I hurried by, nervously passing behind the back of a German S.S. officer. Suddenly I heard shots and people screaming. I quickly squeezed myself through the crowd and ran. When I arrived home, the children were hiding under the plank-beds, trembling with fear. "Get under here quickly!" they said, pulling me under one of the planks. "Where have you been? We worried about you!"

"I was visiting Donia at the hospital. What's going on?"

"Don't you know? The German commander is shooting into the crowd for fun," my roommates informed me with a tone of fear.

"I just saw him in the square!" I gasped.

"You don't know how lucky you are. You just escaped death by a second!"

My God! I exclaimed to myself. Had he turned his head while I was right behind him, it would have been the end for me. One more escape from death. We knew that if the Germans were to discover our orphanage, they would kill us all.

Later we discovered that it was the infamous Major von Breitag, our local German commander, who on his customary strolls through town enjoyed shooting dogs and Jews, inspiring terror. So we hid for a few days under the platforms until the danger passed. We never ventured far from the orphanage because of the constant peril. Only exceptionally brave children would leave the camp, mainly in search of food. Myself, I never saw much of Bershad. I was too weak, and not that courageous. My excursions were limited to a few homes close to the orphanage.

Now word reached us about the mass murders of Jews taking place beyond the Bug River where the S.S. were in charge. Many inmates of Bershad who were sent there for forced labor never returned. We lived in constant fear of suffering the same fate. One day a teenage girl in a cream-colored summer dress with a long braid walked into our room with a look that froze us to the spot. Her name was Fenya, and she told us how she had escaped from one of these mass killings. We huddled together, listening dumbfounded, shivering with fear.

Fenya was born and raised in Ukraine. She and her family had been sent to a Nazi camp where daily executions were common. The Jews, Fenya said, were forced to dig their own graves. Then they were made to line up along a huge trench, only to be shot by the S.S. Each volley caused a victim to fall straight into the trench. Nobody had to even touch them. Nor did the S.S. bother to cover the graves. Fenya, anticipating her turn to be shot, fell into the grave with all the other victims, still screaming and moaning. Realizing later that she wasn't even wounded, she pretended to be dead.

As evening descended, she started to crawl out from under the corpses, and under the cover of night this brave girl ran away, hiding in bushes and cornfields until she reached Bershad.

Similar monstrous accounts reached us often. They were from gentile witnesses who claimed to have seen hills of freshly covered graves stirring within, suggesting that many had been buried alive. In such terror, we continued our daily lives without any sign of imminent liberation.

Finally, came the elating news about the German defeat on the eastern front. This should have been good news, but for us, the children, it meant that the retreating Germans would soon be marching into our camp and that the orphanage might be their first target. Knowing their intent to wipe out future generations, we became very apprehensive.

Somewhat relieved of struggle for mere survival, we realized that we had lost almost three years of schooling.

Although it did not bother all of the children, it did bother me. It enraged me terribly that after having lost my family, my dignity, and my health, I was also robbed of an education. There was nothing I could have done to reverse the other losses, but I felt I could do something about this one. In addition, learning seemed to be a way of lifting myself out of the wasteland.

Several of us voiced our concerns to orphanage volunteers, who shortly came up with a solution. It was decided that Mr. Horowitz, the supervisor of the boys' room and a teacher by profession, would give us lessons. We used the empty hallway where the noninterned orphans stood in line for food distribution. After the last child had left, we, the interned orphans, sat on the floor without paper or pencils and listened to Mr. Horowitz's instruction on science and mathematics. We were one class regardless of age or previous education. It was his goodwill and our receptiveness that made our improvised classes possible. This daily activity was of supreme importance to me, and I tried eagerly to make up for lost time.

Simultaneously the community organized a small private school for those children whose parents could afford a nominal fee. The directors of that makeshift school allotted a few places for orphans. I was overwhelmed to learn that I was among the five or six children from the orphanage our teacher had selected. A dream come true! I felt very fortunate and proud. With my parents and brother gone, it was important to me and to my survival to achieve something. Finally, some normalcy had been restored to my life, some dignity, and I was going to do the best I could to hold onto it.

All this good news was not without problems. Oozing wounds from infected scabies still covered my hands. I had nothing to wear and was terribly ashamed of my shaven head. After all, I was going to be among "normal" children whose families at least had some money, which helped to shield them. We orphans were a different species. I had too much to hide, and at thirteen that did not exactly contribute to my self-esteem. My conflict was between giving up school and conquering these obstacles. With great apprehension, I opted for the latter. At the most critical junction—just before school opened, my "guardian angel" came to my rescue—again.

A week later, as I visited the Korn family, Mr. Korn gave me some wonderful news: a crate of used clothing sent by the American Jewish Joint Distribution Committee for the orphanage had arrived. In a few days he would come to distribute them and let me have the first pick.

For that great event we all gathered in the largest room crowding the plank-beds and the floor, waiting impatiently. The crate, followed by Mr. Korn and his entourage, was brought in and placed on the floor. All eyes were fixed on it as if it were a magic box full of unexpected surprises. As in a ceremony of great importance, with speeches and blessings, the crate was finally opened to the "oohs!" and "aahs!" of the children.

"Ruthi Glasberg, pick the first outfit," Mr. Korn exclaimed. I proceeded to that treasure trove and chose a woolen baby blue dress because it matched the color of my eyes. To cover my bald head, I helped myself to a large handkerchief of the same color. After me, the children attacked the rest of the contents with a frenzy. Boys grabbed girls' blouses, and girls grabbed men's knickerbockers. Tall boys ended up with shorter pants, the girls with a dress too long. We were all smiling, laughing, jumping, eyes shining, our faces lit with delight, faces that had almost forgotten how to express such feelings.

Commotion and high spirits dominated that day. With great satisfaction, we disposed of our rags and replaced them with colorful used clothing, which to us were as new as if they had been recently purchased at the Gallerie Lafayette in Paris. Everybody looked changed, more dignified, more human, and some of us girls even looked pretty. We did not have mirrors but we felt pretty from within, and that reflected itself in the eyes of our peers.

Now I could go to school in a new dress with a blue handkerchief on my head. But hiding the scabies-infected sores on my hands was a big problem. Somehow I got hold of two more handkerchiefs and wrapped them around and between my fingers in such a way that the wounds were not visible.

All dressed up, wounds covered, without books or papers, I headed toward the little improvised schoolhouse, where I entered the fourth grade at the age of thirteen. It was my first day in a classroom in almost three years and also my first contact with children who had hair, were dressed fairly normally, and were not orphans. Right away I felt different, inferior, and insecure. God knows what else I felt, but my heart sank at the thought of being the poor dirty orphan. I would have died had anyone discovered what was going on under my bandages. Though nobody showed signs of noticing anything unusual, my conscience plagued me and distracted me from concentrating during class. I felt like I was camouflaging a criminal act.

Remembering routine check-ups in my school days when children infected with lice and scabies were made the butt of jokes and sent home in tears, I expected the same to happen here. Soon my secret would be revealed and I would be the object of harassment. Luckily, no such inspection ever took place.

But my happiness was soon interrupted by news of the German Army's retreat. Day and night, German tanks rumbled through the main street, followed by soldiers on foot and in trucks. We speculated about our chances of survival now that the town was overrun by Germans. Some predicted our end if more Germans came through our camp. Others thought we would soon be liberated by the Red Army.

There was also a hope that the partisans would help to liberate us. Hiding in the woods, they would carry out heroic acts of sabotage against the Nazis. We knew that among them were Russians, Ukrainians, and Jews, including some from our camp. Many partisans were often forced to hide among the deportees in order to escape detection. Our own Dr. Schrenzel, a lawyer, led a group of partisan youngsters within the Bershad camp. They somehow communicated and often helped the insurgents in intelligence matters.

One day, looking out the window of our "sanatorium," we noticed a human body hanging from one of the telegraph poles. As soon as we ventured out onto the street, we found out that there were several such bodies hanging from all the poles on the main street. To make us believe that these were indeed captured partisans, a placard saying "This is the reward for collaborators!" was attached to each corpse.

Apparently the Germans and Romanians couldn't capture them, so they just killed some Jews in the camp and hung them instead. The bodies were left swaying there all winter.

By now I had seen a lot of dead bodies and had got quite used to them. But to be exposed to those hanging corpses daily was overwhelming. Of course, we inevitably looked out the window, and we had to pass by the main street to go anywhere, so the encounter with the frozen corpses slowly became an everyday occurrence. I talked myself into believing they were scary stone statues adorning the street. Some of the boys, probably out of their own fear, practiced veritable "gallows humor" on some easily scared girls like myself. At the most inappropriate moment they would come up from behind, make grumbling noises, and say, "Look, the hangman is coming! The hangman is coming!"

I was frightened and didn't find the jokes at all funny. I had terrible nightmares about the hanging corpses and often awoke in a cold sweat.

It turned out to be Major von Breitag, the German commander, who tortured and killed almost three hundred Jews, including our Dr. Schrenzel, because of their connection with the partisans.

The pressure on the Romanian camp authorities, caused by the Russian offensive, incited them to execute close to another two hundred Jews in Bershad. And the demoralized Breitag often paced through the ghetto with his loaded gun shooting into groups of Jews as they gathered at the market to buy food. As soon as it got dark, the S.S., under the pretext of seeking out partisans, shot anyone found walking in the streets. Some Jews were held in the command headquarter's cellar without food or water. There they were abused and tortured—their flesh often burnt with red-hot irons to make them reveal the hiding places of the partisans.

Obviously these were innocent victims who had no idea of the whereabouts of the partisans and could not give any information. Nevertheless the Nazis dragged them to the outskirts of town, forced them to dig their own graves, and shot them. They were covered over even though many were still alive.

These latest developments put an end to all activities in the camp, including school. All we could do now was pray and hope for a miracle to happen. And it did.

The rapidly advancing Red Army now began to preoccupy Marshal Antonescu. Under pressure from Jewish leaders and the International Red Cross, in addition to receiving a billion *lei*, he agreed to release five thousand orphans under age eighteen. They would be freed in Romania, and from there they would be shipped to Istanbul, Turkey. From there the Jewish Agency would transport them to Palestine. But he soon changed his mind, allowing only orphans who had lost both parents and were under age fifteen. That reduced the number to fewer than two thousand.

This time we hoped the plan would materialize. Once we heard the news, we could not wait. Travel fever possessed us. Lists of orphans were compiled, and preparations for the trip began with the help of a delegation of Jews from Romania. In a frenzy of excitement, we packed our tiny bundles numerous times and bought food for the trip. But a week later, the food was eaten and we were still in Bershad.

Before leaving, we all went to the cemetery to say good-bye to our deceased families. The monument stood there like a giant protecting the souls of the victims. I read and reread the names of my father, mother, and brother. Reassured that there was at least this obelisk to which I could return one day, I left.

The long-awaited day of leaving the hell of Bershad—our dream of redemption—unbelievably arrived. Once more a caravan of horse-driven carts lined up in front of the orphanage. We mounted them in the order in which the delegates called our names. Again we headed toward Balta. Remembering the aborted trip of two years ago, we prayed hard that this one would go smoothly. One part of me was overjoyed, the other cried inside for the dead we left behind. But as Bershad faded in the distance, so did the thoughts of the past. Instead we began to envision the future as we speculated about the possibility of another fiasco. These tortured thoughts were with us during the whole journey.

Approximately two thousand children from all the camps were gathered into two regional orphanages, Moghilev in the north, and Balta—which included us—in the south. The delegates in charge of this operation, like Fred Sharaga, Dado Rosenkranz, and Itziu Herzig ("Itzhak Arzi") endangered their lives in the mission to rescue us, and it is to them we owe our eternal gratitude.

On several occasions, Adolph Eichmann successfully prevented earlier attempts to rescue the Transnistrian orphans. On March 3, 1943, he sent an order to the German minister of interior in Bucharest, Romania, to block the planned rescue. However the Romanians resisted the order. Thus despite Eichmann's intention, the rescue operation succeeded, at least partially.

This time, Balta was ready to accommodate us. We were placed in orphanages and private homes. A few days later we gathered at a community facility to thoroughly wash ourselves and dress in nearly new clothes and shoes. Clean and clothed, we were then taken to the railroad station.

There were cattle cars again. I panicked. But overcoming this momentary fear I told myself that these cars shouldn't bother me; we were, after all, en route to freedom. Under the supervision of one delegate, about ten of us were seated in each car.

It was a long journey, but we did not mind it at all. There was no comparison with the cattle cars that brought us to Transnistria. This time we had sufficient food and water, and there were frequent relief stops. For the first time in years we were extremely happy. The train soared westbound towards the Dniester as our tumultuous joy knew no limits.

ADDENDUM NO: 17 In the Eichmann Trial
The Chief of the Security Police and of the S.S.
Berlin, March 3, 1943
Heading: SECRET
Number 89/43G
Addressed to the Foreign Ministry,
Legation Council Mr. von Hahn,
Berlin
Rapolenstrasse 11.
Regarding: Jewish resettlement from the Balkans to
Palestine.
Reference: Without.
According to confidential trustworthy information, Jewish officials in Romania are looking through their contacts in Istanbul, to prospectful negotiations with Turkey concerning the issue of Turkish transit visas for a group of 1,000 Jewish children accompanied by 100 Jewish adults from Romania, which in cooperation with "Wagon-Lite" will be shipped via land through Bulgaria and Turkey to Palestine.

We request that this planned emigration, if possible be cancelled.

K207357   By orders of:
                        (signature)
                        Eichmannn

(translated from German
by the author)

Many Loyalties,
Many Homelands

CHAPTER 7

Children Aged in Their Buds
I am near you, those returned
from hell
Who in every fiber of your
worn body
Carry forever the scars of
unlawfulness,
Orphans fearful of the screech
of the door.
For the punishment of the
beast.

Children aged in their buds,
You never knew what evil is,
nor the doll,
Nor the flowers,
Frolicsome you were not.
For you and your parents,
The executioners invented
TRANSNISTRIA.

SHASHA PANA
(translated from Romanian
by the author)

The following day we reached the Ukrainian border town of Tiraspol, from which we were to cross the Dniester River and enter Romania. We were overjoyed at the prospect of leaving the hellish soil of Transnistria behind us, but Romanian officials found a way to ruin even this happy moment.

By checking the lists of names against a roll call and against the pinned name tags of the smaller children, they caught many stowaways—mainly those older than fifteen. Hundreds of older children were denied entry. They were torn away from their friends and younger siblings, put on another train, and sent back to the camps.

The rest of us underwent yet another deparasitation procedure. This time they sprayed us with some white powder (DDT?), gave us another change of clothes, and made us spend the night in a warehouse. Only the next morning were we allowed to board the train again. Soon we crossed the Dniester and headed toward the Romanian border town of Tighina. Three days later we finally arrived at Iassi. About a third of us were to stay here, while smaller groups were taken to other towns.

Although Romania was still at war, and life was unstable and dangerous, at least we were back to some sort of civilization. I was thrilled to be back to a normal city with cobblestone streets, multistoried buildings, electricity, and shops. These long-forgotten images evoked a bittersweet feeling.

Iassi's Jews went out of their way to receive us warmly and to nurture us. Their overwhelming compassion was probably enhanced by their own tragedy. Too soon after my experiences, I got to hear first-hand accounts from survivors about the recent, barbaric history of this city.

Iassi, the old capital of Moldova, was home to many intellectuals. It had a large Jewish population until June 1941, a date marked by the most barbarous massacres in the history of Romanian Jewry. It is sacrilegious to describe this dismal tragedy in a few sentences when entire books could not do it justice. Yet not mentioning it would be an outward sin.

After a merciless slaughter of more than two thousand Jews, thousands more were loaded into about thirty freight cars without ventilation. The "death train" as it came to be known, left for an unknown destination, moving for days slowly and aimlessly from place to place until the poor people inside suffocated. Thereafter, the train stopped at stations only to unload the corpses. About eight hundred Jews miraculously survived that inferno and were interned in a concentration camp from which they were freed a few months later. Their testimonies described in detail the hellish journey to death. At the time I heard the stories the exact number of victims was not known, but later researchers found them to be close to twelve thousand.

After the pogroms, the Jews were ordered to return to their normal lives as if nothing had happened. Indeed, judging by the apparent normalcy of life, it was inconceivable that such carnage had taken place here.

March 6, 1944. The first day of the childrens' freedom coincided with the Jewish holiday of *Purim.*

We were brought to a former home for the aged, and led to a bright, elegant dining room. Dozens of tables displayed a variety of delicacies: Challah! Haman ears pastries! Cookies!

My reaction was like that of a blind person whose sight has suddenly been restored. The lights were too bright for me after three years of darkness. The abundance of food set on sparkling white tablecloths was an incredible yet, in a way, a disturbing sight. Oh, God! Delicious, unrationed food! In unlimited amounts! It was overwhelming. For a while I stood motionless at the door of the dining room.

"This is a dream," I said to myself. "Don't get carried away. Soon you'll awake to the horror of the past three years." I never ate a bite.

The well-meaning community had prepared a feast for us. They couldn't possibly have known the reaction of starving children to such abundance. We needed some kind of decompression process similar to what divers go through before they surface. The majority of the children had the same reaction as I did—they couldn't swallow a thing. But there were some who not only stuffed themselves but hid food under their clothing and in their pockets, afraid there would be none the next day.

After dinner we were shown to our new quarters, the girls on one floor, the boys on another. The rooms held rows of bunk beds with sparkling white bedding, warm blankets and soft pillows. It was heavenly, strange, and almost too cozy. But we adjusted quickly and absorbed all that luxury and happiness. Yet underlying that happiness was a feeling of terrible guilt that we had survived while the remains of our families rotted in a far and distant place.

At least we, the surviving children, might realize our parents' goal of going to Palestine—the land my father had eternally dreamed of, the ultimate fulfillment of every Jew. Papa had told me enchanting stories and had taught me Zionist songs, so I had a vague idea of what it might be like to live there in the land of milk and honey. That image fulfilled a need, a hope, a desire to be part of something, to be absorbed or adopted by a people, *my* people and *my* country. But the war was still going on, and even though I was no longer in the camps I could not shake off my fear of a reversal of events.

During the few months of our stay in Iassi, many Jewish couples started to adopt children by a unique and unusual process. The orphanage would gather the children in the dining room for a talent show, in order to show us off to them. At one end of the room was a bare stage on which we presented our performances. We, the Bershadians, reorganized our choir, though we clearly missed our choirmaster. Some sang, some danced, and some read poems in various languages.

The audience consisted of people from the Jewish community, some of whom came to select a child of their liking—something we did not know beforehand. The prospective parents had an opportunity to observe the child and assess his or her talent without being too obvious. And based on that observation, they made their selection.

To have some talent was important; it was a way of standing out from the crowd. My solo singing and ballet dancing apparently made me a desirable candidate, with the result that three families wanted to adopt me. I was flattered, but I politely declined, explaining that at thirteen I couldn't accept anyone as a parent and I could never call someone else "Papa" or "Mama." Besides, the need to belong to a group that had experienced the same fate exceeded that of being a lonely adopted orphan.

One of the families gave up trying to adopt me, but the other two were relentless. As a solution, I suggested alternating weekly between the two families. They agreed, and I left the orphanage to stay first with the Aronowitzes.

There I enjoyed the warmth and coziness of a family that served delicious home-cooked meals on a nicely set table, accompanied by a *Gespritzter*, white wine with a spritzer of seltzer straight from a siphon bottle. It was through them that I was introduced to this beverage, of which I am still fond.

Then it was the other family's turn to take me to their home. To show me off to their friends, they often asked me to sing, which I did gladly as a gesture of gratitude. I continued to live with them until something unusual happened in their house.

One day they invited me to one of their weekly gatherings they called a spiritualist séance. Six to eight people sat in total silence, with palms touching the edge of a round table. I thought it was a game and watched carefully for the outcome. The hostess, my foster mother, asked one of the female participants for the name of her deceased husband. She then called on his spirit and explained that if he responded it would make the table rise. That was a strange and scary experience and I tried to leave, but they insisted that I stay.

Suddenly I saw one edge of the table rising slightly all by itself. I was dumbfounded. I got goose pimples listening to the woman's conversation with the spirit, who supposedly responded by lifting the table several times. Perhaps it was because of what had happened to my family that such spooky tinkering with spirits made me uneasy, so much so that I asked them to return me to the orphanage.

April 1944. The Red Army advanced deeper into Romania as the Axis forces hastily retreated. Aerial attacks became a daily occurrence, forcing us to hide in bomb shelters. Even though this time they were Soviet attacks, they nonetheless hit indiscriminately and intensely. And in view of the danger they posed to us children, it was decided to evacuate us into the center of Romania. Our guardians broke up our group into several smaller ones and dispatched us to various towns. Some children were fortunate to go to Bucharest, but I was among those destined for Buzau.

The poorly organized Jewish community there was totally unprepared for our arrival. They housed us in a synagogue where thirty to forty children to a room had to sleep on floors covered with straw mats. The food was scant and tasteless, but things improved somewhat when later they placed us in an empty house with those eternal plank-beds along the walls. We would have considered all this sheer bliss compared to Bershad, but after the short, pampered stay in Iassi we deeply resented this lower standard.

The food also became more acceptable and we were less crowded, but life was not pleasant because the attitude of the community leaders.

We were all becoming more anxious about emigration to Palestine, so from time to time we inquired of the community president when the next transport would be going to Palestine. "Next *Purim*," he would sarcastically reply.

Our shoes, not new to begin with, started to fall apart, so we sent a group of older children to ask when we would get new shoes. "About the time of the horses' Easter," which was a Romanian saying to indicate *never.*

With the exception of a few families who invited us to their homes for a meal or two, nobody cared about our emotional needs. I was fortunate to be the frequent guest of the noble and kind Abramovitz family, in whose home I was treated like a queen. They fed me and clad me in their older daughter's dresses. I also became friends with their son, Isaac (now Professor Itzhak Ohad), an exceptionally gifted and refined young boy to whom I was drawn because of his violin playing, which, as always, brought back memories of my lost brother.

Upon arrival in Buzau, a list of our names had been made available to the local Jews, and soon many families came to the orphanage in search of relatives. To my great surprise, a gentleman came looking for me, introducing himself as a "Laufer"—my father's family. Indeed I did have such relatives in Czernowitz—my Aunt Toni and Uncle Simon Laufer. After so many years of isolation, meeting a family member, even a distant one who knew my parents, was a very pleasant feeling.

He visited often. Then one day he invited me to come and live with him and his wife. I didn't think there was any harm in it; quite the contrary, I thought it was a kind gesture considering that, being refugees themselves, all they had was a small room. However, it turned out to be a disaster.

At that time I had a bad cough, so I looked forward to the care I would receive in a private home. But his wife was a grouchy and jealous woman, who made me uneasy. My coughing at night disturbed her sleep. She then blamed her husband and caused scenes of such magnitude that I begged him to take me back to the orphanage. Although we slept on plank-beds, there we at least shared our miseries and did not burden anyone.

On day while walking together, he said, "You are a pretty, young girl, and soon boys will be courting you. You know what might happen next?"

I kept silent, ashamed even to listen to such talk.

What he tried to convey was a warning against pregnancy. I was physically and sexually undeveloped, flat-chested, had no menstruation, and looked like a ten-year-old child, and here was this man talking to me about sex and pregnancy. I nodded my head in gratitude, not knowing what to do with this new information. In any case, my mind was on other topics in those days, mainly emigration to Palestine. Compiling the child-emigrant lists seemed to take forever. Smaller groups had left from time to time, but the majority of us waited impatiently for our turn.

Days passed in exasperating boredom, interrupted only by the occasional visit of some dignitary, for whom I would be asked to perform. The stage was our plank-bed, on which I had to dance ever so carefully so I would not fall off. Singing a song was no problem, but for my ballet solo, I had to sing a Strauss waltz while at the same time dancing. My singing repertoire was abundant, but my most acclaimed song was "My Yiddishe Mama." Everywhere else such presentations worked in my favor, except here in Buzau. This became obvious when I noticed that the organizers repeatedly failed to put me on the list to go to Palestine. I became suspicious about the delay, since I had registered at the same time as a group that had already left. I had someone from the community inquire about it. He was told that they had to place a local girl on the list so they postponed my departure until the next sailing. That made me furious. How could these people play favorites and give my place to a girl from Buzau who had not even experienced the camps?

I felt extremely disillusioned to learn that people in the higher echelons were corrupt and could play with the destinies of such downtrodden children. The next list had also been completed, but I still didn't hear from them. I again asked someone to talk to the community president about me, which he did.

"Ruth Glasberg? Who is that?" asked the president.

"You know her very well. She's the girl who always dances ballet and sings at performances for visitors."

"We don't need dancers in Palestine. We need *chalutzot*—pioneer girls—to work the land," he answered indignantly.

Indeed, the organizers gave priority to young Zionists who wanted to build new collective settlements called *kibbutzim*. Being taken off the list seemed like a tragedy at the time, but in retrospect it saved my life.

Because Palestine was under British mandate, legal entry of Jewish emigrants was limited. The overwhelming number of refugees from Nazi persecution gave birth to a new enterprise, an illegal emigration network known as "Aliah Beth."

To smuggle these Jews into Palestine, all sorts of vessels were purchased. Three of them, the Turkish steamers *Mefkure, Bulbul,* and *Morina,* were supposed to sail in the summer of 1944 with thousands of refugees from various countries. The Emigration Office allotted a quota of two hundred and three children from the Buzau orphanage. They left by train to Constantza, the Romanian port on the Black Sea, from which they embarked. We later heard that the *Mefkure* was torpedoed by a German submarine and burst into flames. All three hundred and six passengers, including ninety-six children from Transnistria, drowned.

In the meantime, the war continued unabated. The Soviets advanced, bombing the Romanian towns in their path. Machine-gun battles took place on the outskirts of Buzau. Sometimes bullets flew over our heads, forcing us into shelters where we spent many sleepless nights. Although we took comfort knowing that the Red Army would enter any day, it was a trying time for us.

Summer 1944. The Soviets finally captured the town without much resistance from the Romanians. Anarchy reigned. Russian soldiers intruded into many homes, broke store windows, and looted the contents. They mostly looked for food and liquor, something they had been deprived of for months on the battlefield. The local people hid in their homes or cellars in fear of the invaders.

Since most of us orphans spoke Russian, the Jewish townspeople took advantage of this asset and used us as interpreters in exchange for food and lodging. Ironically, these same families that would not take in an orphan before suddenly came begging us to stay with them now that their property was in danger.

One family that owned a cellar full of expensive vintage wines took me into their home to play both interpreter and diplomat to distract the soldiers from finding the cellar. A few uneventful days passed before a group of soldiers knocked on the door. I greeted them in Russian, which immediately took them aback. In a very polite way they asked for alcohol and food. I translated the request to the landlady, who hurried to bring out wine and delicacies, which the hungry Russians quickly devoured. In the meantime they asked me many questions related to my presence there and my knowledge of the Russian language. Listening to a short résumé of my life, some had moist eyes. The good Russian soul surfaced in these war-hardened soldiers as they hugged me and wished me well. We ended up singing Russian songs together, which made them forget the search for the wine cellar.

Once my mission had been completed, I was sent back to the orphanage, which, like the whole town, was also given to anarchy. Some children took advantage of this lawlessness and went out to loot the stores already broken into by the soldiers. My friends tried to persuade me to join them, but I resisted. "It's not right for us to do such shameful things," I preached. "We didn't break into the stores, the Russians did," they retorted defensively.

"This is *their* business. We should not participate," I said. One cynical boy snapped, "The Communists are going to confiscate the stores anyway, so why shouldn't we get something for ourselves?"

Under continuous pressure, I caved in. But by the time I finally made my daring appearance, all the shops had been broken into and the merchandise taken out. I found myself in a looted jewelry store surrounded by empty boxes and scattered trays.

In this chaotic litter, I spotted something shiny on the floor. It looked like a ring. Overcoming my inner conflict, I picked it up and ran out to show it to my friends. They took a good look at it and burst into laughter. It was a metal ring mold, a totally worthless item. What a disappointment! Yet it was a relief to my conscience.

As the anarchy continued, we got word that it would be best for us to move to Bucharest if we still wanted to emigrate to Palestine. A few older boys formed a committee and went to the Soviet commander to ask permission to leave. He granted us the favor, and so we traveled by train to Bucharest, now occupied by the Soviets. There our small group happily rejoined the children who had left Iassi previously. We were housed together in a large orphanage, awaiting our final trip to Palestine.

August 23, 1944. In view of their defeat, the Romanians decided to break away from the Axis and sign an armistice with the Soviets, quickly changing from fascism to communism. That change indirectly affected us Transnistrian orphans who were originally from the reconquered provinces of Bukovina and Bessarabia. By law we were now official citizens of the USSR, which took jurisdiction over us.

The new communist government immediately designated two buildings for the fourteen hundred orphans, one for girls and another for boys. We were placed two to three children per room and settled in with regular beds and other comforts. Food was served in abundance in a huge dining room, and schooling in real classrooms with professional teachers soon started. We were truly schoolchildren again. Our social life was enriched by parties and visits to the boys' orphanage located a distance away.

The Soviets launched an aggressive campaign in an effort to draw all the orphans to their side. We were shown propaganda films about Soviet heroes and heroines. One of them, Zoya Kosmodemianskaya, a woman partisan, made a special impression on me. She became one of my first feminist heroines. In spite of the most cruel and heinous torture, she refused to reveal the location of her comrades and died for her country.

The point of all this was to indoctrinate us with communist ideology, and all our teachers and leaders did their utmost to achieve it. At our age they didn't have to work too hard. In our eyes, the Soviets were perceived as liberators, protectors, and friends. And with Stalin being portrayed as the father figure who adored children, there seemed no need for worry.

We were told that in a few months we would be returned to our "homeland"—Russia. They did not mention that our homeland was really Bukovina and Bessarabia, which they had reconquered from Romania—nor did they ever mention Palestine.

The communists discouraged Zionist activities and the Zionists' plans to mold us into farmers. Instead, the Soviets promised to educate us; we could become doctors, teachers or engineers. One should not waste human potential, they argued. But by the same token, the Soviets drafted many of our orphan boys as young as thirteen into the army, indifferent to the trauma they had suffered during the previous three years. Nevertheless, the Soviet arguments appealed to the younger ones among us who had not been indoctrinated by Zionist ideas. We were chiefly seduced by the promise of a free education and an idealistic future.

We were about eight hundred girls divided into classes according to the last grade we were in. At this point I was fourteen years old yet only in the fourth grade. That humiliated me enormously. Again, my eagerness to excel and to undo the harm of having lost years of education turned into an obsession.

One of my teachers was a young woman and a dedicated Communist. I do not remember what exactly caught her attention, but a few days into her science class she asked me to stay after school because she needed to speak to me. Thereafter we met almost every day. She asked me about my experiences in the camps, but I wasn't ready to talk about them. One day she asked me: "What would you like to be when you grow up?" I was surprised at such an inquiry; this was a topic I did not dare to even dream about due to the huge void in my schooling.

"A writer or a doctor," I replied after a long pause.

"I noticed your curiosity in class. At your age, you could benefit from some supplemental subjects."

"What do you suggest?" I asked, wondering what she was leading to.

"Well, I could help you after school," she suggested.

I couldn't believe my good fortune. I grabbed the offer with great enthusiasm and gratitude. This wonderful human being was volunteering her free time exclusively to me! We used to sit down in different locations, in class, on the building stairs, in my room, in any quiet corner where she would lecture me for hours. The main topics were Communism, Darwinism, and literature. She certainly found in me a curious and eager student, and we developed a close relationship. She was to be extremely influential on my philosophy of life and even managed to persuade me to become an atheist.

I was proud of my Jewishness and would have never renounced that rich historical and cultural heritage, but the idea of God was irrelevant to my life at that point. By learning about evolution and correlating it to the absence of God during the genocide, my eternal questions about His presence had been finally answered in a logical way. I adhered to the ethical values of the Ten Commandments and did not feel the need to pray to an invisible old man up in the heavens. These values, which had been imbued in me as a child, molded me into an authentic human being who worshiped the ideal of truth and social justice. Mainly I had a well-developed conscience, strong enough to show me the difference between right and wrong.

Here and there, in a private moment, my teacher would very diplomatically ask a few questions about Bershad and, in doing so, extract a few painful episodes. She seemed markedly moved.

A short time before our departure to the USSR, my teacher-mentor appeared in my room holding a new notebook and a pencil in her hand. She seemed quite glad to see me. "Glasberg," she said. "Would you do me a great personal favor and write down on paper your memories of Transnistria?"

I looked at her incredulously, as if she had asked me to climb Mt. Everest. "How do you suppose I could write all that down with my limited education?" I responded.

"It doesn't matter how you write; just write in your own words," she assured me. Convinced that she wanted a souvenir from an enthusiastic student, I didn't question her motives. Supplied with paper and pencil, I began to write in Romanian, in spite of only three years of elementary grammar. Despite this handicap, I described my experiences in Bershad as best I could. When I finished, she took me to an office to have the manuscript typed.

A few days later, my teacher brought me a few carbon-paper copies of the typed manuscript and thanked me sincerely for my effort. (I now have the published article and an anthology in which it appeared.) Embracing each other, we said our adieus.

While we prepared in full for the return to our "Russian homeland," other children who were not lured by the Communists' promise remained in the city under the guidance of Zionists who continued organizing emigration to Palestine. I had friends in that group, many of whom wanted to win me over to *their* camp. They tried desperately to convince me of the Zionist dream. But by that time I was not only scared to defect but also convinced that Russia was the right place for me. The Communist ideal burned brightly in my soul. Nothing could persuade me otherwise.

I had a full, interesting life in beautiful Bucharest, which, in spite of the war, was bubbling with life and entertainment. Contributing to this good life were distant relatives who, somehow, found out about my existence, and invited me to their homes. Most of them were themselves refugees.

One was my father's cousin Joseph Greif. Until this day I can't understand how people communicated across those long distances. How did all these relatives, many I had never heard of, suddenly find out about my survival and come forward offering their assistance: my father's cousins, my mother's cousins, cousins of cousins? Everybody seemed rather shaken by the past events, but to see a surviving orphan must have really touched them.

A cousin of my mother's, Dory, took special interest in me, and visited me often. Soon we became quite attached to each other. So much so that I confided in her a secret that seriously bothered me: I was fourteen and had neither developed breasts nor menstruated. I was so convinced that I was not normal as a result of the trauma that this problem almost became an obsession. I even thought that I could provoke the start of menstruation by rigorous physical exercises. Where this idea came from, I don't know; perhaps it was just intuition. Every time I visited Dory, I ran up and down the six flights of stairs to her apartment numerous times. Result: nil. Dory didn't take it seriously; it rather amused her.

Shortly the preparations for our return to Russia accelerated amidst rumors that our final destination would be the Donbass coal mines or the city of Odessa. I knew about Odessa, the beautiful port on the Black Sea, through songs and literature. But Donbass? That was new to me. I could hardly imagine what they would do with us there.

We were each given a suitcase full of clothes: felt boots, underwear, and a winter coat. The highlight of the girls' wardrobes were the *valienky*, typical Russian boots made of white felt trimmed with brown leather—truly beautiful and very warm. With that small trousseau, we were ready to face the harsh Russian winter. I proudly embarked on the trip to Mother Russia without the faintest idea of what awaited us.

December 1944. Another repatriation, another homeland.

The authorities gathered all the children at the boys' orphanage, and from there trucks would take us back to Iassi—to the same railroad station we had arrived at from Transnistria almost a year before. And just as then, a long train of cattle cars was ready for us. I wondered if cattle-cars were forever my destiny. And the irony of returning on the same route, back to now-Soviet Ukraine, did not escape me either.

Faced with this déjà vu, I had to keep on reminding myself that now we were not persecuted and that Odessa had been recaptured from the Nazis. Nevertheless, we had an uneasy feeling.

What intrigued me most were the chameleon-like Romanians; changing their colors depending on the company they kept. Just three years earlier, people of the same nation had humiliated, abused, and killed the Jews. I had a hard time believing that their ideology had changed overnight. Which is not to say, that all Romanians were Nazis, but neither were they all communists. Therefore, I had some doubts.

At last the trip started. About twelve boys and girls occupied each car. We had enough food, water, and stops for the use of toilets. Accompanied by friendly escorts, both Romanian and Russian, the trip was almost comfortable.

After several days we reached the city of Odessa. Judging by the column of trucks and the number of officials approaching the train, it was obvious we had been expected. Officials would go from car to car asking children under fourteen to leave the train and mount the trucks that would take them to a specially created orphanage.

We were a close-knit group of friends of all ages, so parting with the younger ones was very sad. But orders were to be obeyed. The rest of us remained inside the train, wondering about our own fate. Again the Donbass issue came up. Now we were told that we would study, but also work without pay in the coal mines—a patriotic deed for our newly adopted Motherland.

Darkness descended upon Odessa, engulfing our cars and the railroad station. We were settling down on the floor for the night when suddenly a heated discussion erupted about my staying with the older children.

"How old are you, Ruthi?" one of the older boys asked.

"Fourteen and a half," I answered.

"You look like ten, and you don't have a birth certificate to prove your real age. You should have gone with the younger kids."

"I don't want to lie," I snapped.

"Look at yourself. You won't survive the harsh life in the coal mines. You're just a kid," another boy suggested.

Suddenly everybody got involved in the argument. They only wanted what was best for me. Their concern was heartwarming. I realized that they perceived me as being much younger than fourteen, though I refused to accept the fact that it was caused by my being underdeveloped. They had always accepted me on an intellectual level which made me feel comfortable in their company. I hated parting from them.

All their talk finally convinced me of my mistake, and now the fear of perishing of hard labor in the mines really scared me. What could I do? It was too late. Or was it? The discussion abated, and we soon fell asleep.

Suddenly, in the middle of the night, we heard the car door being opened from the outside. The silhouette of a tall man appeared in the door frame. The contours of his figure were discernible by the dim light of a lantern he held up against a backdrop of the blacked-out station. He was cloaked in a long coat, and on his head he wore a typical Russian fleece hat with long earflaps that dangled down to his waist. As he brought the lantern closer to his face we could make out his distorted features, his mouth totally twisted—a Quasimodo-like image that inspired revulsion and fear.

"Are there any children under fourteen in this car?" he asked in Russian. Apparently he was responsible for finding those underage who might have been overlooked the previous day.

I could not believe my ears. Was it possible that I would be saved from what seemed like potential death in the mines? Was I really so lucky?

At first I didn't step forward, still grappling with the conflict between my conscience and my will to survive. When the others saw me immobilized, they gathered around me and practically pushed me out the door.

At that point I raised my hand and shouted "I am!" The ghastly man took a good look at me and gently asked, "Why didn't you leave with the others?"

I shrugged my shoulders in silence. I was scared of him and could hardly imagine that this creature would serve any good purpose. Yet I followed him toward a solitary truck across the railroad. There, to my pleasant surprise, were another twelve children, all collected at the last hour. We were so happy to see each other on that dark and unfriendly Odessa night that we hugged and chatted incessantly until the truck's loud motor started to roar. Nobody told us where we were going. We assumed that we would probably be joining our eighty friends in that special orphanage to which they had been taken that morning.

We traveled in total darkness along the shores of the Black Sea. Even though we heard the waves breaking on the shore and smelled the salty air, we couldn't discern the sea. By peeking through the slits of the canvas that covered our military truck, we determined that we were not going to Odessa. To our great disappointment, we realized that we were traveling outside the city. That worried us. "Where are they taking us?" we asked anxiously.

Nobody had an answer. It seemed an endless journey alongside the sea, through scattered little settlements here and there. We must have traveled a couple of hours before the truck stopped in front of a primitive peasant house in the middle of nowhere. Clearly we were far from the city of Odessa. Our guides announced, "We have arrived, children!"

"Arrived where?" we wondered, without speaking out loud. Suitcases in hand, the thirteen of us walked in, hoping to meet our peers. Instead we were met by a friendly supervisor who explained that the house was an orphanage for *bezprezornye*, generally delinquent children. There were boys and girls of all ages, both Russian and Ukrainian, none of them Jewish.

We were deeply disappointed not to be reunited with our friends. And to be categorized as delinquent children was a strong aftershock only nine months after our liberation from the horrors of Transnistria. The realization that the Russian leaders had so little knowledge and understanding of our vulnerability was very disturbing.

When we inquired were about the fate of the larger group picked up that morning, all they told us was that there was no more room in the other orphanage so we had to be brought here. The living conditions were horrible and the food consisted mostly of pickled cucumbers, sauerkraut, and substitute egg powder. After our last few months of a fairly comfortable life in Bucharest, this was terribly disappointing.

To add insult to injury, the Russian children had under the influence of the Nazi occupation, become overtly anti-Semitic. They neither knew what a Jew looked like nor what it meant to be one, but they had certainly picked up the Nazi methods of humiliation. Once they heard that we were Jewish, they verbally attacked us with profanities and mockery and imitated a supposedly typical Jewish, guttural, rolling *r* by calling the girls *Sar-r-rochka* and the boys *Abr-r-ramchick*. It was an insult that often culminated in fist fights. And so this was the good life and freedom the communists had promised us.

I felt trapped, disoriented, and once more fearful for my life in that godforsaken place. The disappointment, in addition to the gloomy winter months of 1944–45, did something to me. For the first time since I had been orphaned, I threw up my hands and tried to accept the fact that I had no further links to anybody or any place—so much so that I actually blocked out the memory of any living relatives at all.

However, when faced with a situation beyond my power, I would always try to make the best of it. The Russian girls were more tolerant than the boys. And because I was blond and blue-eyed and spoke a nearly accent-free Russian, they accepted me as one of their own. Consequently, they treated me with more respect than they did the rest of the Jewish children. Instead of dwelling in self-pity, I tried to adapt to the life-style of the Russian girls.

This small, primitive house had neither running water nor toilets. Ten of us shared a room where we slept two to a narrow iron bed. But, more important, we also shared our insubstantial lives. We sang together and told stories, yet the most interesting of all pastimes was our "dream interpretations."

Every morning before dressing to go to school, we would stay in our dirty beds for a while and tell our dreams. Each of us would offer an interpretation of the other girls' dreams. The positive and optimistic interpretations were the ones I especially clung to, for they nurtured my wounded soul. We became experts at this and took it very seriously.

The harsh winter made it difficult to keep our bodies clean. About once a week it was bath time in the kitchen. Water had to be brought in from a faraway pump and heated on the stove. In a large tin basin we washed ourselves in succession, about five or six girls in the same water. The supervisor would oversee the whole ritual and also decide the order in which we would bathe. When my turn came to step into the basin filled with dirty, brown water from the previous bathers, I had to repress feelings of nausea. I just made believe it was muddy river water.

How I dreaded those baths! Sometimes I was lucky to be first or second, and only then did I feel that I really got a good sponge bath. But that seldom happened. By now my hair had grown back which made me very happy, but the lack of hygiene brought about lice infestation . . . again.

As if my endless curse of hunger, dirt, and lice wasn't enough, I now had to endure anti-Semitic slurs from Russian boys my age. I blamed myself for having been naive and idealistic instead of having listened to the Zionist call to go to Palestine. But it was too late. Now I had to figure out how to get into school and at least get some education.

Although school was compulsory for all of us, not all the Jewish orphans wanted to risk being beaten by local children. Some preferred to stay in the orphanage, where they felt more protected. I decided to take on the challenge because I had already lost too much schooling and felt that losing more would destroy my mind.

The only school in that village, the name of which I don't recall, was intended for the children of collective farmers and the orphans. These *kolkhozes* were located along the seashore and were identified by numbers; ours was number eighteen, I believe. The population consisted of a few hundred peasants who worked on the collective farms and whose houses were scattered around a small perimeter.

To reach school during winter meant wading through deep snow. Fortunately, I did have the knee-high *valienky* boots. When I walked into the fourth grade, I was the only non-Russian child in the classroom, for that matter in the entire school.

It was not easy to overcome my self-consciousness. I was once more the oldest in my never-ending fourth grade. But I was determined not to let anything interfere with my studies.

Surprisingly, I kept up with the rest, considering my interrupted schooling. I was surprised that German was one of the subjects. The teacher, an old man with a long white beard, was equally surprised that I spoke it. This resulted in lengthy conversations about my personal history. He showed such genuine concern for me that I confessed to him my fear of being attacked by local hooligans in the schoolyard.

He was disturbed by the situation and kindly offered to give up his lunch hour to stay in the classroom with me during recess. The real danger was on my way to and from the orphanage. Then I had to run as fast as I could.

As soon as I had assimilated into this new milieu, another twist of fate turned my life around.

By some strange coincidence, we discovered the location of the larger orphanage where the younger children had been taken to. They were a group of more than eighty or one hundred living in a nearby village. We asked for, and were granted, permission to visit them. To reach their orphanage we had to walk many miles through deep snow and biting cold. But the joy of seeing all our friends, whom we had considered lost forever, was worth the effort. It was a celebration hard to describe.

That reunion came to play a crucial role in my life. A few weeks after, I was called into the supervisor's office. Scared as I was about every little thing, I imagined the worst. Perhaps they had discovered my real age and were going to send me to the Donbass mines. With jittery knees I entered the office, where I was greeted by a Russian officer.

"Are you Ruth Glasberg?" he inquired in Russian. "Yes, I am," I replied, somewhat suspiciously.

"Do you have an aunt called Anna Rosenberg?" he asked. I heard that dear name, but for a while could not make a connection. So I asked: "Why do you need to know that?"

"Well, because I am going to take you home to her. She has filed papers for your adoption," he explained.

Sensing my consternation, he started to speak to me in German. He told me that he was a Jewish officer from Czernowitz serving in the Red

Army and that his daughter was in the other orphanage. She was one of several children who, posing as orphans, had been smuggled out of Transnistria. He had come to bring her and the others back to Czernowitz.

Now that many of the families had returned from Transnistria, they wanted to be reunited with their children whom they had disguised as orphans. Documents had to be shown to prove the relationships. With more distant relatives like nieces and nephews adoption papers had to be filed, and that was what my Aunt Anna had done.

I was so moved that I broke into tears. My dearest Aunt Anna wanted me to be her child just like my mother had predicted: I would have a family and a home again at last. A beautiful dream had come true.

The officer waited for me to pack my belongings and to say good-bye to my friends. That wasn't easy. I felt lucky to be adopted yet sorry for the other children who had not been. As much as I hated to be pitied, I abhorred even more being envied. I wished all of my friends could find families to adopt them as well, but it was not in my power to change the situation.

So we said good-bye, and the officer and I left in a military vehicle.

Home Again?

CHAPTER 8

We drove to the larger orphanage, picked up a group of children including the officer's daughter, and left for the Odessa railroad station. Under his supervision, we boarded a train en route to Czernowitz.

This was my fourth time crossing the Dniester River to and from the Ukraine, each under different political circumstances. The first one was in 1941, at age eleven, as a deportee from fascist Romania to occupied western Ukraine, called Transnistria. The second one took place in 1944, at thirteen, when I was repatriated to former Romania. The third occurred the same year in December when I was repatriated from Soviet-dominated Romania to Ukraine, recently liberated by the Red Army. I was then fourteen. On this, my fourth trip out of Odessa, I was on my way to my hometown, Czernowitz, where I was going to be adopted.

All my previous trips had been in cattle cars. This time I was sitting in a cozy compartment on a passenger train like a human being, and I was exhilarated.

I was going home! Home? Not really, for I had lost mine forever, but at least I was going back to my hometown. My emotions soared as I envisioned reunions with relatives and friends, then plunged when I pictured myself there without my family.

What would I say when I arrived? How would I feel? Would anybody recognize me? Would they treat me as an orphan? Which of my friends and neighbors would I find again? Many thoughts churned in my mind as the train sped through the countryside nearing our destination.

"Next station *Chernovtsy!*" the conductor shouted, pronouncing the town's name in Ukrainian.

My heart started racing and somersaulting; goose bumps covered my skin. When the train rolled into the station, I gazed out the window, eager to see the familiar railroad station, but in the moonless night it was impossible. After descending from the train and walking through the buildings, I recognized it, and joyous memories of the past were rekindled.

We drove to the house of the rabbi from Seculeni, who had opened his home to the returning orphans. The night seemed endless as I nervously waited for sunrise to confirm that I was back in Czernowitz and would indeed see my relatives.

The next morning a gentleman came and took me to Aunt Anna.

March 1945. The streets of my beloved Czernowitz were deserted on that early, cold winter morning. A strange sensation overcame me at well-remembered sites: nothing had changed—except me.

As we entered the narrow, curved Masaryk-Gasse that led into Aunt Anna's street, I recognized many buildings, and my anxiety increased markedly as I remembered the times I had walked here to visit her after school. Turning at the right corner, I found myself in front of her building. In a moment I would see Aunt Anna and Lucie!

As soon as we began climbing the staircase toward the fourth floor, I heard a duet of excited screams: "Ruthale! Ruthale!" The voices of Aunt Anna and cousin Lucie merged as one. I rushed into their outstretched arms for a tearful reunion. His mission completed, my chaperon took his leave.

I imagine how shocking it must have been for them to see me again, particularly the way I looked, a reminder of the horror and yet also a miracle of survival. Many years later they told me that I looked like "a small child with an old woman's face."

Both my aunt and Lucie tried to make me feel at home. They understood what was stirring in my soul, and that was what counted most. I appreciated their tactfulness in not asking me about the events at Bershad. In due time I briefly told them about it, and the subject was never brought up again.

On the other hand, my father's sisters, Toni and Cilli came to see me and burst into hysterical crying. They made me uncomfortable, turning me into an object of pity—an attitude I abhorred. Still I was glad to see them. My sentiments toward Aunt Cilli were tempered with resentment because of their failure in preventing our deportation, but she was my father's sister and I still felt affection for her.

Both aunts wanted to know everything that had happened to me in Bershad. I politely gave them the facts without details or emotions. They sobbed loudly, while I remained cool and collected. Afterwards, Aunt Cilli suggested that I come to live with them. I tactfully declined because I felt more at home with Aunt Anna.

Later, Lucie told me that when they had asked Cilli to help pay for the adoption papers, she agreed but failed to deliver. And so my poor Aunt Anna, who had little money, sacrificed a significant sum for my sake. That was more reason for me not to live with the Zloczowers.

Aunt Anna's always austere financial situation had worsened. Because of Soviet regulations that allotted a limited number of square feet per person, she had to give up her only income from the rented living room to let a Russian family live in it for free. Under the circumstances, I expected to be asked to sleep on their bedroom floor. Instead, they invited me to share their double bed.

That selfless gesture moved me to tears. I wanted to accept, but a pang of conscience prevented me from doing so. While I longed for the cozy, white bed and for the physical closeness of the two who loved me, the fear of infesting them with lice clashed with my desire. I would have rather slept on the floor, but they insisted.

Just before bedtime I took a sponge bath and Aunt Anna helped me wash my hair, which by now was shoulder-length. She did it so lovingly, I almost felt as if it were my mother's touch. Dressed in a clean nightgown, I climbed into their bed. Snuggled under the eiderdown, my head on soft feather pillows, and with these two dear ones on each side, I felt sheltered and protected for the first time in years.

The next morning I woke up late. For a moment I did not realize where I was. "Good morning, daughter, did you sleep well?" my aunt asked with her loving, sweet voice. When I heard the word *daughter* I could have died of happiness. I was so comfortable under the eiderdown that getting up required a great effort. But her call for breakfast spurred me to overcome my laziness.

Since Aunt Anna showered me with love and attention, it was natural for Lucie, her daughter, to be jealous. But she never showed it. I became an integral part of the family without ever feeling that I was an orphan or a burden. They shared the little available rationed food, their bed, and their privacy. Weeks later I was relieved to find that Aunt Anna's special shampoo with kerosene had finally taken care of my lice, for neither she nor Lucie ever got infested.

She never disciplined or criticized me; perhaps there was no reason to do so, or she was afraid to hurt me. So much consideration. So much love. She had a way of making unpleasant things seem funny.

Word of my return spread quickly, and many people came to welcome me back. The most important, though, were my dear friends Litty and Reli. Their presence helped me put together a few of the broken pieces of my earlier life; their friendship was a fragment strong enough to lean on. Fortunately, both girls returned from Transnistria with their families intact. They were in another camp where the survival rate was greater. Some of my other friends never returned at all.

I sensed a feeling of pity on the part of many adults, and that was one thing I could not deal with. Among the people I had encountered over the years, few ever inquired about the tragedy. To hear about it made everyone uncomfortable, including the survivors. For that matter, I was equally reluctant to talk about it. I used my renewed vitality like a shield to ward off questions.

My instinct told me that the best way to be accepted, especially by other teens, was to act like any normal fourteen-year-old. Determined never to show my sorrow, I projected an often assertive and eternally cheerful attitude. But hiding beneath the mask of normality was a scared and hurting child. The other life haunted me every waking moment and caused me terrible nightmares.

Over the next few weeks, I slowly recovered from the physical ordeal of the past four years. I felt invigorated and ready to enter the mainstream of that relatively normal life in wartime.

After a few days of rest, it was again time to think about my education. Being fourteen, I would have to enter the eighth grade, according to the Soviet ten-year school system. I had several discussions with cousin Lucie on this subject as we debated my choices. She wanted me to start at the sixth-grade level, but I was scared because I only qualified for the fourth grade. I did not want to be ridiculed in case I was not able to catch up with the rest. However, with Lucie's unyielding persuasion, and with much apprehension, I courageously plunged into that adventure. Because it was wartime and recordkeeping was chaotic, it was easy to convince the authorities to register me in the sixth grade. Again being the oldest in the class made me self-conscious, but I adjusted as best I could.

Things became further complicated because the school was a nonreligious Jewish one and the primary language of instruction was Yiddish; Russian and Ukrainian were taught as separate languages. I had to learn everything in yet another language, one whose Semitic alphabet written from right to left was completely new to me.

I made the adjustments under extreme stress. School was free, but supplies were not. Lacking money, I often borrowed books from my classmates.

Under the Soviet system, both sexes attended the same school, and the interaction between them in sports, political, and social activities greatly appealed to me.

My favorite subjects were Russian language and literature. I loved poetry, which I easily learned by heart and often recited. My teacher, a Mr. Weizmann, would always say, "*Dietochka*! (Kidlet!) Show the class how it's done." I excelled in other subjects and soon received all "excellent" report card grades. Success in education was my revenge. I could not afford any defeat. I had to excel.

Under the skilled guidance of our director of social and sports activities, Mr. Stanger, we performed patriotic songs and marched in parades with all the other schools of Czernowitz. We also carried red flags and placards with slogans and pictures of Lenin and Stalin. Like a spiritual experience, all this evoked in me a sense of elation—a feeling of devotion to a good cause, one that would make the world a better place in which to live. I even envisioned a world without borders. In my eyes, Stalin was the father figure I so much needed. I choked with emotion whenever I saw him kissing or hugging a little girl, and I secretly wished I were the lucky one.

At the same time the situation at home was not rosy at all. Aunt Anna was so poor that staying with her troubled my conscience. I would have liked to contribute monetarily, but how could I? I was fifteen years old, without any skills, and legally not allowed to work. On the other hand I had nothing of value to sell that might bring in some money, except for the set of silverware I had carried with me since . . . and with that I would never part. Being dependent frustrated me.

Food was scarce and unhealthy, which concerned my aunt, who knew I needed better nutrition. She wanted to pamper me, but in those times all she could get were a few ounces of a horrible, sour, stone-hard bread made of whole kernels of cornmeal and rye. For that small ration we had to stand in long queues for hours. Meat and poultry were unheard of, let alone butter or fruit. She could not afford to pay for black-market products. The situation deteriorated to such an extent that my aunt, out of despair, traveled to Milie for the first time since the massacre to ask her father's former partner for some flour and oil.

On the train she accidentally met Aunt Cilli, an opportunity she seized to plead for help on my behalf. Cilli insisted I should come and stay with them if I needed better nutrition. When Aunt Anna told me about their conversation, I was ambivalent. In the end I could not bring myself to leave that loving environment just for the sake of food. Although I opted to remain with Aunt Anna, I did compromise by accepting an offer to lunch once a week with the Zloczowers.

At that time their younger son, Guido, lived with them. He was a rather aloof teenager and never asked about my experiences in Bershad. Their older son, Marcel, was more sensitive, but he was in the Red Army fighting the Germans. I was especially anxious for his return, because ever since we were children I had had an infatuation for him.

Because we all missed him, he was the topic of conversation on my weekly visits. When news reached us that he was wounded, we were terribly upset. To our great relief, he later returned completely recovered.

Before my weekly visits to Aunt Cilli, I was given well-meaning instructions by Lucie and Aunt Anna to bring up the subject of our household goods. Every time I was there I felt like a spy, constantly alert to every object in the household, prepared for the accidental discovery of something that might once have belonged to my family. But I spotted nothing. And after each visit Lucie questioned me, and I always had to answer in the negative. I lacked courage.

I was convinced then that the Zloczowers either never expected me to survive or thought that I would not remember the transfer of our household goods to their house. One day I finally gathered all my inner strength and confronted Aunt Cilli. In a defensive voice she told me that they had sold everything and sent the money to me in Bershad.

Did she think I was retarded or that I had lost my memory? The money they sent me was probably the value of one tablecloth. And the one package contained Guido's used clothes. Now she expected me to believe that it was the total worth of our assets, Uncle Sammy's carpets included? I was furious!

I swallowed my anger and boiled inside. To cope with the situation, I told myself that Aunt Cilli, after all, was not a bad person, that it was her husband who had coerced her.

What was I going to do now that I needed money for some really important reason? Years of starvation and disease caused my teeth to decay, in particular my front incisors, causing me much embarrassment, but I had no means to pay for dental work. Whether Aunt Cilli did not notice this obvious blemish, or chose not to, I did not know. In any case I brought up the subject during one of our friendly chats. I must have done it on one of her especially vulnerable days, because she promised to talk it over with Max to see if he would agree to help. Shortly after our talk, she offered to pay for the dental work.

My happiness knew no limits. Unfortunately the result was worse than the defect. The new gold-framed teeth did not exactly enhance my beauty, nor did they boost my vanity. Neither did Lucie's frequent teasing help. She was a pretty twenty-one-year-old, my role model, yet with all her love and good intentions she sometimes deeply hurt me.

On the positive side, she really became my surrogate sister just as Aunt Anna became my surrogate mother. Both helped me in the healing process even without a father figure, which I never found among my uncles or other male relatives.

Despite everything, life was good to me. I was happy with the few pleasures that those austere days had to offer. But gnawing fears persisted that, contrary to my hopes, I might not have escaped without harm, especially since I was not developing breasts and had not had my period by age fifteen. I was too embarrassed to talk to anyone about this problem. After months of torment, I finally divulged my secret to Aunt Anna. She suggested we visit my former pediatrician.

We did, and after a thorough examination, he said, "Ruthi, the years of deprivation and illnesses have taken their toll. But with proper nutrition and enough time, nature will do the rest. Be patient."

That did not alleviate my fears. I actually harbored the idea of not being a normal human being, and particularly not a normal teenager, compared to other girls my age. While I might have lacked feminine attributes, I was most certainly mature on an emotional and erotic level. Unable to project my femininity to attract the opposite sex, I sublimated by portraying myself as a tomboy.

As time passed, I learned to cope by finding compensations for my unfulfilled desires through reading, studying, and school activities, none of which was ever too much or too tiresome. Still that was not enough. I wanted more.

I wanted to learn English and French. I voiced my wish to Aunt Cilli, who once more showed a streak of generosity and offered to pay for private lessons once a week.

There was a well-known teacher, Mrs. Kern, whose specialty was art history, but who was also well versed in many other subjects, including languages. Since my friend Litty had already been taking lessons with her, she introduced us.

What a treasure I found! This middle-aged lady with kind eyes and a simple yet elegant air about her immediately captivated me. We talked about my needs and wishes, taking into consideration my ardent desire to learn both English and French. Because the budget allowed for only one hour of instruction, she suggested splitting my hour-long lesson into two halves. After a while she noticed that I was better in English, so she advised that I drop French and dedicate the entire hour to English.

No detail about me escaped Mrs. Kern's sharp eye, including my handwriting. It was that of a child with meticulous calligraphic nuances, not appropriate for a fifteen-year-old, she said. "We have to do something about your longhand. Try at least to print the capital letters so they don't look so childish, and then we will work at other changes."

Mrs. Kern observed every letter of mine, and through them she believed that she could analyze my character. Revealing her expertise in graphology, she suggested that I exhibited an "exaggerated goodness" by writing very rounded letters: "Don't be so good! Be a little bit bad and make your letters more angled."

Another of Mrs. Kern's odd remarks was about my punctuality. I did not own a wristwatch, something few people had at the time, so I relied on the kitchen alarm clock at home and the tower clock in the main square. But above all I had developed the most reliable of all, my inner clock. I could feel time, and therefore I was always punctual. I had never given it any thought until Mrs. Kern brought it to my attention. "How is it that you are always on time, to the minute, without a watch?" she asked.

"I honestly don't know," I said.

"That says a lot about your character," she added without offering any further comment. Thus there was no explanation to what it all meant.

Realizing that my schooling had been halted four years earlier, this highly intellectual and wonderful teacher took it upon herself to guide my academic development with great sensitivity. Gradually she led me from fairy tales to classic literature, from a child's penmanship to longhand, bringing me up to the level where I belonged.

She related to me vignettes, stories, and novels. Observing that my comprehension was good, she lent me first a small German book, *Kabale und Liebe* by Schiller, followed by plays and short novels by Goethe and Heine. Then she promoted me to the next level: long and difficult novels translated from French and English into German.

The most memorable were *The Forsythe Saga* by Galsworthy and *Romeo and Juliet* by Shakespeare. Then came the great French writers Dumas, Hugo, and Balzac. That was the beginning of my passion for the classics, the window that opened and allowed me to discover a new, exciting world of knowledge and adventure. I found books everywhere, in Russian, Romanian, Yiddish, and, of course, German. Books became my friends, teachers, guides, and counselors. They were also my refuge from haunting memories. This teacher planted in me the seed of love for literature and languages, poetry and philosophy; she helped me educate myself by opening my eyes to the vast world found in books.

My best friend Litty studied art history with her and sometimes shared with me what she had learned. We were close and did not move without each other; I also felt at home with her parents. We met daily in school, and in our free time we went together to movies and to soccer games— of which we became great fans.

I did not tell Litty about my tragedy in detail, nor did she ask; that fact reinforced my denial and helped me project the image of a normal teenager that I hoped to maintain. The only person other than my aunts who was intrigued by my survival was the Russian woman who shared the apartment with us.

One day she asked me if I would tell her how I managed to survive as a child. I related to her a small fragment of my experience. With every sentence I spoke, the woman turned paler and paler as tears streamed down her face. I got scared and stopped talking. She knelt at my feet crossing herself several times and said, "My child, you are a saint. People ought to pray before you. Don't you know? Only a saint can be saved by a miracle."

I felt bewilderment as this compassionate Russian soul, bestowed saint-

hood on me. Afterward, the idea of my being immortal started to cross my mind with some regularity.

I never realized that my story sounded so incredible because until then I had been surrounded by children who suffered the same fate. But now being in a family environment, I became some kind of oddity. It was obvious that not too many double orphans my age had made it back. On the other hand, my lucky friends Reli and Litty not only survived with their families but even got back their apartments.

Just as before, Reli was living across from our former apartment buildings. Not wanting to be faced with the past, I seldom visited her. On the rare occasion that I did, I would stand at her bedroom window and stare across the street toward my old apartment, remembering happy family scenes. Strangers now lived where I had once led a normal, happy life. That realization was sheer torture. My lost childhood pierced my heart. I was flooded with all the memories of my carefree years in the bosom of my family.

Just as our townspeople had returned from the liberated camps of Transnistria, so later did thousands of Jewish prisoners liberated by the

Soviets from the extermination camps in Poland. They streamed into Czernowitz, the streets filling with those sad, emaciated prisoners in striped uniforms that hung loosely on their frail bodies. This pathetic scene was hard to forget, as were the first horror stories about the efficient extermination machine the Nazis had built for the purpose of the "Final Solution."

I must confess that I had no idea that such camps existed.

The prisoners were Jews from different European countries, with whose experiences I could well identify. Our townspeople took them into their homes, while others helped with clothes or food until the Red Cross transferred them to Displaced Persons camps throughout Europe. Some chose to return to their native cities in search of family members.

Soon I was notified that a group of my peers had returned from Odessa and the Donbass mines. At the same rabbi's house, amid laughter and tears, we enjoyed a tumultuous reunion. They told us of their horrible life in the coal-mining Donbass province, where they had lived in a communal house, worked eight hours a day without pay, and received none of the promised schooling. When I heard that, I was certainly grateful for their encouragement to stay in Odessa with the smaller children.

May 7, 1945. "Pobeda! Pobeda!" [Victory!]. The loudspeakers on the main square blasted the news of the long-awaited day of peace. People poured into the streets shouting, singing, and dancing with joy. I took part in the jubilation, rejoicing in the victory. But at the same time I felt an enormous void that obstructed the free flow of pure happiness.

Even today that pattern seems to repeat itself. In moments of joy an alarm seems to go off, reminding me that my loved ones are not here to experience it; therefore I feel more sad and lonely on holidays or other festivities. Although I love parties, they make me feel alone. And while I project a cheerful facade, I often cry within.

People usually consider a survivor to be lucky, but in reality it is often a heavy burden, loaded with guilt and excruciating memories that cannot be erased. It's a sense of not belonging, of having no roots, no family, and, in my case, harboring a secret feeling of being partially dead or not totally alive.

One way to defeat this feeling and to avoid facing myself was to immerse myself in a frenzy of distracting activities. I got involved in every kind of event.

To celebrate the end of the war, schools choreographed parades and performances for a scholastic Olympiad at the National Theater. For that occasion my teacher, Mr. Weizman, suggested to the organizers that the Olympiad be opened with the poem "Borodino" by Lermontov. This poem hailed the Russian victory over Napoleon in much the same way as we were now hailing the Soviet victory over Hitler. I felt honored to have been chosen to recite by heart the poem of about fifteen stanzas— it was extremely challenging. With Mr. Weizmann's coaching and my patriotism, I had no difficulty reciting it with genuine pathos. I was ready and proud to represent the Jewish School. But I also had to sing in the choir and participate in several dances for which I borrowed dresses and otherwise improvised.

I had performed many times before but never on a stage of a real theater with such a large crowd. I was supposed to recite the poem and then immediately change into a costume for a Ukrainian folk dance. After that I had to change for an American jazz dance and finally change once more for the choir. It was sheer madness.

Olympiad Day arrived with all its excitement. For the recital of the poem, I had to wear the typical Communist Youth Organization uniform of a dark blue skirt, white blouse, and red triangle necktie. I stood backstage waiting my turn.

As soon as the lights went down in the hall and the floodlights illuminated the stage, the master of ceremonies stepped out and announced, "We hereby declare the Olympiad of schools opened with the first number, 'Borodino' by Lermontov, recited by Ruth Glasberg, a sixth grader from the Jewish School."

And I thought I had known stage fright before! This was the real thing. My knees almost buckled and my mouth was as dry as the Sahara. For a second I thought that I would never overcome the fright, but the moment I stepped in front of the curtain I conquered the fear, only to confront a new calamity. Never before had I faced a microphone and floodlights aimed directly at my face. Totally blinded, I could not see the audience.

I panicked for a moment but collected myself and quickly started my first verse. I was convinced that I had overcome all obstacles; then I noticed to my horror that my voice sounded strange, and droplets of saliva danced scintillatingly in front of my eyes. I was sure that everybody noticed it—it almost paralyzed me. Once more I swallowed hard and continued my recital without hesitation. Judging by the applause, I must have done a good job. It was a reward I badly needed.

I hurried off and changed for one of the group dances, but in my haste I did not close my skirt properly. As if fate wanted to prevent me from having any delusions of grandeur, when I approached the center of the stage, my skirt fell down, and the audience roared with laughter. I felt like crawling into a hole and dying, but instead I ran behind the props.

There was no time to lose. The whole dance would have been disrupted. It seemed an eternity until someone helped me close the skirt with a safety pin. In a matter of seconds, I took my position, and the dance was performed without turning into a major disaster.

I could have continued to reap the fruits of my successes, were it not for my conflict with the Zloczowers. To put an end to it, one day I finally gathered all my courage and confidently demanded from them every item left of our belongings. It worked. Aunt Cilli brought out a few crystal liquor glasses, towels, a bedspread, and some other knickknacks. I recognized them all, and it devastated me to see the pitiful remains of what used to be a complete household.

With a lump in my throat, I took the few remnants and left in anger. Now I started to make plans to sell the few items I had gotten back. Because the Soviet system had put an end to normal business transactions, I had to sell everything in a makeshift flea market on the outskirts of town. Whoever had some kind of a display table or bench was considered a real merchant, but amateurs like myself had to display the goods on a newspaper spread on the ground.

Now I became a child-entrepreneur who at age fifteen joined adults in this odd way of bartering. Instead of spending Sundays with my friends in pleasurable activities, I spent them at the market. But in a way it was fun. Unfortunately my merchandise did not attract too many customers; it took many weeks to sell a small item. The meager proceeds I proudly offered to Aunt Anna, who categorically refused them. I kept the unsold odds and ends: two crystal champagne glasses, a silver-plated fruit basket, and an old dress and purse of my mother's. A shoemaker created a pair of loafers from the leather purse, and a dressmaker altered the dress for my figure.

I was happy with very little and grateful to be in my hometown among family members. But fate played yet another trick on me.

International political pressure on the Soviets made them issue a decree in late 1945 by which all Romanian Jews living in the territory of Northern Bukovina and Bessarabia were free to leave for now-Communist Romania. This sudden change was good news for the majority of the Jewish population, who intended to emigrate to Palestine via Romania. But for others it posed a huge predicament.

In our household, fierce debates took place daily. Aunt Anna wanted to leave, while Lucie and I did not. I was totally shattered at the thought of yet another uprooting. Suddenly I saw my new life falling apart. Disappointed as I was in many of the communists' ways, I remained faithful to the cause.

Lucie, of course, was opposed because her fiancé, Willy, was a staunch Communist. To him the idea of leaving the USSR was totally unacceptable. As a result, the three of us united into a solid front against Aunt Anna, who insisted on leaving. Poor Lucie was torn between her loyalty to her mother and to Willy.

By the fall of 1945, most of my relatives, friends, schoolmates, and teachers, including Mrs. Kern, started to leave. I really had no desire to go anywhere else; I was happy in my hometown. How many times in my short life was I supposed to start a new school and a new social life? But my wishes and opinions did not count. My only alternative, if I decided to stay, would have been to live in a communal trade school, which was a home for orphans and abandoned youth. That idea did not appeal to me. Besides, what would that town be like without Jews and without my friends?

In the end Aunt Anna won the argument by convincing us that we would all have a much better future outside the Soviet Union and that Willy might change his mind and follow Lucie later.

As the exodus approached, a commercial frenzy began. All the Jews who were about to leave were permitted to sell their household goods. Prices were ridiculously low. Those who had returned from the camps in Transnistria and were able to repossess some of their goods were now forced to part with them again. The others who had remained, like Aunt Anna, faced this problem for the first time. It pained me to see her suffering as she had to get rid of her lifelong possessions, only to end up with just a few suitcases and bundles. Ironically, I was spared that pain. All I had was a single suitcase and tons of memories.

After selling the goods, there was another problem: how to smuggle out cash over and above the legally authorized amount. That meant hiding it in inconspicuous places, mostly within body cavities. This reminded me of previous experiences that made me eternally fearful of customs and border controls. Even though this was a time of peace, with the Soviets in charge, and a whole different proceeding, I could hardly control my anxiety. My aunt had given me a small amount of paper bills to hide in my underwear, assuring me that they would never do a body search on a girl my age. I was not convinced, and, feeling guilty, I practically froze in panic at the border. Fortunately there was no body search for me. On trucks, we safely crossed the border over the Seret River into Romanian territory.

Farewell again, my native land.

From Communism
to Zionism

April 12, 1946. We entered communist Romania as one of the last groups allowed to leave the Soviet Union. Thousands upon thousands of Jews from North Bukovina, now reoccupied by the Soviet Union, had been flooding into Seret since 1945, creating severe lodging and food shortages.

These people, in dire economic situations, became nuisances to the Romanians. To rid themselves of this burden, the government opted to close an eye to those escaping through the western borders into Hungary and Yugoslavia. But it was complicated to establish contact with the clandestine networks of the Mossad L'Aliyah Beit, the organization responsible for emigration (not to be confused with the current name for the Israeli Secret Service). Meanwhile, the refugees had to survive on dwindling reserves or depend on social welfare which was practically unavailable. Those who did manage to escape were guided by the emissaries of the *bericha* (escape) organizations toward the D.P. camps in Germany, Austria, and Italy from where they would eventually be taken to Palestine.

Aunt Anna was lucky to have maintained contact with Yona-Itzhak, our relative who had escaped the Milie massacre of 1941 and who had arrived with an earlier group. He took us into the tiny room he shared with another six refugees and offered us the bare floor to sleep on.

The situation was so desperate that I couldn't stay with Aunt Anna and Lucie any longer. But where would I go? Without a penny in my pocket and without any skill, I faced a new personal torment. Nonetheless, it was time to say good-bye.

Amidst that turmoil my guardian angel remembered me again. I got notice from my Aunt Toni that David Greif, one of my father's cousins, was living in the town of Roman; he agreed to put me up for a while.

But I had no money to pay for even the cheapest fare, which was by passenger truck. The drivers charged a small sum per person, and to increase their profits they often filled the truck with up to twenty passengers. Luckily, Litty's family was headed in the same direction, so her parents offered to take me along and pay my fare as well.

Although we had never met, the Greifs received me with exceptional warmth in their large home; they even gave me my own room, a luxury I had never experienced before. I enjoyed a few weeks of pampered life in a small town that had remained relatively untouched by war.

During my stay in Roman, I met an eighteen-year-old boy. We instantly were attracted to each other. He invited me to movies, dances, and promenades in the park, all of which I enjoyed and which aroused a strange but pleasant feeling. Then one day he tried to caress me. Actually I wanted the physical contact, but at the same time it embarrassed me, because I had not yet developed breasts and did not want him to know. So I did not let him touch me. I was in a terrible predicament, feeling like a woman yet not really being one. Still, we had a few pleasant weeks together. Unfortunately, this little infatuation came to an end when the time came for me to move on to my Aunt Toni's family in the town of Targu-Neamtz. I stayed with them another few weeks until I was shipped to Aunt Cilli and Uncle Max in Buzau, which—ironically— was where I had lived in an orphanage just two years before. I felt like a soccer ball being kicked from one corner to another.

I was treated like an object without soul or feelings, but I had both and both ached in despair. The Romanian saying "You can't escape that

Buzau, 1946, "The Happy Gang." (Top to bottom) Litty, Jenny, and I.

which you fear" applied precisely to my situation. I had always dreaded living with the Zloczowers, but now I was forced to do just that.

It probably was not easy for them either, even though in those times sharing was more natural than it is today. The four of them occupied a small room with only two beds. Sometimes I slept on the hallway floor or on other occasions with my aunt and uncle in the same bed. My male cousins, Marcel and Guido, shared the other bed.

Although they let me sleep in their bed, when it came to the sensitive issue of treating me as one of their own children, their attitude was different. At every opportunity they would reinforce my feelings of being an orphan, especially Uncle Max. For instance, he would constantly give his sons pocket money but never offered me a lei. At mealtimes I always got the smallest portion or the poorest quality food. These acts hurt and humiliated me profoundly.

Fortunately, many refugees from our town had settled temporarily in Buzau. Among them was my best friend, Litty. She was a blessing because I could share my feelings with her, and when I could no longer bear the Zloczowers I would sleep over. I confided to her my distress at feeling trapped and my desire to run away. But where to? By what means? And how could I do it?

One idea was to join a Zionist youth organization. But embracing such a life-style would mean the sacrifice of any future education. Two years earlier I had resisted going to Palestine, but now that I had to abandon my hometown Czernowitz and couldn't stay with my relatives I convinced myself that becoming a socialist-Zionist was not a bad alternative. It was what I had always dreamed of and what my father had instilled in me as a noble cause until communism supplanted it. At the same time, it offered me the opportunity to be self-sufficient.

Toward that end, some of my friends tried to lure me into their Zionist youth organization, the politically middle-of-the-road Hanoar Hazioni. Being a member of such an organization entitled one not only to participate in a camp but also to join a preparatory commune called a *haksharah*, to which the Jewish Agency gave emigration priority. That would offer me the best chance to get to Eretz Israel—the pre-1948 term used by Jews to refer to Palestine. But in order to remain faithful to my socialist convictions, I opted for the more leftist party Hashomer Hatzair.

Soon enough, I started to miss my friends who were constantly trying to convert me to their cause. Torn between my ideology and friendship, I eventually gravitated toward the latter and joined them.

In 1946, I was sent to a two-week summer camp financed by our organization. It was an unforgettable experience. There I learned that during a previous summer camp, four members of our organization had decided to form a haksharah, whose goal would be the creation of a kibbutz in Palestine. They immediately started to recruit members and requested from the Central Committee a place where the group could practice working the fields. Their ideal was to return to the land—the source of life. Ultimately, they saw these communes as the basis of the future Jewish state. And so these pioneers took their first steps in preparation for *aliyah*, emigration to the Land of Israel.

The group was assigned a piece of land in the small farming village of Colentina, near Bucharest. Twenty youngsters initiated the commune, naming it *L'hagshamah* (Toward Realization), Group I. Soon afterward

Group II formed, and later both groups left for Palestine via Italy. Within a year a third group was formed.

That was my chance. After Litty and other friends from our organization helped me contact Group III, and after an informal series of conversations, I was accepted. To make it easy for me to get to this tiny village of Galautzash in Transylvania, they assigned a member of the commune to meet me at the train station upon his return from a vacation.

The young man arrived, we recognized each other by the description I had given to him in a letter, and together we traveled toward our destination. A sudden feeling of independence overwhelmed me. I was sixteen, my hopes were high, and my mood ecstatic.

The next morning the train arrived at a tiny Galautzash station where a few representatives of the commune awaited us. They took us in a horse-driven cart to the outskirts of the village, where they lived in an isolated one-story house with two large rooms, a kitchen, and an outhouse.

Living in human "herds" and sleeping fifteen girls to a plank-bed was not new to me. What *was* unusual was the social structure in a group of youngsters brought together by idealism and a common goal, not by necessity or destiny.

The thirty or so commune members greeted me cordially and made me feel welcome. Their ages ranged from seventeen to twenty-five. Most had led relatively normal lives, because they were the lucky ones who lived in Old Romania and were spared deportation. Even here I felt different as the youngest, the smallest, and the very last to join.

I was also one of the few with a grim past.

I later learned that two other members of our group were also survivors of the camps, but we never spoke about it. We were too busy creating new lives, filling every minute with activities and dreams. It was inconceivable to expose our nightmarish stories to others.

We worked hard and shared equal rights and benefits. We made decisions by majority vote taken at general meetings. In short, we were a miniature cooperative putting socialist theories into practice. That fascinated me.

Another novelty was the rather intense intermingling between the sexes. Although at night the segregated accommodations were respected, after work and on Sundays there was a great deal of socializing and necking, despite the lack of privacy. Without the slightest experience of fondling or lovemaking, I was uncomfortable in this new situation. I was not used to this close interaction between boys and girls.

Although, I was the youngest and the only physically underdeveloped female, I did not lack admirers. Most of them, surprisingly, were willing to accept a platonic friendship after I made it clear that I was not interested in any kind of physical closeness.

All of us worked at a large timber mill that employed mostly local people. Our commune managed to work out a deal whereby we were able to get jobs for free room and board in lieu of salary. We did it mainly for the experience. And what an experience that was! We worked in three shifts under physically taxing conditions. Never having done arduous labor for eight continuous hours, I had a hard time keeping up with the rest of the group.

On the day shift our job was to lift the heavy logs and load them onto wagons on tracks. Working in pairs helped, yet the physical drudgery eventually overwhelmed me. Ironically, I was doing the work that my father's laborers used to do at the mills he managed.

On the night shifts, we had to fill wheelbarrows with sawdust in order to feed the burning furnaces. The only advantage was the opportunity to warm up on cold nights and to broil bacon-wrapped lumps of dark bread.

I liked our communal life in which everyone was equal and equally possessed nothing. Our group was not homogeneous; it consisted of a mishmash of Hungarian-speaking Transylvanians, Romanian speakers of the Old Kingdom, and a few German-speaking Bukovinians like myself. But in spite of it, we were compatible. The challenge of creating togetherness—bound by the same dreams and goals—added substance to our lives.

Our group leader, Maiciu (now Meir Shamir), helped create that togetherness. He was tall, good-looking and broad-shouldered, with a thick shock of dark blond hair. Because of his wisdom, charisma, and leadership, we thought he was the oldest of the group. Only decades later he revealed his secret—he had been only seventeen at the time. Every female had a crush on him, including me, but he was engaged to a girl named Bertha, who had left Romania with Group II, and he remained faithful to her.

After months of hard work and consolidation, we were notified of the imminent date of emigration to Palestine, where we would join Groups I and II of L'hagshamah. We were given a few days off to say good-bye to families and friends. I went to Bucharest, where Aunt Anna and Lucie lived. The conditions in which I found them saddened me deeply: a tiny cubicle of a room and hardly any means of sustenance. It was heartbreaking for me to have to leave them for God knew how long, and I felt very guilty about being unable to help them in any way.

Next I visited one of my father's cousins. As soon as he saw me, he asked, "Did you read your story in the local newspaper?"

"What story? What paper?" I had no idea. He took me to the newspaper building. There he asked for a specific edition. In no time someone brought out a newspaper from the archives and handed us a copy of the *Romania Libera*.

I read it and was so overwhelmed that I hardly recognized my own story. But it was mine, all right. It was a shortened version of the nine-page manuscript I had written in 1944. The banner headline read, "Awaiting the trial of war criminals. For years Transnistrian children have lived in misery, hunger and terror."

Now I understood. That was why my teacher at the Bucharest orphanage had requested that I write about my experience in Bershad. I never thought my story would serve as a testimony.

I was going to safeguard that newspaper for posterity; it might one day serve some useful purpose. (It appeared in an anthology in 1991.) Originally I had three carbon copies of that 1944 manuscript. One I kept; the two others I gave to my aunts for safekeeping. It was important to have such testimony documented soon after the experience because many adults doubted children's recollection of events.

While in Bucharest I also visited all the families that had been kind to me in 1944. One of my relatives told me that my story had been broadcast on Romanian state radio. At the conclusion, the reader said, "Ruth

Glasberg, wherever you may be, rest assured that we will avenge you."
I was puzzled as to how they got my story, and why they read it.

I was touched by both the radio program and the newspaper article. Unfortunately, I did not have the time to get a copy of the radio program, because I had to return to my commune.

After saying my farewells, I boarded the train for Galautzash where all the planning, packing, and organizing for our trip to Palestine had resulted in travel fever. My suitcase was filled mostly with precious mementos: a few photos of my family I had painstakingly collected from relatives, my school yearbook, my manuscript, the published newspaper article relating my camp experiences, and of course my sentimental set of silverware.

All the commune members had returned from bidding good-bye to their parents and relatives. They told stories of sad fathers and sobbing, heartbroken mothers. Ironically I had been spared that particular hardship. "Happy me who is an orphan," I thought, as I remembered one of Shalom Aleichem's stories. It pained me to part with my adoptive family, but it did not compare to the pain experienced by my friends who had real parents. I marveled at their idealism which was so strong that they were able to overcome separation from their families even without the prospect of an early reunion. We knew of our final destination but only vaguely about how and when we would get there.

Shipwrecked

November 1946. Palestine was still ruled by a British Mandate. His Majesty's government was worried about the breakdown of law and order between the Arab and Jewish communities following the postwar influx of Holocaust survivors. Claiming that Jews had exhausted their yearly quota in December 1945, the British allowed only a small number of immigrants per month.

By that time Europe was full of displaced persons camps, occupied mostly by Holocaust survivors and some Zionist youth organizations awaiting immigration to Palestine. Their numbers far exceeded the limited quota. Because of those circumstances, the Jewish Agency formed an organization called *bericha* (escape) that infiltrated the camps in Italy, Austria, Germany, and France and worked cunningly behind the scenes to organize illegal immigration.

Members of L'hagshamah Group III were among thousands of others undertaking such a risky venture. Our activities were shrouded in secrecy and in endless hushed rumors. We left Romania via train to Yugoslavia; from there we were to go by boat to Palestine, and both trips were to be clandestine. Unfortunately we had to quell our joyous mood for fear of being discovered by the border police. I panicked at the thought of another checkpoint, but the train crossed the border into Yugoslavia without incident. However, I could relax only when it stopped to let us out in Belgrade. Having crossed numerous borders for four years, I hoped this time would be the last one I would cross in Europe. I was sailing to another continent altogether.

A convoy of trucks stood ready to take us from the capital to the city of Zagreb. From the rolling trucks that rushed us to a holding camp, we barely caught a glimpse of either of these two beautiful cities. But we were part of a secret operation and careful not to be discovered.

We reached the refugee camp on the outskirts of Zagreb. It was a large area of tents and corrugated tin barracks erected to house hundreds of refugees and emigrants in transit to Palestine. People of various nationalities ambled around the grounds, curious to learn about the new arrivals. Our commune had to settle into one crowded barracks with up to two hundred people of both genders. Hearing the various languages, one had the feeling of being in a new Tower of Babel. At night it turned into a din of snoring. In addition to that, winter was setting in and we had little protection against the cold. But our enthusiasm to emigrate was so great that we endured the temporary chaos and misery with optimism.

The whole aliyah pilgrimage was led and supervised by astute, well-trained men from the underground Jewish army in Palestine called the *Haganah*. They were responsible for organizing the emigration to Palestine and were called Mossadniks. They kept in constant touch with representatives of the various youth organizations, who in turn relayed any pertinent information to their members. The liaison for L'hagshamah was our leader, Maiciu.

A few weeks later, the good news came that it was finally our turn to leave. It was the long-awaited moment of truth: emigration to our homeland at last.

At the end of November, a transport of about eight hundred people, our group included, traveled by train for many hours toward an undisclosed port. Looking out the window and admiring the breathtaking scenery, we also spotted the sea, an exciting view that reassured us that we were indeed heading toward the embarkation point. From books I had read and movies I had seen, I envisioned rosy pictures of a grand sea voyage.

As the sun started to sink slowly below the horizon, it gradually turned darker and darker until night engulfed us. No moon, no lights, just a cold, tenebrous night. The train came to a halt, and we were instructed to get out. All eight hundred people, well-drilled, descended in deadly silence. Soon some guides with flashlights appeared and whispered orders for us to follow them. I could see little in that murky night, yet as I approached the vessel I instantly understood that it was anything but a passenger ship. At best it resembled a cargo or fishing boat; in neither case was it fit to accommodate eight hundred passengers. In fact, another deck had been built above the original top deck to squeeze on more people. My hopes sank to an abysmal depth.

These boats used in the illegal operations had been purchased from different countries and sailed under a variety of flags. Their original names were changed to a Hebrew code: Ours became *Rafiach,* even though it was originally called *Atinai.* Both the crew and the ship were of Greek origin, but the people in charge of the emigrants were the Mossadniks, mainly young men from the kibbutzim, idealists who performed an extremely dangerous and patriotic task.

(There is good documentation of illegal immigration to Palestine at the Naval Museum of Haifa, Israel, including replicas of some of those boats. About 118 illegal boats made their way to Palestine in 140 sailings with 107,000 immigrants from 1934 to 1948, when the State of Israel was created.)

We were led into deep and dimly lit holds without ventilation or portholes. The entire space was taken up by two stories of wall-to-wall plank berth onto which we had to pack ourselves like sardines with just barely enough height to lie down. I had to slide in horizontally and share the space with dozens of other women. One could not sit up. To make things worse, the toilets were upstairs on the deck, and to reach them was quite an undertaking. When all the human freight had been packed into these "luxury cabins," the ship's noisy motor started with a dreadful roar and an obnoxious belch of fuel. The odor alone caused me instant nausea. The overloaded ship began rocking mercilessly, and most of the passengers, myself included, became seasick.

Once I started vomiting, there was no end to it. I moaned and vomited and cried and vomited some more. Mealtimes were the worst. They distributed some canned fish whose odor, fused with that of vomit, made me desperately ill. It so exhausted me that I could not even make it to the upstairs toilets. I just wanted to die. Suddenly Solo, one of my admirers, came to my rescue.

We had been friends from the time I joined the commune. He came down several times a day to help me to the toilet, at other times keeping me on deck where he and the other boys slept. The vessel was so skimpy that, from time to time, the captain had to order the crowd on deck to move from one side to the other in order to keep the ship balanced.

While my brief stints on deck provided some relief, I would get sick again on returning to the hold. Sometimes I was so weak that Solo had to carry me to the toilet in his arms. Were it not for him, I probably would have not made it through the ordeal.

We lost all notion of time and circumstances. One day, deep down in the dark hold, sick and in great distress, we passengers were unaware that our boat was fighting its way through a fierce storm. Worn out and lethargic, I could not have cared less what happened to me, but Solo did. He came to take me out onto the deck and kept vigil over me while I was asleep.

That afternoon I was jolted out of my sleep by creaking, thunderous noises that sounded like falling tree trunks. The noise grew louder, followed by hysterical screams of "Help! Help!" echoing from hundreds of voices.

In a flash I sat up. Still confused between dream and reality, I was petrified to see a huge rock looming beyond the railing. Around the boat leapt wild, high waves of an angry sea. Swells of water splashed onto the deck. Bewildered, I watched the panic-stricken passengers yelling and running aimlessly.

Above that chaos a voice blared from a loudspeaker: "Attention! Attention! We've hit a rock! Keep calm! Keep order!" I picked up only bits and pieces of the orders that followed: we were to jump onto land when the waves brought the boat close enough to shore.

Pandemonium!

Hysterical passengers crawling out of the holds were swarming on the deck, pushing, shoving, and screaming. People jumped from the ship to save their lives. The lucky ones who had been on deck and could reach the railing leaped first. Solo could have done the same, but he wanted to rescue me. Only I could not move. Sweeping me up, Solo shoved his way through the agitated crowd and placed me on the railing in preparation. As I stood shivering, holding onto a post, he gave me instructions about how and when to jump.

In my state of mind, I could not make sense of all the garble, from which I picked out words like "Jump! Watch out!" Only after several repetitions did I realize that Solo was actually directing these words at me.

During the few seconds that the boat came near the shore, desperate people tried to throw themselves onto the barren, rocky island. Some did it at the appropriate moment, while others failed and were crushed between the boat and the rock.

Furious waves savagely pushed and pulled the sinking boat to and from the shore. A dozen or so brave crewmen who had managed to get off in time pulled on a rope they had previously tied to the stern and tried desperately to keep the boat from drifting away too fast. That gave people more time to abandon ship.

Standing there petrified, I was unable even to think of jumping. To me it would be a death leap, but Solo insisted and repeated his instructions. "I'll go first," he said. "Wait for my signal, then you jump and I'll catch you in my arms. Don't be afraid."

All around me frantic, shrieking people continued to leap overboard, some hitting the rocky ground, others the water. The creaking boat, the high menacing waves, and the screaming all but paralyzed me with fear. "I'm scared! I can't swim! I'll drown!" I cried.

One last time Solo repeated his instructions. Then he leaped off, unharmed. With arms outstretched in a gesture of encouragement, he yelled,

"Now!" I continued standing on the railing, clutching the post, numb with fear. Seeing people drowning and being crushed below me, I couldn't gather the courage to move.

The chaos continued unabated, the screams increased; some confused people actually returned to the holds—already full of water—to salvage their belongings, unaware that time was running out. Some met their death down there.

Solo's patience ran out but not his ingenuity and determination to save my life. He pulled out his trouser belt, constantly coaching me. "I'll hold one end of the belt, all right? You take hold of the other end when I throw it to you, then I'll pull you off at the right moment, all right?"

"I'll try," I shouted back, unconvinced.

The boat continued to be swept toward the island by the strong waves and to be pulled far away from it by the force of the tide. One part of the boat was almost under water, drifting lopsidedly back and forth. My first attempts to catch Solo's belt were unsuccessful. Then the sinking boat was once more dashed toward the rock. This time I was finally able to snatch up the end of the belt, and before I knew it Solo pulled on his end. That swift motion yanked me off the railing onto the rocky surface. I felt as if I had broken a leg, but it turned out to be just an injured ankle. I was safe! I was alive! My guardian angel had saved me once again.

I must have been very confused or even in a state of shock because, recovering from my fall, I found myself all alone. Solo had vanished along with everyone else, disappearing as if swallowed up by the earth. They must have scurried to find shelter before nightfall. With hardly any strength and limping, I was unable to go far.

Meanwhile, the sea was quickly devouring the tiny old boat. It took no longer than about twenty minutes or so before the brave men who had been pulling the rope had to let go. There was nothing else to be done. Sinking with it were an unknown number of souls and the meager belongings of the emigrants.

I was left with nothing but the clothes on my back. With great difficulty I climbed up the rocky cliff in search of a familiar face, but I found none. Instead I encountered a rather ludicrous scene. A few shabby-looking shepherds with rifles dangling from their shoulders descended from the top of the rock as if they were ready to fend off invaders. To their dismay, they were to witness a human tragedy that changed their role from fighters to rescuers. It must have been the biggest event in their otherwise secluded, monotonous lives. They quickly climbed up the rock to alert the others, and soon all of them got involved in feeding and sheltering us.

Before night had descended, the ship was swallowed up by the ferocious Adriatic Sea. Shortly, a cold, torrential December rain gushed down on that desolate island, adding more misery to our already desperate situation.

Everybody climbed the rock as if there would be some salvation at the top. Lacking the stamina to climb, I sought out a tall rock nearby to lean against and to protect myself from the rain.

The stunning suddenness of the tragedy had me overwhelmed and totally mystified. Why was I left alone by my group and by Solo in particular, after all he had done for me? The fear and loneliness in that rainy, ghastly night were absolutely devastating.

Standing there glued to the rock, my thoughts raced from past to present. Stripped anew of all that tied me to my past, I mourned over all the items I had so laboriously collected in the last two years: the few photographs of my family, mementoes acquired from my aunts after the war, my one beloved set of silver cutlery, and especially the original copy of my article published in the newspaper *Romania Libera*.

Alone in the darkness, drenched to the bone, my thoughts were interrupted by occasional yells, calling out names in an attempt to find lost friends and family members—but not my name. My anxiety grew, as did the fear of perishing in that madness.

The rain wouldn't stop. In my dripping wet clothes, I shivered both from cold and fright; I wished deep down within me for someone—anyone—to call my name and find me.

After being on land for a few hours, I was free of my seasickness, but now, for the first time in days, I was desperately hungry and thirsty. From my protective boulder, I saw a few people wandering around and bending down from time to time. At first I could not see clearly what they were doing; only after a while did I discover that they were collecting rainwater in cupped hands from puddles between the rocks. I followed their example, but it tasted salty and did not quench my thirst. I felt such an intense hunger after days of constant vomiting that I would have ingested anything edible. But there was nothing. I searched in my immediate area until I discovered a tall plant resembling a green onion. Happily I pulled it out from the soil, root and all, and put it in my mouth; I ate it though it was as tasteless as grass.

Without a watch I could not tell exactly how long I had been standing there, hoping for the miracle of a search party. It must have been hours. I feared I would spend the whole night alone under the boulder.

And then it happened! "Ruthi! Ruthi! Where are you?" a voice called from a distance. Could it be? Perhaps I was already hallucinating? Was it wishful thinking? Or had someone indeed missed me?

"I'm here! Over here!" I shouted continuously, with such force that I was sure the very rocks would vibrate. I was astonished by the surge of energy that enabled me to scream so loudly.

A tall silhouetted figure emerged from nowhere, repeatedly calling: "Ruthiii! Ruthiii!" Then he stood before me. It was Maiciu. Sobbing, I threw myself into his arms, grateful to have been discovered. He held my soaking, shaking body and reassured me that all was fine now. He took off his wet coat and helped me put it on. It was so heavy I almost collapsed under its weight, yet it warmed my body and protected me from the incessant rain. With his help, I clambered up the rock to a tiny church built of stones to which the old and infirm had been taken. I rested there for the few remaining hours of the night.

Before daybreak, Maiciu returned and led me to an area with some shallow caves that normally sheltered sheep. This time they provided refuge for hundreds of desperate, shipwrecked Jews. Not all the people fit into the few caves, and many had to content themselves with sitting in a ditch, molded into each other's spread legs.

Screams of delight erupted from the throats of my L'hagshamah comrades as I walked in. Solo was among them, and, with hugs, I expressed my gratitude to him for saving my life. When I asked where he had disappeared to, he told me that he had jumped back onto the ship to help rescue a group of Hungarian children. My group had survived without a single loss. With my comrades again, I felt safe and protected. Huddled together, we started to reconstruct events, share information and rumors, and speculate on the outcome.

The most encouraging piece of news was that our Mossadniks had saved the Morse transmitter and were continuously sending out S.O.S. messages in the hope that someone, somewhere would intercept the signals and send help. In what form a rescue mission would arrive or when were the big questions. The tragic news was that many people had lost their lives. Eight bodies were pulled out of the sea or washed onto the rocks and lodged beneath the stones. We never knew how many others perished. We were stranded on a barren, rocky, sparsely populated Greek island named Sirina in the vicinity of Rhodes. A strategic island in the Aegean Sea, Sirina was guarded by a large family of shepherds and fishermen who lived in a crude stone house and in some of the caves. The Greek government maintained them with food provisions and a few armaments. Through the interpreting of the Greek crew, communication was established with the islanders. They did everything in their power to help us. It was they who indicated the location of the caves for shelter.

The next morning everybody ran out to see for themselves the aftermath of the tragedy. A cool, clear day greeted us, as if nature had completely forgotten yesterday's tempest. We were now on another side of the island, facing a different shoreline than the one where the ship had sunk. Almost devoid of vegetation, the island did have a tiny field of alfalfa and a small church. Our representatives met with the crew and bombarded them with questions. We found out that the *Rafiach* had been a small 650-ton cargo vessel without any lifeboats or other lifesaving equipment, unfit for such a large human cargo. The survivors were repeatedly assured that the crew had signaled our location by Morse code and that help would soon arrive.

Our hunger and thirst on the second day were becoming intolerable. Many people, out of despair, tried to offer their jewelry or other belongings to the islanders in exchange for food. When our Mossad leader, Gad Lasker, became aware of their intentions, he immediately stopped it in a very astute way. He told the Greeks not to accept the individual offers because the rest of the hungry crowd might kill them and their sheep. Instead, he gave the natives some gold coins he had stashed away for just such an emergency. The islanders accepted the payment and prepared food for all. They slaughtered sheep and cooked soup in a large iron cauldron. The ingredients of the soup were difficult to ascertain: the broth contained some meat and bones, but mainly it was a clear, salty hot liquid, a welcome delicacy after that first cold rainy night.

The queue was endless. Most people lacked cups or spoons, so they had to borrow from those who managed to salvage some. When my turn finally came, I was so famished that it no longer mattered to me if the soup were made from stones, as long as it was hot and salty.

The second night, we nestled close to each other, trying to sleep, happy at least to have that musty cave for a shelter. Twisted and entwined, with our heads propped on each other's backs, thighs, or bellies, some actually managed to sleep. A few fortunate ones who had salvaged some bundles used those instead. Coat owners were lucky not to have to lie on the moist soil of the cavern. I wanted to use the coat Maiciu had given me earlier, but because it was made of paper fiber, a World War II fabric substitute, it fell apart from having absorbed so much rainwater.

Sleep eluded me because of the uncomfortable position and the brooding over all my precious belongings, now disintegrating at the bottom of the sea. As happy as I was to have escaped alive, anguished thoughts about my destiny kept me awake. But I was also aware that at the end of that bleak tunnel there flickered a spark of hope that allowed me to be consoled by fantasies. I thought that now for sure there would be a great compensation for having survived yet another tragedy. Somehow these naive thoughts helped me through another long night.

Our third morning on the island, with only the previous night's food in our stomachs, found us in a dispirited mood. We assembled outside with ears and eyes alert to any sight or sound that might indicate potential rescue, but to no avail. There was nothing on the horizon except for an occasional solitary bird. We grew more apprehensive, thinking that we might perish from starvation or dehydration on the godforsaken rock of Sirina. Rumor had it that a small group of people had even attempted a mutiny against the Mossadniks, trying to take away the Morse code transmitter. Patience had grown thin.

The leaders suggested we light bonfires so that we might be discovered should a search party be on its way. But the lack of trees and the wet vegetation made this task difficult. Most of the young men scoured the small island and managed to collect enough material to light several fires. Soon smoke rose to the sky from multiple locations. Scattered around the fires, groups continued their vigil in complete silence. At the slightest noise or sight, everyone scrutinized the sky and instantly interpreted. But all were false alarms.

Slow, anxious hours passed, sending us into deep despair. Nobody saw the smoke and nobody picked up our S.O.S. We were doomed to another long night plagued by burning thirst, hunger, and cold, with only a cave for shelter.

Momentarily somebody broke the silence whispering: "Shush! Shush!" cupping his ears and turning them toward the sky to hear better, and we all followed suit. "I can hear a buzzing noise, this time for sure it's a plane!" the herald said in an authoritative tone. Discerning a faint sound, with eyes screening the sky, we almost stopped breathing. A dark dot became distinct. "Another bird," shouted the skeptics, dismissing the appearance with a shrug.

Soon this "bird" circled the island several times, each time lower and lower until there was no doubt anymore; it was indeed a plane. We jumped and rejoiced in that miracle of miracles! As if in a rehearsed choreography, we waved with whatever piece of cloth we could get hold of or with our bare hands. We had been located at last!

Seeing the plane fly off, we began shouting and screaming at the top of our lungs, "Come back here! Come back here! We are here!" as if we could be heard up there, an absurd assumption based on a desperate fear of being abandoned forever.

That they did not hear us we knew, but that they did not see us and took off leaving behind eight hundred wretched souls thoroughly robbed of hope was devastating.

But that same afternoon the long-awaited salvation arrived. On the horizon a few planes appeared and flew low over our heads, circling the island several times.

I had never in my life seen such a spectacle. Out of the blue sky, dozens of parachutes opened in mid-flight. I stood there transfixed. With my mouth wide open, I followed those gigantic umbrellas gliding slowly lower and lower. Now a new hysteria mounted as the mob ran toward the anticipated spot of impact. The parachutes descended with what we thought were parachutists, but as they plummeted onto the rock, we realized that these were crates instead of human beings. It was disappointing. We expected some contact with people who would bring us good news. Then we quickly realized that the plummeting crates *were* good news: they contained food.

Exhilarated, we ran toward those boxes, many of which had split open on impact. The manna from heaven continued to fall, and the starving crowd rushed toward it like hungry animals in pursuit of their prey.

The strongest, the fastest, and the most unscrupulous lay hands on the open boxes, ready to pilfer their contents. Fortunately, the leaders were able to disperse the mob and distribute an equal amount to everyone in a quick and orderly manner. The boxes contained *matzoth*, chocolates, canned goods, blankets, and medicines, and the Hebrew labels indicated that the drop was a Jewish operation out of Palestine. The pamphlets dropped from the planes swirled like confetti over our heads. As we picked them up, we were thrilled to read a comforting message in Hebrew: "*B'teavon!* (Bon appetit! Enjoy!) Rescue boats on the way." Signed: "Courtesy of Kibbutz Yagur."

Now that we had been found, we hoped that Jews from Palestine would come to our rescue and take us safely to the shores of our homeland. With those expectations, we scrutinized the sea for signs of any vessel approaching the island. Nothing. At dusk our hopes vanished, giving way to anguish about the possibility of spending yet another night in the caves. Now at least we had fortified our bodies with solid food. Water, on the other hand, remained a critical issue. Many gave up the vigil and, exhausted, entered the caves to spend another miserable night.

On day four, the early morning quiet was abruptly pierced by shouts and commotion. Hundreds of people spilled out from the caves to see what was happening. From a distance we could discern the form of a small ship, which turned out to be Greek. It came to rescue only the Greek crew members but also took the Jewish sick and injured and their families. The captain informed us that they had picked up our S.O.S. and so had others in the area, so we would probably be rescued soon.

December 12, 1946. At dusk we saw two gray ships approaching the island. The screams of joy were uncontrollable. We hoped—no, we were almost convinced—in our naïveté, that they belonged to the Haganah and would take us to Haifa.

They appeared to be destroyers hoisting flags whose origin we still could not identify. As they approached the island, it became obvious that the flags were British. That did not deter our collective euphoria. We rationalized that since Palestine still lay under the auspices of a British Mandate, the Jews had to use these flags. We were told by our leaders that the ships had come to rescue us and would take us to Palestine. Finally my wishes had come true . . . I thought.

The destroyers anchored far from the rocky island. A fleet of lifeboats that would ferry people to the island arrived with a group of British Royal Navy officers. We were deeply disappointed; still we greeted the crew with enthusiasm, considering them to be our saviors. The officers held a few preliminary discussions with a select group of representatives, not the Mossadniks, who had to hide so as not to be captured by the British. The officers invited the shipwreck victims to board the two destroyers. A friendly, polite crew of sailors greeted us, offering food, blankets, and pillows. Our L'hagshamah group stayed together and descended into a large, deep hold that was far more comfortable and spacious than the accommodations on the *Rafiach.*

The sailing was infinitely smoother, and I did not get sick this time. There was no doubt in anyone's mind that these polite and friendly Britons would take us directly to the port of Haifa.

The destroyers sailed for hours, during which the Mossad leaders, who now hid their identity and made believe they were common immigrants, charted our course. Some hours into the journey they realized that something was terribly wrong and started to investigate.

They soon informed us that we might not be going to Haifa after all but to the island of Cyprus. Cyprus? What and where was that? Few people had heard of such a place. A short briefing followed, one that had a devastating effect on everybody's mood. Our leaders explained that camps in Cyprus had been established earlier in 1946 by the British Mandate in Palestine to detain all captured illegal Jewish emigrants. They would later be released on a basis of "first come, first go" in groups of fifteen hundred as part of the legal quota for entry into Palestine.

The crowd lost hope and became angry. I personally refused to accept my inimical fate. For the first time, the rebel in me was ready to fight. On the other hand the frightened child in me was silently praying: *Please not another concentration camp! Not another betrayal. Not another humiliation! Not again!*

We decided to put up passive resistance in protest against the forthcoming imprisonment by staging a hunger strike, which lasted for about a day and a half. We sat hungry and vexed, hoping for a change of heart that never came.

Suddenly the ship's engines went silent. We speculated that we might have arrived at a port, but from the holds we could not see anything. Then we heard a voice blasting through the loudspeaker, "Everybody up on deck!"

Our leaders ordered us not to move. We remained standing frozen in place like statues. No one said a word. No one moved. The voice ordered again: "Out! Or we will force you out with tear gas!" This time it sounded threatening.

Refusing to move, we felt very brave and patriotic, but not for long. The sailors did what they had been instructed to do—they blasted us with powerful water hoses. When we continued to resist, they tossed tear gas canisters into the hold.

When the coughing and gasping for air became unbearable, we succumbed. Blinded by the intense burning and itching in our eyes, we scrambled onto the deck. Bewildered people ran into each other in chaotic disorder, while some still resisted leaving the vessel. But the British soldiers intervened and eventually we all had to abandon the destroyer. Surrounded by armored cars, the soldiers loaded us into military trucks and Jeeps mounted with machine guns. Shrieking sirens pierced the air, heralding the conquest of less than eight hundred helpless, unarmed, ship-wrecked Jewish refugees—a clear-cut victory by His Majesty's Royal Navy and the mighty British Empire.

The trucks first stopped at the inspection barracks. The British authorities checked us for infectious diseases and for weapons. Then we were supplied with a cot and a blanket per person, as well as some personal items. Finally, they ordered us back to the waiting trucks. As we continued on the last leg of our trip, we could clearly see the high barbed wire fences and searchlight towers at each corner, manned by armed British soldiers. My heart stopped for a few seconds. This painful reminder of recent horrid experiences under the Nazis made my blood boil. Why? Why? A silent, swelling cry of protest from within threatened to burst my chest. This unsettling injustice of being deprived of freedom yet again cast a pall even on my usually optimistic personality.

After having survived the setbacks of Balta, Bucharest, Odessa, and Sirina, I hoped to be treated with tenderness in a sheltering, loving environment that would help me heal my emotional wounds and protect me from further trauma. Instead, I was faced with another calamity.

With the war over, and the Nazi goal of annihilating the Jewish race, the existence of a detention camp for Jews who wanted to go to their homeland was totally incomprehensible to me. Although the British intended neither to kill or to persecute us, they were, nonetheless, our oppressors.

The convoy came to a halt in front of the camp's entrance. The trucks rolled into Detention Camp 62, Caraollos, Cyprus, known also as "The Summer Camp."

Cyprus

CHAPTER 11

Once inside the camp, a panorama unlike anything I had ever seen emerged: a wide, arid, sandy area as far as the eye could see, totally covered by row upon row of small tents amid which thousands of refugees milled about.

Among those refugees were our comrades from Group I and II who arrived via Italy and whose boat had been captured a month earlier. Somehow they found and immediately integrated us into their ranks to form a single L'hagshamah commune. That welcome was the only positive aspect in this whole trial. With their help we pitched our tents, unfolded the canvas cots, and settled in for a good night's sleep.

We arranged the tents in the form of a closed square with all the doors opening into a central yard in order to achieve a certain measure of privacy from the thousands of other inmates. To create a large dining/meeting place, we joined two tents together. There we assembled for a general meeting, attendance being mandatory. A long briefing session brought us up to date on current affairs.

We were informed that the camp was run autonomously by a committee of representatives from the various communes and other detainee groups. No armed British soldiers were ever allowed entry. The bad news was that food was scarce and consisted mostly of poor quality canned goods like "corned beef" (supposedly made of camel meat), sardines, and hash brown potatoes, and a strict daily ration of water was distributed from special trucks. Because of the water shortage, personal hygiene became a real problem. A few compounds shared one latrine, but there were no showers.

There was one small, unfenced area leading into the seashore which was, nonetheless, carefully watched. This opening to the sea gave us a feeling of some freedom, illusory as it was.

The compounds and tent-lined alleys were grouped together by nationality or political affiliations. The overwhelming number of people, who had been there for many months already, were mostly survivors of the Holocaust.

Delegates from the Haganah helped the inmates in every way, especially in the administration of the camp. Disguised as refugees, they sometimes posed as members of youth organizations. These secret soldiers maintained contact with Palestine via hidden ham radios. They smuggled themselves in and out of the camp in the most ingenious ways and represented the only link between the Palestinian Jews and us. These brave men buoyed our spirits by setting up an array of community services and activities. They told stories about our homeland and taught us Hebrew songs and folk dances.

A view of the Cyprus internment camp.

Me in Cyprus, age sixteen.

L'hagshamah, meanwhile, conducted its own internal activities, led by a skillful leader named Diczi, whom the group nicknamed "The Philosopher." I stood in awe of his knowledge, his quiet diplomacy, and his soft voice. Mainly, he succeeded in instilling confidence in those of us who had neither schooling nor sophistication by giving us opportunities to develop our natural potential. If it were not for the support system the commune provided, I don't know how I would have dealt with this new loss of liberty.

On a less serious level, we tried to have as much fun as was possible under the circumstances. For the Purim holiday, when it is customary to wear masks and costumes, we decided to have a party. Some creative girls designed costumes by transforming items from practically nothing, so that we had some kind of bal masque. As I always wanted to be a dancer, I asked them to make me a ballerina costume. From a white sheet they fashioned a tutu and—presto!—I had my wish fulfilled, if only for one night. Little did I know that the outfit would get such raves, especially from the guys. Only later did I realize that it was neither the costume nor the ballet I performed but the exposure of my bare legs and thighs that created such a furor. I was unaware that I had developed at least *one* feminine attribute, and it hit me that I was no longer a child or a tomboy but a young woman. "So why hadn't I gotten my period?" I asked myself. My perpetual preoccupation with the fear of abnormality continued.

Still, that did not deter several admirers from being attracted to me. One of them, a tall, handsome, athletic, green-eyed, twenty-year-old named Marius, was especially persistent. I reciprocated his overtures of courtship, and slowly we fell in love. The feeling was unlike any other I had ever experienced: a medley of excitement, novelty, eroticism, pleasure, and apprehension.

Blinded by love, I didn't see his defects. My male friends warned me of his frivolous and immature personality, but I took their warnings as a sign of jealousy and listened only to my heart, indulging myself in the pleasure of loving and being loved in return. My only apprehension stemmed from my deftly kept secret of not being a fully developed woman and whether, or when, Marius would find out.

After many agonizing weeks, I decided to talk about it with one of my girlfriends. She agreed that at sixteen and a half I really should be menstruating. Her advice was to see a "woman's doctor" at the little clinic set up in a prefabricated shack staffed by Jewish volunteers from Palestine.

There a male physician greeted me and asked, "Do you speak Hebrew or Yiddish? Because these are the only two languages I speak."

"I speak Yiddish," I answered, happy to be able to communicate with him. Otherwise it would have required the help of an interpreter, which would have caused additional embarrassment.

I told the doctor that I was going to be seventeen soon and was still lacking many signs of feminine development, mainly menstruation. He fired questions in a way that made me feel humiliated.

"Are you married?"

"No."

"Did you sleep with someone?"

"Sure, with many people, for many years on plank-beds."

"No, no. I mean did you sleep with a *man*?"

"No, never," I said, angrily dismissing such a suspicion.

"Did someone touch or kiss you?"

That last question I denied vehemently, hoping that it would not show. "Aha!" I said to myself, "I must have done something wrong by letting Marius kiss me his way."

Once the questioning stopped, he asked me to undress and get up on the table for a physical examination. I was scared to death he might not believe that I was a virgin, but he did. After the examination he declared that there was nothing wrong with me and all I needed was to take some pills. I sighed with relief. Feeling degraded and ashamed, I approached the camp pharmacy to fill the prescription.

Halfway there, a sharp cramp in my lower abdomen made me change my route and go instead to our compound. Slowly I dragged myself to the latrine, where I could take a closer look. I could not believe my eyes! I got my period! What a joy and a relief! I was a normal woman after all!

I wondered if my strong reaction to the humiliating interview could have triggered this minor miracle. I was so excited, I quickly spread the news to all my girlfriends, who shared my happiness and offered advice about how to handle the new situation. I welcomed the monthly annoyance as a normal, healthy, yet necessary evil.

The assurance that I was normal, like people who had never endured the camps, gave me a boost of self-confidence that lifted my spirits and energized me. As a consequence, I got deeply involved in a series of strenuous physical tasks.

The Haganah members selected the strongest, ablest boys and girls for the *Shurat Hameginim* (The Line of Defenders), a sort of paramilitary training. Marius was among the first from our commune to be recruited. Soon after, they selected me. This clandestine training went on in several locations of the camp away from the watchtowers and the barbed wire. While the British may have suspected these ongoing activities, they chose to turn a blind eye.

Every morning we marched and ran in formation, climbed trees, and learned hand-to-hand combat called *kapapp* (a form of stick-fighting similar to fencing which, for lack of wooden clubs, we performed with short broomsticks). A few weeks into training, I became an expert in this type of combat and was soon promoted to the rank of group leader, teaching kapapp to about twenty girls. Later, a judo expert came to our commune and taught us another art of self-defense.

The position of leadership in the Shurah brought me popularity and recognition, but the ultimate reward was the feeling of security that, if attacked again, I could defend myself without arms. I was a child no more but a strong, athletic young woman, determined not to let any force corral or humiliate me.

Several weeks after our arrival some bad news struck us like a lightning bolt: the monthly immigration quota to Palestine was suddenly cut from 1,500 to 750. Anger and indignation led to protest marches, and we threw blazing rags over the fences at the British, who in turn barged into the camps with armored cars.

In an admirable act of heroism, my Marius lay down in front of the first armored car. Everybody stopped breathing. Holding onto each other in an atmosphere of highly charged tension, we anxiously waited to see what would happen. The car continued on, coming to a stop only a few inches from his sprawled body. There was a sigh of relief.

An officer ordered the vehicles to turn around, and exit the camp. We cheered wildly. Marius's heroism was paramount in preventing the British soldiers from moving in. Adventurous and daring, Marius became a hero in the eyes of the prisoners.

To help ease the tensions created by the reduced quota, Golda Meir, then head of the Jewish Agency, came to visit the camp. In her honor, all the communes paraded carrying the Jewish national flag. Normally this honor was given to a man, but my commune chose me to be the flag-bearer.

Later at a meeting, Mrs. Meir asked that the adult detainees renounce their quota privileges in favor of children and babies, a request that was not favorably regarded. In the end, a separate youth quota was established to include children, their families, and orphans; thus peace returned to the camp.

After his heroic act, Marius became more and more involved in the Shurah. Then one day he decided to leave the commune and live altogether in another compound. Although he came to see me daily, assur-

I'm carrying the flag for L'hag-shamah in a parade.

ing me that once we arrived in Palestine, he would rejoin us, I was doubtful and terribly disappointed.

Meanwhile, the protests continued. We marched, shouted slogans against the British government, and hurled stones at the barbed-wire fence not far from an abandoned military hospital. It occupied a corner of the camp area but was separated from the rest of the camp by an additional barbed wire fence. Eventually some of our members noticed that the hospital compound was totally devoid of British personnel. We came up with a plan for our commune to take it over. After several exploratory surveys, we began the invasion. At night our men would cut the barbed wire. Then the rest of us would quietly dismantle and carry our tents over for the men to put up.

We had discovered paradise: an oasis in the sandy desolate desert that was the camp. Across from a grove with green grass, trees, and bushes stood a one-story concrete building consisting of a few rooms. Close by, a tin shack with showers and a latrine facilitated our hygienic needs. What a relief it was to be far away from the choking crowds of the sandy main campsite! We hoped the British guards would never drive us out—and they never did. We became the camp's elite and envy. But even this paradise was not immune to the devastating winter rains that so often flooded our tents. Some nights we would be startled out of our sleep by the cold rainwater that rose above the level of our canvas cots, soaking us to the bone.

The long, rainy winter months gave way to the welcome spring of 1947, but no word came about our quota. This wait naturally took its toll on the inmates, who out of boredom became desperate. To counteract our lethargy and depression, our commune came up with innovative activities for its members.

One was to start a photography lab with a single camera and an improvised darkroom. With supplies smuggled from Palestine and the expertise of some of our members, we developed a busy enterprise. People from throughout the camp came to have their pictures taken or just purchase souvenir-type photos of the various camp sites. Although of poor quality, these snapshots had great sentimental value.

Another activity was stone carving. Some of our explorers found a stone indigenous to that island which, in the hands of a few artisans, was soon turned into an assortment of objets d'art: picture frames, ashtrays, album covers, and candlesticks. We put them on our small wooden night stands made of crates to embellish the primitive interiors of the tents.

Driven by a desperate need for clothing, we began to rip apart the extra tents for fabric. The tents had four layers of canvas, khaki, white, blue, and yellow. As soon as the Jewish Agency provided us with a sewing machine, we created a "mini-garment industry" under the guidance of our own seamstresses and tailors and soon had an array of new clothing to wear.

We, the *Rafiach* survivors, were finally able to have a change of clothing. Even though the canvas was rigid and felt coarse and prickly to the skin, the joy of having a new skirt, a halter, a pair of shorts, more than compensated for it. Coincidentally, we were clad in the national blue and white colors of Israel.

Although these cottage industries helped a lot to combat the boredom and monotony of imprisonment during the day, they did nothing to ease the dark, gloomy evenings. In the dining tent we did have the luxury of one Petromax kerosene lantern with a sophisticated mechanism that produced a relatively bright light. After dinners or meetings, we would take it into our tents on a rotating system. The lucky tent with the Petromax instantly became the center for gathering and socializing.

Without the Petromax, the only flicker of light inside the tents came from improvised lamps made by filling an empty food can with kerosene, sticking in a piece of fabric, and then tightening the opening to hold the improvised wick. After the other girls in my tent fell asleep, I would take the light to my nightstand and read classic novels (supplied by the Jewish Agency) into the wee hours. In the morning I would look like a chimney sweep, my face and nostrils covered with greasy soot. It was hard to wash it off, but it was a small price to pay for knowledge. While I had totally erased from my mind the idea of ever going back to school, due to my commitment to kibbutz life, books still remained my main source of information, education, and companionship.

Sometimes, instead of going to the dark tents, the entire commune would stream out into the yard for a round of *hora* dancing. Every so often we would stage small performances for other communes to enjoy. Mostly we sang and performed Russian dances choreographed by me.

L'hagshamah's cultural and social programs gained such a reputation among the other communes that many party officials came to visit us to learn something from our experiments. Our reputation reached as far as the Haganah who decided to hide its clandestine headquarters in our compound. "Avner," one of their members, was the sole occupant of that secret tent, complete with a ham radio and other devices, which nobody was allowed to enter. That order was respected even though we were dying of curiosity.

As more and more illegal vessels were captured, the number of Jews brought to Cyprus increased. That overburdened the workload of the British, who requested help from within the ranks of the camp community. The leaders recruited one English-speaking member from each Zionist youth commune to work outside the camp to distribute supplies to the new prisoners. I was to be the one from L'hagshamah.

To say that I spoke English was an overstatement, as all my knowledge consisted of the few private lessons with Mrs. Kern back in Czernowitz. Still, the official tested me and said my English was good enough for that purpose. About ten or twelve of us were let out every morning through the camp's gate and escorted by two armed soldiers to British headquarters. There, in several corrugated tin barracks with convex roofs, supplies were stored. Our task was to sort and prepare packages of clothing and other necessities for distribution to the incoming refugees.

Leaving the confinement of the camp for the day was not exactly freedom, but it carried the illusion of it. For me it was also a welcome change to work with a group of people from different countries and of different ideologies, although it was at the cost of my position as "leader" in the paramilitary.

Now and then, officers paid us sporadic surprise visits. But most of the time we worked unsupervised, which created an opportunity to steal some goods. It seemed almost heroic to cheat on the British oppressor for the benefit of the entire commune. I had never stolen as much as a pin in my life for my personal gain, but now I did it with gusto for L'hagshamah. In the process we all became skilled thieves. Convinced that all the items were British property, we thought nothing of tricking them out of some of it. (We learned later that they were from the American Jewish Joint Distribution Committee.)

In the afternoon, as soon as we were left alone, we would start our operation. While one would stand watching the door, the rest would stuff their armpits with socks, put on several pairs of men's briefs, and wrap their bodies with many yards of fabric, and then put on their own clothing. On our way back to the camp we looked like blimps. The walk was not long, but under the hot Mediterranean sun—with our bodies insulated by the extra layers of stolen goods—it seemed endless. Amazingly, neither the escorts nor the guards at the gate seemed to notice the drastic increase in our sizes from morning till afternoon.

Upon my return from work, my comrades greeted me with anticipation and beamed with approval when I started to peel off all the hidden layers of clothes and fabric. Everybody benefitted from this "heroic" act of theft, turning my crime into a blessing.

All the British officers were polite toward us, yet one particular officer treated me in an especially cordial manner. He was unattractive, in

his late thirties, and I called him the "old man," since that was how I, at age seventeen, perceived him. He was the one with whom I had the most direct contact.

He would come into our barracks under any excuse in order to talk to me, often bringing me little gifts. Sometimes it was cigarettes, even though I did not smoke; at other times it was sweets or chocolates. In a subtle way, he almost seemed to be courting me, but I treated him more like a nice uncle. My coworkers and my commune members had their share of entertainment at the expense of my "sugar daddy." But at the same time, the members enjoyed sharing the goodies I received from him.

April 1947. Four months after the shipwreck, the British granted permission for women and children survivors of the *Rafiach* to emigrate to Palestine ahead of the others. That entitled us, the girls of Group III, to leave almost immediately. But after many heated debates, our leaders felt that it was not in the best interests of the commune to let us go now, as the first groups seemed better prepared for farm work and life on a kibbutz. The general meeting voted that we should stay and that some twenty-seven members of Groups I and II should go first.

As a result, my group, and sixteen from the other two groups stayed behind. In our naïveté and idealism, we were convinced that we had made a worthwhile sacrifice. However, that decision by the general meeting prompted many members to leave the commune altogether, causing a serious crisis and lots of disappointments.

The lucky twenty-seven pioneers left Cyprus and were later assigned by our party in Palestine to live on Kibbutz Usha for one year of training in preparation for the establishment our own kibbutz.

Soon after the pioneer group's departure, Marius also decided to leave Cyprus, having succeeded in getting himself on an early quota. To my great sorrow, the day of his departure approached all too quickly. The thought of separation from him, for any length of time, devastated me. We promised to write to each other three times a week and made wedding plans, vowing eternal love and faithfulness.

Shortly before his departure, I dared to request from my British supervisor an unusual favor: to let me accompany Marius to the ship. Not expecting a positive response, I was utterly surprised to receive written permission, in addition to an offer of an uniformed escort to accompany me and bring me back to work. Marius and I traveled in a truck full of people who probably were wondering about the unusual presence of an armed escort. Everybody was in an elated mood: after all, in only sixteen hours, they were to be free.

At the sight of this real passenger ship, I gasped. Even if it was not a luxury liner, compared to *Rafiach* it was huge. I was allowed to board it as a guest, and, as we were walking, holding hands, Marius tried to convince me to escape with him as a stowaway. I would not hear of it, even though my escort stood nonchalantly near the truck, looking the other way, perhaps expecting me to make a dash for freedom.

Embracing in one last furtive kiss, I bid farewell to my love and returned to the truck to watch Marius and the others sail off. The soldier helped me onto the truck, now empty of passengers, and dropped me off at the barracks, depressed and lonely.

Marius left Cyprus on May 19, 1947. That very same evening, I decided to start a diary to alleviate my pain. Later, when I got his first letter and address, I transferred my entries into real letters, still keeping the diary. Aside from private matters, I also wrote about events that took place both in our commune and in the camp. Here are just a few excerpts from my diary notes, which I have translated from Romanian.

* * *

May 19, 1947. I spent all afternoon crying at work, so they let me leave early. When I returned to our L'hagshamah gate, Sammy greeted me with a joke to which I reacted with apathy. He tried to console me by patting my shoulder and saying, "You have to be strong." At these words a new stream of tears began. Some friends were surprised to see me because it was rumored that people saw me boarding the ship, assuming that I left. But others assured me of their complete confidence in my loyalty to L'hagshamah. They were convinced that my idealism and commitment to the commune came before my personal interests. That was pleasant to hear. I kiss you. Your Ruth.

May 23, 1947. My English has improved a lot as a result of constant conversation. The "old man" presented me with two extraordinary gifts: a Petromax lamp for my tent and a puppy. What a pleasure it is to enter the tent and find it glowing and full of friends who come to share the light. It is incredible what a bright environment can do for the mind. Adding to my elated mood is my cute puppy, with whom everybody wants to play. He has become the center of attention since he's the only animal allowed inside the camp, so I feel rather privileged. Kisses. Your Ruth.

May 28, 1947. There is a lot to write about today. It is the long-awaited date of the double wedding of Mira and Ivan, Cilli and Singher. The Mossadniks seized this opportunity to carry out one of their clever schemes. They gave me the unprecedented mission of trying to get some key British officers, like Major Pie, to attend the wedding. I didn't question their intentions, even though I knew it was absolutely unheard of for the British to socialize with the inmates. I made use of whatever charm and good relationships I had, and surprisingly they accepted.

At 4:00 P.M. the officers arrived at our gate, to the astonishment of the camp's inmates. Leading the entourage was Major Pie in Bermuda shorts and a Panama hat and carrying his ever present swagger stick. Following him were the captain, the lieutenant, and other officers, all slightly intoxicated already. Diczi and I were selected to be their hosts. Major Pie gallantly kissed my hand and offered me his right arm to rest mine upon. In that pose we walked solemnly toward the brides' reception place. You should have seen that absurd, pompous procession of the old, proper British officers led by a sixteen-year-old inmate. In a distorted way, it seemed as if I were living just for one day in the period of Emperor Franz Joseph. The officers kissed both brides and wished them well, after which we all went out into the grove to await the religious ceremony.

Our artists did a marvelous job decorating the arbor where the *chuppah* (canopy) stood. The day was glorious, the spirits festive. At the end of the ceremony, we all stood at attention for the singing of the *Hatikvah* (the Jewish anthem). The officers mimed the words, trying to hum the melody. It was hilarious to watch. While we prepared for dinner the officers left, but they returned at 9:00 P.M., just in time for the feast. Where all the food and wine came from, I have no idea. Perhaps for that special occasion, the British or some Jewish organization provided it. At any rate, we ate and drank to our hearts' content and were in an excellent mood.

Suddenly Dudu, the Mossad guy, asked me to try and get the British drunk so he could get one of them to sign some important documents. Since I was in charge of their entertainment, I did as asked, although I wasn't very happy to have to cater to the old drunk officers.

The entertainment began with Bertha's solo singing, followed by dancing. Later I was asked to sing my solos. I didn't feel like it at that moment, but when the major begged me to do him a favor and sing I felt I had to please him, so I did. After a few drinks, I got into a better mood and even performed my Russian-Cossack dance.

A few minutes later Dudu approached me again and whispered, "Take the old man out for a dance." I did what I was told, knowing that it served some secret purpose. The old officer turned out to be a wonderful dancer. When Dudu felt that the major was drunk enough, he approached him and in perfect English requested some signature. The ma-

jor complied without question. Victory! We continued singing and dancing and having a good time, long after the British left. I hug and kiss
you. Your Ruth

June 8, 1947. It is Saturday, and I played a little trick so as not to go to
work today. I had previously tried to convince all the people who work
with me that we shouldn't go in on Saturdays since we were Jewish, but
they were all afraid of Bacalu, the supervisor. I'm not. He's just another
inmate who speaks better English, so he became the boss. My protest,
which my coworkers called a "revolution," achieved its goal, and we
don't have to work on Saturdays anymore. Everybody congratulated me
and jokingly said that I probably have some Russian revolutionary blood
in my veins that enables me to do daring acts. Love and kisses. Your
Ruth.

June 19, 1947. We discussed the deterioration of the commune's esprit
de corps and the need for self-discipline to preserve our sanity in this
desperate monotony. It's easy to become depressed if one does not keep
busy. This morning we got up like lightning and washed and dressed to
be ready when the coordinator would come to our tent. Sara, who was
in charge this week, was speechless at our self-discipline. Out we went
for our morning exercises, which Diczi usually leads, but he decided
someone else should take the leadership. The group suggested that from
now on I should be the one. Some of the men jokingly protested against
a woman climbing to power and threatened not to participate. But it
seemed to go pretty well. Kisses, Ruth.

June 21, 1947. Today I turned seventeen! On such an important date,
I have the desire to be hugged, kissed, and wished well by one dear, sincere, and beloved friend whose presence I miss today more than any
other day. How much I long to spend this day with you and to be completely happy and free!

When I woke up, I found on my nightstand a white envelope and two
stone booklets, products of our workshops, but nothing from you. Dis-
enchanted, I refused to touch anything. Instead I went out to wash first.

Upon my return, Shoshana stopped to wish me a happy birthday. Then
the rest of the girls followed suit. I was deeply touched by the sincere

caring we have for one another. My tentmates had written a lovely note. The stone miniature albums contained a series of camp scenes mixed with a few snapshots of our group, and one of the two of us.

In the afternoon we went to the beach to swim. The sea was tranquil and warm and, as usual, had a calming effect on me.

At dinner, Maiciu announced that it was my birthday and everyone congratulated me. After dinner, I found one more note on my cot, which informed me of a gift I was supposed to have gotten in your name. How sweet of you to have thought in advance about me and my birthday! Thank you, my love. Your Ruth.

July 24, 1947. The commune has made a daring decision at one of our general meetings. It has to do with getting to know each other better and with improving the relationship between the married and unmarried members. We are undertaking an unprecedented social and psychological experiment in line with our goals to eliminate any individualistic tendencies. We are not content just sharing the "wealth," eating and dressing the same. Now in addition to the material, we want to share our spiritual and emotional aspects as well. Should be interesting.

For this endeavor, we have dismantled all the tents and combined three of them into a large one for the women, another for the men. We crowded the cots together so that all eighteen chattering ducks sleep a breath away from each other.

The daily routines continue as usual, except in the evenings, when we present a short résumé of our lives, after which we do a self-criticism. Once this is done, the others comment and give their feedback. That practice helps us to get to know each other better, to improve negative traits in a nonthreatening and caring environment. All we want is to better ourselves, hence perfecting the group as well. I like the feeling of togetherness and openness, since I always strive for perfection.

The married couples, meanwhile, are having a two-week "vacation" from their spouses, which they take with humor on the whole. A few grouchy couples try to ignore the rules and meet in hidden corners of the compound, hugging and kissing. Naturally, not everyone is happy with the experiment. The notoriety, though, has attracted the attention of an American psychologist who came to visit us. She's doing a study of this innovative system of creating a society void of conflict.

Despite all this activity, I miss you. I picture how pleasant it would feel to be with you in a normal room in a real apartment with doors and windows, sitting on a real chair, listening to music from a radio.

Oh yes, the newest additions to our tents are four little kittens who adopted us, me in particular, since they chose to sleep on my cot, as if they knew how much I adore cats.

Enough for today! I kiss you many times. Your Ruth.

July 27, 1947. I completely forgot to tell you that Avner the Mossadnik who lives in the secret tent was caught and imprisoned for a few weeks. Thanks to my indirect intervention, he is free now. It seems I played some sort of a Mata Hari role when I persuaded the British officers to come to the wedding. Apparently the document signed by the drunk major was crucial to Avner's release. When Avner returned to his tent near ours, he brought a gramophone and some records, a real treat.

A fierce sandstorm swept through the camp, spoiling everybody's mood. The heat is unbearable and makes us all lethargic. To top it off, we have a critical water shortage. To quench my thirst, I've learned not only to suck the juice of lemons but to eat the pulp as well.

Toward evening the storm let up and we were able to enjoy some music Avner played for us. We listened to arias from the operas *Carmen* and *The Barber of Seville*, as well as folk songs from Eretz Israel. All those put me in a melancholy mood. I've been daydreaming of you.

Our weekly "Wall Paper" edition put out seventy-five pages, a success to which I am happy to have contributed.

Lately, I am suffering from some intestinal problems. Tonight I felt so bad that my friends had to carry me out into the arbor in order to be able to join a gathering. I fell asleep, but my friends woke me up so I wouldn't spend the whole night there! Love, Ruth.

September 21, 1947. How can I express in a letter the overwhelming emotion I felt, and still feel, thanks to the telegram you sent me for the holidays? One more proof that you do think about me and my wishes; that gives me a dose of hope and strength to overcome the six weeks that still stand between us. I don't know how to thank you. Today I am a happy girl. The whole commune shares that happiness with me; even Diczi came to congratulate me and planted a kiss on my cheek. Did I tell you that I got a dress made of the fabric I had stolen from the warehouse? Well, a lot of girls got the same, and it will come in handy for my vacation in Palestine. I am sick and tired of wearing these garments made of tent canvas. It is unfair to a girl of seventeen to look like a beggar. Do you have enough clothes? I mean real clothes. Are you still working in the construction job? Love and kisses. Your Ruth.

October 20, 1947. I guess that this will be the last letter you receive from me. The day of our departure nears; by the time you will have received this letter, I might be in Palestine already. I constantly dream about freedom in my own land, the land of my father's dreams and my brother's hopes, and now of our reunion. My heart is filled with hope for a better life devoid of anti-Semitism and persecution. Soon I will meet some of my relatives, and perhaps later Aunt Anna and Lucie will come too. I miss them both very much.

Unfortunately I am the only survivor of my family who will carry out my father's dream, but the idea that I will toil on the land and contribute to the creation of a Jewish state gives meaning to all that happened. To be part of a new society is another proud feeling, that of carrying out a mission. A thousand kisses and hugs. Your Ruth.

*   *   *

We were buoyed by the exciting news of the UN's proclamation that partitioned Palestine into Jewish and Arab states, but this historic event had no bearing on the immigration procedures.

The six long months of our separation passed in anguished yearning, until the quota lists for our commune arrived. Someone read the names aloud, but to our great astonishment they were short by two—my friend Elise's and mine. We rechecked several times, but there was no mistake. We were dumbfounded. Soon a representative of the Jewish Agency came to explain what had happened. They had filled the monthly quota with people eighteen and over, leaving the younger ones to emigrate on a separate Youth Emigration quota. As Elise and I were not yet eighteen, they filled our places with two adults and we would have to wait yet another two months for the next youth list.

I couldn't believe this new, evil destiny. It was too much. Unable to accept the unfairness of that decision, I rebelled in a peculiar way. Remembering my poor mother's bout of hysteria when the communists tried to occupy our apartment, I copied her performance.

It was not difficult as I had already been crying and shaking for hours. All I added to the real anguish was loud screaming and more forceful shaking of the body. My tantrum was so impressive that my friends helped me to lie down and called a doctor. He immediately diagnosed my affliction as a case of hysteria, gave me some pills to calm me down, and left. Later drowsiness led into a deep sleep. From then on, I don't remember the sequence of events, except that I achieved nothing and felt ashamed for having made a fool of myself. While the group was in high spirits, I felt a deep sadness and a savage anger. No words of comfort or sympathy penetrated my hardened defensive shell. Elise was upset too, but not to the same degree; she was not a Nazi camp survivor, and she did not have a boyfriend waiting for her in Palestine.

With Elise at my right, disappointed at not being allowed to leave the Cyprus internment camp for Palestine with the others.

My depression must have caused some sort of amnesia because I have no recollection of the days after the entire L'hagshamah group left and of how the two of us had survived alone for the next two months.

What I do remember is the date of December 29, 1947, when a leader of the Youth Emigration came to take us to the gathering point for all the other children under age eighteen. From there we were taken via trucks to the port of Famagusta.

The same ship I had seen when Marius left awaited us. We were given a blue certificate issued by the Immigration Department of the Jewish Agency for Palestine. Our passport to freedom.

Elise and I shared a cabin during the voyage to Haifa. I couldn't quite believe that I was indeed going to the Land of Israel. The fear of some reversal constantly lurked in the back of my mind, but at the same time I could hardly contain my emotions—bittersweet as they were. A dream was coming true.

The Promised Land

CHAPTER 12

January 1, 1948. Just before daybreak, after a calm voyage, our ship approached the shores of Palestine. Coincidence or fate turned my dream into reality right on time—New Year's Day.

The morning was cool and hazy as we made out the faraway silhouette of Mount Carmel. Haifa lay asleep beneath a silky cover of fog, like a beautiful bride waiting for the groom to lift her veil. As the ship slowly made its way into the harbor, the sun's heat dissipated the fog and the city, built on three levels somewhat like San Francisco, presented itself to us in its most impressive regalia.

The excited children crowded onto the deck in anticipation of the tumultuous moment. Choked with emotion, my friend Elise and I hugged, unable to say a word. In a short while I would be free in the land of my forefathers— my new homeland. No more camps, no more persecutions, no more wars. I was home.

Immediately after disembarking and passing through some formalities, we were loaded onto trucks and driven out of Haifa to an area of open fields. And once again my heart sank at the sight of huge tents in the middle of no- where—a transition camp.

Elise and I settled down in a tent with approximately twenty other women, not knowing what was in store for us. Exhausted, we fell asleep.

Suddenly I was awakened by wails that sounded like children being tortured. Listening, carefully, I heard it again. The screams were real. Petrified, I woke Elise and the other girls to listen to the cries. They heard them but did not seem alarmed. It was only my wild imagination associating those cries with tortured children. Later I learned that the area was inhabited by jackals which—when hungry—emit a howl like a child's cry. What a frightful experience on my first night in freedom!

A few days later we were taken to the Athlith transition camp, which was surrounded by barbed wire and armed British guards. At that point it seemed to me that there would never be an end to imprisonment. My vision of a much different reception in this land of mine rapidly vanished.

I sent telegrams to Marius and my relatives announcing my arrival, and shortly afterward he came to visit me. Our reunion was wildly emotional, just as I had imagined it would be; we behaved like two playful children. He twirled me around like a baby, and I giggled happily, forgetting for a few hours all the pain of separation.

Just as Elise and I began to float on a cloud of happiness, our friends from Kibbutz Usha came to visit and brought us back down to earth. They told how the Arabs had attacked Jews on all fronts and had besieged towns and villages. And although they were repelled by the Haganah, they still posed a great danger. Kibbutz Usha, to which Elise and I were finally released, was near the Lebanese border and had often been attacked. The perils of a new war dampened the joy of my newfound freedom.

Tensions increased, and so did my anxieties and fears. This explosive reality did not make allowances for the emotional frailty of a seventeen-year-old survivor of the Holocaust.

In the months prior to our arrival, the first L'hagshamah group had already completed its military drills; therefore Elise and I had to begin ours with another group. For several weeks we trained at Yagur, a neighboring kibbutz. At the completion of that military course, we all gathered in a solemn ceremony to pledge our loyalty to the Haganah on the Bible and the gun, an emotional, patriotic, and proud moment.

Simultaneously, we had also trained in a new and difficult language (Hebrew), in a new arduous vocation (agriculture), and in a totally new and unique life-style.

The political situation in Palestine was becoming more volatile. The Arabs attacked and blocked roads, making travel a dangerous adventure. In precisely that period, Marius paid me a surprise visit. Beaming with adoring pride, I listened to his recounts of the risks he had taken to come and see me. We hugged, kissed, and talked incessantly, exchanging thoughts and filling each other in on everything that had not been covered in our letters.

My tactful tent-mates left us alone for a little privacy—the first in our relationship. We certainly took advantage of that luxury, getting physically closer than ever before. At one point Marius wanted to "go all the way." In the burning passion of that moment, it took enormous effort for me to remain in control and not to give in. I was unyielding in my principles concerning virginity and marriage. He tried to persuade me by playing the guilt game, about having risked his life to see me, therefore deserving me as a reward. That attitude angered me. In my naïveté I felt blackmailed. Even though he left disappointed, our love prevailed.

At about the same time, my commune had completed the first phase of training. We now prepared for phase two, called "independence," meaning that we were to be on our own, to find jobs and relinquish the salary to the communal account. In the following months I worked as a dishwasher, a laundry worker, and a candy maker in a halvah factory. During this time, we lived in a few plywood shacks erected on an empty plot assigned to us in Kiriat Benyamin, a suburb of Haifa.

From our camp, we had a full view of beautiful Haifa, but getting there was dangerous. To enter the city from our side of the highway, one had to go through an Arab neighborhood, where snipers constantly attacked passing vehicles. A few armored buses made that route on an erratic and infrequent schedule. In one of those, despite great fear, I made my first trip to Haifa.

Besides working, during these months, I got in touch with some of my mother's relatives: Drs. Emma and Norbert Lustig and their parents, the Nagels, all four survivors of the Milie massacre. Through them I met other distant cousins of my mother, originally from Milie, who had lived in Haifa since the thirties. As usual these meetings evoked a lot of sadness, yet the relatives' kind and helpful attitude gave me strength and support.

Four months after my arrival, I witnessed history in its making—this time the independence of my new homeland.

May 14, 1948. Kol Israel Radio (The Voice of Israel): "We hereby proclaim the establishment of the Jewish State in Palestine to be called the State of Israel. We extend our hand in peace to all neighboring states and their peoples, and invite them to cooperate." The announcement was a long and emotional one, touching on every aspect of Jewish history, suffering, and persecution, culminating with the extermination of six million Jews during the war.

But the tumultuous celebrations came to an end as the whole nation braced itself against the sudden Arab offensive. Claiming false victories as they vowed to throw the Jews into the sea, the Arabs launched bombers to destroy the cities of the new state, and Jerusalem was under siege as fierce battles raged in the corridor leading to the city. Most of the Arabs living in Israeli territory fled to Jordan. The British abandoned their headquarters, making way for the Israeli armed forces.

A few months into the bloody fighting, the Arab invasions were stopped by the elite fighting unit called the Palmach, aided by heroic acts of many kibbutzim. Eventually the United Nations effected a temporary truce, which gave our nation some breathing room. Only in September 1948, after a second truce was achieved, were we allowed to settle on a piece of land in the Judean Hills, given to us by the Jewish National Fund.

This was the last phase of total independence for L'hagshamah. Everything was packed, the shacks dismantled, and our first group of twenty left for Tel Aviv. Then, in a convoy of trucks, we began our long, adventurous journey.

Because the junction at Latrun fell into the hands of the Arab legion, access to Jerusalem via the main road was blocked and an alternate path had been improvised by the Israeli Army. They lined this steep, narrow path with iron mesh to prevent vehicles from skidding on that winding, muddy path. It became known as the Burma Road.

The trucks of our convoy stalled often as they tried to climb that steep, narrow path. We were forced to get off and help push them out of the mud. The roadside bore testimony to recent battles: burnt Jeeps, over-turned tanks, trucks, and armored cars, all lying in ditches like abandoned skeletons. These scenes, combined with the noise of shootings and explosions in the distance, dampened our excitement. I was very scared.

When we reached the abandoned Arab village of Saris, at the foot of the mountain where we were supposed to settle, the sun had already set and it soon would be night. It was therefore suggested that we wait for the next day to start our ascent. That was fine with us. We built a camp-fire and picnicked, sang, and danced the hora the whole night, oblivious to our exhaustion. We celebrated our historic moment, the achievement of our goal. Before the fire died out, we all stood at attention and sang our L'hagshamah anthem. In this elated and deeply emotional mood, we watched the sun slowly rising above the peaks of the Judean Hills, heralding the arrival of a new day and a new beginning.

Kibbutz L'hagshamah

CHAPTER 13

September 28, 1948. In the early morning we climbed anew onto the trucks and continued on the last leg of our journey up the winding, precipitous dirt road. We had to stop several times for our guide to check his map, but after a few wrong guesses he announced, "Right here! Right here!" and pointed with the index finger of his outstretched hand.

The caravan stopped abruptly. We jumped out onto a desolate, arid field and unloaded the trucks. Red-eyed, we looked around at the breathtaking view of the surrounding hills and into the depth of an enormous valley coming alive under the rising sun. Yet our campground was barren and rocky. I felt a spiritual resurgence, as if I were the first human being to step upon that virgin soil and was witnessing the recent creation of the world. I scrutinized the landscape and wondered what we could do here and how we would survive.

We pitched our tents between two abandoned Arab villages, Saris (now Shoeva) down at the main road and Beit Machsir (now Beit Meir) at the top of the mountain. The outpost L'hagshamah was born! From that moment on, we became a new strategic settlement, a new dot on the map of our young and tiny motherland: Israel.

It was a solemn moment in my life, facing a mission I was determined to fulfill. Hand in hand with sixty other idealistic comrades, we would turn this sterile, rocky soil into a fruitful garden, building a home on this abandoned piece of land. Perhaps there was a purpose to my survival after all.

For the next three months our camp was bustling with arduous activity: putting up prefabricated Swedish shacks for a dining room and living quarters, connecting water pipes and electricity from the village below, and erecting an outhouse and a showerhouse from corrugated tin.

Eventually we purchased a few dozen chickens and a few cows. My specialty, acquired during training in Usha, was raising poultry, so most of the time I tended the chicken coops. Later I was assigned to a tree-planting project for which we were paid by the Jewish National Fund.

Five of us girls worked without relief for many months planting seedlings on the bald mountainside. It was a hard, back-breaking job, yet an important one for a country where every tree is a planted one.

On another mountain slope, our agricultural experts guided a different group of comrades in preparing for the planting of orchards by building garden terraces. They planted an assortment of fruit trees, including prune and peach, and the famous Muskat and Hamburg grapes. We all worked tirelessly, but we knew that this was our own—our very own—land so nothing was too hard or too much.

At night an armed male-female patrol, on a rotating schedule, would stand on the lookout for Arab marauders and thieves trying to steal our only water pipe. It became our responsibility to maintain surveillance over the main road and the surrounding area.

Several months had passed without news or a visit from Marius. Because he was still serving in a mine-disabling unit, I was worried. And sure enough my premonitions came true. Informed that he had been wounded in the leg, I immediately traveled to visit him in a Jerusalem military hospital. What a relief it was to learn that it was a minor wound compared to the injuries of many other soldiers in the same room!

During that emotion-filled visit, Marius still tried to persuade me to leave the commune and live with him in Jerusalem, but I stood my ground. Finally, he promised to rejoin L'hagshamah, provided we would live together as a couple until we decided to get married. I reluctantly agreed, and with this promise I returned home to reevaluate my feelings, which were not in total harmony with the plan. While I enjoyed Marius's company, I had my doubts about marrying him.

An inner voice warned me against committing myself to Marius, yet the thought of not being with him was absolutely inconceivable. Sometimes I tried to visualize us separated, passing one another on the street like strangers, the scene made me shudder. I couldn't imagine my life without him.

Apart from that conflict, I was content with my life. I was going on nineteen, a beautiful age, particularly when one is filled with enthusiasm, idealism, and faith in humanity. Belonging to this large, wonderful surrogate family of the commune helped me grow and feel part of something grand. It almost completely fulfilled me.

Most of our comrades had acquired a trade, some had natural talents, and a few had both. All these served to meet the commune's needs. Although trained for agriculture and aviculture, my natural interest gravitated toward people, their well-being and their problems. I cannot recall the circumstances under which I became the commune's healer without any training or any experience in the medical field. All I had was a natural tendency to help. Whether with a small bruise, a cut, or a broken heart, many turned to me, and I did the best I could to help them.

Once I reached the unofficial status of "healer," the group actually appointed me to be their medic, a job I exercised with my only tools: common sense and good will. But having no training, I felt quite incompetent, and after a while I asked to be sent to at least a first-aid course. The commune granted that request.

We made contact with a certain Dr. Abeles, a member of our political party and director of the *Kupat-Cholim* (Labor Medical Fund) clinic in Jerusalem. He came to our commune to assess the necessity for a skilled medic; then he interviewed me and approved the request. He offered me a three-month training program in his clinic. I was elated.

Having to stay in Jerusalem represented a problem. I had no one except my Aunt Toni and her family there, and they, like all new immigrants, lived in the most primitive conditions. She, her husband and their twenty-six-year-old son, Isaia, lived in a tiny room that held one bed and a narrow sofa. There was no kitchen and they had to share the only bathroom with a family of three. Still my relatives welcomed me with open arms. I slept on a blanket laid out on the tile floor, grateful for the space and the little food they so graciously shared with me.

When I presented myself to Dr. Abeles, he took me to the outpatient surgical department and entrusted me to the head nurse, a heavy-set, middle-aged woman. Fortunately, she spoke Yiddish so we could understand each other. Elated, I put on a starched white apron and began my observations.

This was my element. There was something inspiring about the white nursing uniform and cap of my instructor and in the environment of glass jars, instruments, and white cabinets. It was almost like a divine calling.

There was much to learn in that short period, and I soon picked up the basic first-aid procedures and routine treatments. Shortly afterward the nurse allowed me to treat patients under her supervision, and later I did so by myself. That was so rewarding and fulfilling that I wanted to know more and more. By the end of three months I was qualified to give injections, to bandage, to sterilize syringes and instruments, and to organize a small infirmary.

In Jerusalem, I had many opportunities to be with Marius, now released from the IDF (Israeli Defense Force). He was staying with his sister there and working in construction, earning a nice living. He continued to make plans for us, some of which I did not fully agree with. I still could not shake off the uneasy feeling that he wanted us to live together *before* getting married.

This life-style was common in our group, and many of my friends thought that my moralistic attitude was rubbish. But I could not convince myself. To me, my virginity was something sacred, not to be easily given up, especially not under pressure. I returned to L'hagshamah as a slightly more knowledgeable medic to whom a small clinic had been entrusted. After my full-time job at the kibbutz, I held daily clinic hours in a small shack. Once a week a doctor came from the neighboring kibbutz for those cases I could not treat.

Between work and our social activities, of which I was the hostess, I was a busy girl, and happy at that. Adding to my happiness was the arrival of my cousin Lucie, who like the majority of Romanian Jews were now legally immigrating to Israel. Willy, her fiancé, had been in Israel awaiting her arrival and they got married a few weeks later. One day Lucie came to visit me at L'hagshamah. We rejoiced in our meeting amidst tears and laughter. She explained how she had to leave her mother behind when an opportunity to emigrate presented itself.

She brought me a dress she had sewn herself. It was a lovely light blue cotton fabric sprinkled with tiny pastel flowers, a gift I cherished for many years. I proudly showed her the kibbutz, explaining our life-style and our ideology. Unimpressed, my pragmatic cousin tried to show me how foolish and naive I was. To make a strong point she said, "Can you see yourself wasting the best years of your life as a peasant? With your brains you can do better."

"I don't want any other life. I'd be the last one to leave L'hagshamah," I responded.

And so it went, on and on, until I started to get angry with her for not supporting me in my noble cause. Yet after we parted, a gnawing uneasiness crept into my thoughts. I began to picture my future and was no longer 100 percent convinced that I really wanted to remain a "peasant" forever. But leaving was out of the question. Now there were two important people in my life who wished I were not so hung up on the commune: Lucie and Marius. But that did not discourage me at all; on the contrary, I persuaded Marius to rejoin the commune, and he consented.

In a state of apprehension, I awaited his arrival. The moment I saw him, suitcase in hand, my happiness was so overwhelming that it completely obliterated any previous, negative thoughts. This is one of the pitfalls of youth. He was officially reinstated into the commune at a general meeting. Later many of my friends, who were opposed to his return, told me that they voted in favor, not for his merits but for my sake.

In a kind of unofficial marriage ceremony, we proclaimed ourselves a couple. The general meeting acknowledged our committed relationship and approved our request for a couple's room, but they were all full.

That problem could be solved only if a married couple would voluntarily give up their room. Since my friends Maiciu and Bertha were going on vacation anyway, they offered us their quarters. The whole issue was so much in the limelight and so embarrassing that I felt like crawling into a hole to make it all disappear.

Night fell. Marius and I retired to our temporary accommodations. I felt uneasy and tense. Unlike our other romantic encounters, this time Marius behaved differently. Gone was all the tenderness I had experienced before. Instead of trying to calm me down and make me feel relaxed, his crude and insensitive approach only heightened my anxiety. It seemed as if he was taking revenge for all the years I had refused him. Oblivious to my emotional condition and my physical unreadiness, he proceeded to claim a conjugal right.

That night the lovemaking I had dreamed about and saved myself for turned into a disaster. My bad conscience, my naïveté, my supersensitivity and lack of knowledge, led me to believe that he alone was to be blamed. That bad experience renewed my doubts about being a normal woman and carried into my future relationships with men. In addition to his previous insensitivities, this one helped me in the decision to break off this relationship with Marius. As if blown away by the wind, all my love and strong feelings vanished, leaving me in an emotional trauma. Besides the renewed preoccupation with my feminine "abnormality" and a new secret to keep, I was also faced with the problem of dealing with the reactions of the commune and of some others on the outside.

To my great relief I encountered so much love and support among my fellow commune members that it eased the burden considerably. It seemed like everybody was on my side, but I was depressed and wanted to be left alone.

For a short while, Marius continued to be a member of the commune. And even though I did not want to talk to him, he pursued me, declaring his love and his desire to marry me. It all fell on deaf ears. Only then did I permit myself to see him with an objectivity I hadn't possessed before. Suddenly I realized how incompatible we were and what a mistake it would have been to marry him.

But he did not give up easily. He even managed to get into a fight with one of my admirers, and in his jealousy he threatened to kill the man if he did not leave me alone. The poor guy disappeared for a few days, which allowed Marius to calm down. As I remained unresponsive to him, he finally gave up hope and left the commune. Relieved of that pressure, I began to resume my normal life at last.

My work in the health field became more demanding and posed more problems as the group increased in size. Many married women became pregnant, and the newborn babies were entrusted to my care. More serious medical problems required professional knowledge beyond my capability; therefore, our members had to travel to Jerusalem to be treated. My ignorance of medical science bothered me; I felt that I needed to become a registered nurse to really do a good job. But that was only possible by entering a three-year program in a nursing school which required living in the dormitories. I presented the issue to the general meeting and emphasized the commune's need of a professional nurse in view of current and future demands. After many discussions, the majority voted against the idea, saying that the time was not appropriate: "Now our priority is to work the fields and plant trees, for which every pair of hands is precious."

Defeat was something I did not take well, especially when I felt strongly about an issue. At the same time, I was not ready to leave and start the program without the approval of my group. Again, I was faced with a difficult period of soul-searching.

My strong desire to become a nurse was motivated by many factors, one of them being a genuine desire to help the sick and another a craving for knowledge. But without a high school diploma or even the equivalent, entering a nursing school was unthinkable. These motivations propelled me into a frenetic action toward the achievement of an otherwise unobtainable goal.

As no single soldier can win a battle, neither could I do this without appealing for help. The only person I knew who could help me was Margalit Laufer (called Zitta), my cousin Israel Laufer's wife.

Zitta was an admirable woman with whom I soon became good friends, despite her being much older than I. She was warm, sensitive, and compassionate. Within Israeli circles she was a well-known actress and radio announcer, and as such she had many good friends and connections in the upper echelons. Zitta was the only person who took a genuine interest in my experiences during the war and to whom I once dared to relate a painful episode. When I finished, she looked me straight in the eye, grabbed my shoulders, and shook me as though rousing me out of a dream. "Ruthi!" she exclaimed. "Is this true? Or is it a product of your imagination? I've read a lot about the atrocities, but I have never heard of such a story. Besides, you were probably too young to remember."

That did it! From that day on I never told my story to anyone, realizing that it was too weird, absurd, and painful for people to believe. Why should others believe me when I myself had difficulties believing that I had actually been there and gone through that nightmare? So I buried that secret together with the others. Besides, what difference did it make?

Though Zitta may not have entirely believed my stories, she did believe in me. She spoke with the dean of the Hadassah Nursing School, whom she knew personally, about what was required for a candidate to be accepted into the program. What she discovered came as no surprise: I would need to present a high-school diploma and a record of perfect health. This was disappointing, as I possessed neither. "Forget about it," I told myself.

In the following weeks, I evaluated my situation and struggled with two options. One was to stay in the commune and forget about my desire to better myself by pursuing the nursing profession and living independently in the city; the other was to give up my goals in the commune, my friendships there, and the life-style I was so accustomed to. I opted for the former.

Slowly, I recovered from the calamitous fiasco with Marius and the refusal of the commune to let me go to nursing school on their behalf. And in spite of the arduous work, I was still very happy with my simple life among my friends in the kibbutz.

One special moment of happiness came when my dear childhood friend Litty arrived from Romania with L'hagshamah Group IV to join our commune. After a short time, she became engaged to Eli, another member from Buzau.

Many things, however, had gradually changed in our commune since the days of our highest aspirations. As long as we lived isolated from our families and city life, all was well and we could strive to become a "perfect society." But in reality, human nature tilts toward individualism, a natural trait which we had tried to change. We got along socially, tolerated each other's idiosyncrasies, and lived in harmony until faced with the tempting circumstances of having to share gifts and personal possessions. Some less idealistic members were even unhappy about not getting any salary for their work.

All these problems started a wave of defections, further weakening the structure of the commune and causing an internal crisis. Even Litty and Eli, who by now were married, decided to leave. Their departure had an effect on my own decision to leave.

For a long time I stubbornly clung to my belief in our idealistic social system. Eventually, however, I came to understand that the total sharing of one's possessions with the whole group was unrealistic and unnatural, even if the concept was beautiful and noble. This came home to me when I received an inexpensive wristwatch from Aunt Toni and needed the approval of the general meeting just to wear it because it was considered the commune's collective property. This bordered on the ridiculous. I foresaw a major shake-up as a result of the latest developments. Now, becoming a nurse was more than a "divine calling"; it was a matter of having a profession that would enable me to survive independently anywhere.

Once I came to grips with the new reality, disappointing as it was, I felt more comfortable planning my nursing career. How and where to start my first steps toward this difficult goal were the big questions. All I knew at this point was that a high school diploma was a must. But I did not even have proof of my six years of education.

During one of my visits to Zitta, I brought up the subject and she again promised to help me. In a short time she succeeded in obtaining an appointment for me to be interviewed by the dean of the Hadassah Nursing School. The mere thought of meeting the key person petrified me. I thanked Zitta but refused to go. "What should I go for, if the first thing she would ask me is to show her a high school diploma?" I asked with skepticism. Zitta did not agree with me at all. "You don't know that for a fact," she said. "There is no harm in meeting her and hearing what she has to say. She is a very nice person and, incidentally, is also from Romania." "I will think about it," I promised. A week later, I decided to take a chance and traveled to Jerusalem for the interview.

At that time Jerusalem had been divided between Jordan and Israel, and in that division Mount Scopus, which lay between the two countries and housed the Hadassah Hospital and Nursing School, was called a no-man's-land. Under these circumstances the hospital had been forced to evacuate and relocate in downtown Jerusalem, in scattered small and large buildings totally unfit to serve as hospitals. Nonetheless they had to suffice for the next twenty years. At least all the dwellings were on and around one street. The nursing school was housed in a wing of St. Joseph's Monastery, opposite the main hospital building. The nuns ran their Catholic school and religious activities in one wing, and the nursing school operated in the other.

With great apprehension I walked into the monastery, looking for the dean's office on the second floor. A secretary asked me to sit in the waiting room. Finally, I was led into the office. Behind a desk, a slim, distinguished-looking uniformed nurse greeted me smilingly and introduced herself as Mrs. Margalith. She opened the dialogue in Hebrew, which I only partially understood. "So you are the girl from the kibbutz who wants so badly to become a nurse," she said.

"Yes, Mrs. Margalith, but I don't understand Hebrew very well," I answered apologetically.

"No problem, we can speak Romanian, Russian or Yiddish, whichever you prefer," she offered.

"Romanian, please, if you don't mind," I said.

"Tell me a little bit about yourself and your motivation to become a nurse."

I gave her a short synopsis of my life and then explained many of the reasons for wanting to become a nurse. From the expression on her face I could detect a profound empathy, which almost made me feel guilty. Our dialogue continued in a friendly and relaxed manner until the dreaded question surfaced.

"Do you have a high-school diploma?"

"That's it," I told myself, "here comes the degradation."

As usual, my instincts rushed to my rescue. My inner voice told me that it was a decisive moment in my life, one that would mold my future, for which it was worthwhile lying once more.

"Yes, Mrs. Margalith, I completed the *dyesyatilietka* [ten years of schooling] in Russia, the equivalent of high school in Israel, but unfortunately my diploma as well as all my other documents are at the bottom of the Adriatic Sea." I was surprised at my own chutzpa.

"Glasberg," she said. "I am sure that you will be a good nurse, and I would like very much to have you in my school. But without a diploma, it is out of the question. I am very sorry."

I swallowed hard to prevent tears of disappointment from flowing down my cheeks. I thanked her for her interest and left the office.

Outside, on the patio of the monastery, student nurses in their long, blue uniforms, stiffly starched collars, white aprons, and shoulder-length white caps moved busily in and out. At that sight, a pang of envy overcame me, and a deep feeling of humiliation pressed heavily on my spirit. With the sad news, I ran to Zitta, who listened sympathetically, still trying to give me some hope. She promised to look into the problem and find a solution.

I realized again and again how, even after being liberated, that the effects of the war continued to haunt me, even threatening to handicap me intellectually for the rest of my life. I was a person, yet a nonperson, without a family or a home, or a document to identify me, with no birth certificate, no report cards, no diploma, no passport to prove my existence, only my new Israeli identification card.

Then I had what I thought was a brilliant idea. I would have to track down at least one of my teachers from Czernowitz among the thousands of recently arrived immigrants, which was comparable to looking for a needle in a haystack. It would require some detective work to find one and convince him to give me a written testimony of having completed the ten-year curriculum. But my determination was so strong that nothing could discourage me. After my regular eight hours of hard physical work in the kibbutz, I set out on my quixotic adventure. The first on my list was Professor Weizman, my Russian language and literature teacher. I only hoped he would remember me and perhaps even lie for me. One has to bear in mind that a telephone in those times was a luxury few possessed. Mail was out of the question, since all the new immigrants settled temporarily without addresses in transition camps or in abandoned Arab neighborhoods. Thus, one had to go personally and search for a particular party by asking friends, acquaintances, and family for assistance. Since Litty lived in the area, she found out that Professor Weizman was indeed in Israel and lived somewhere in Jaffa.

One would have had to know Jaffa in 1948–49—an abandoned Arab town, a small port with narrow alleys and twisting roads without names or numbers—to understand what it took to track down the precise apartment of anyone. With only a vague description of his residence, I went from pillar to post, knocking on many wrong doors asking for him. In those days it was not unusual to get nebulous direction. A resident might say, for example, "Go to the next corner; after the little white house at the right near the post at the left, go three doors down; it's the one with the blue window."

Finally, I knocked on one particular door, and before me stood my beloved, respected teacher. He presented a lamentable sight. It was mind-boggling to see that old, tired, gray-haired man, dressed in shorts and an undershirt, standing bent in the low door frame, looking stupefied at his unexpected visitor. The image of the once dignified, well-dressed professor that had remained engraved in my memory was shattered. I felt pity for him.

"Mr. Weizman, don't you recognize me? I'm Ruth Glasberg from the Jewish school in Czernowitz," I managed to get out, afraid he might not remember after four years.

He wrinkled his forehead and exclaimed: "Dietochka [Kidlet]! How could I forget? You were the one who recited poetry so well," he said, his eyes lighting up at the memory.

Relieved by his recall, I told him what I required. He gladly agreed to grant it. He must have forgotten in which grade I was, for I doubt that he would have told a falsehood for me otherwise. We went inside his humble room, and on a simple piece of notebook paper he wrote down that I had completed ten years of studies and was indeed his former student. I thanked him fervently and headed back home, happy to have at least one piece of paper to show.

Equipped with that "document," I returned to Mrs. Margalith, proudly showing her proof of my story. She took a good look at it, shook her head, and said: "This is very good, but not enough."

"What else can I do?" I asked her in a broken voice.

"We need more proof. Let me think about it, and I'll let you know through your cousin."

As I left, I wondered how I could have believed that such a statement would help me enter nursing school. I had a very naive view of bureaucracy.

Weeks of uncertainty and anxiety passed until Zitta again found a solution. She managed to convince an acquaintance in the Ministry of Culture to give me an appointment to see a certain Mr. Perlman. He was willing to test me orally in the subject I knew best: Russian literature and poetry. Upon his approval, Mrs. Margalith would allow me to enter the nursing program.

To this day I cannot understand how I could have been so frivolous to present myself at such an important exam unprepared. I was totally oblivious to the fact that for the past three or four years I had never come near any Russian literature books in the original language and that during those years my brain had functioned under duress, completely blocking out whatever I had known. In my enthusiasm I had not thought of testing my memory. It was not so much frivolity as blind faith in the power of the will to succeed. Innocent, I took advantage of my only opportunity to prove myself, even though the man who was going to test me was a Mr. Perlman, an important person in the Ministry of Culture.

He was an older, gray-haired Russian Jew with a kind smile, who received me cordially in his office. To make me feel relaxed, he conversed with me in Russian about this and that. In doing so, he was probably testing my proficiency in the language itself. Finally he asked, "Which is your favorite poem?"

"'Borodino' by Lermontov," I replied without hesitation.

"Recite it for me, please."

I started to recite it, but never went beyond the first stanza. Nothing came to my mind. Seeing my anguish, Mr. Perlman kindly tried to give me a second chance by letting me recite a different poem. I frantically searched for the name of another of my favorites and remembered one by Pushkin. But, except for one line, neither the name nor the content came to mind.

To my astonishment, Mr. Perlman finished the job for me by reciting the poem from beginning to end, as I sat there nodding in approval. It was Pushkin's "The Lay of Oleg the Wise." When he finished, he ushered me out, promising to talk to Zitta. Humiliated, I walked out of his office, choking back tears of anger. That was it! I had blown my last chance. The humiliation was too much to bear. "Now what?" I thought. "Return to the kibbutz and stay there forever in complete mental vegetation?"

No! After a few moments of dejection, I rebounded and resolved to continue my struggle. I would fight with all my resources to undo all the harm the war had caused me. I was going to achieve my goal of becoming a nurse so that I might help preserve life and serve humanity in my own little way. With this determination, I wiped my eyes dry and walked toward the main road to hitchhike back to L'hagshamah.

A week later, still expecting a miracle, I went back to Zitta to hear Mr. Perlman's verdict. I could see in her eyes that it was bad news. She hesitated for a few moments and then quoted him.

"The girl is a *bur*" (ignoramus in Hebrew) were his words. As much as I hated to admit it, he was right, considering my performance. But to be labeled as one was so degrading that my spirit was crushed. I wondered what Zitta may have thought about the whole situation and how she would tell Mrs. Margalith.

Apparently, Mrs. Margalith *did* believe in my potential in spite of the bad report. Sometime later she informed Zitta of an alternative: a high school equivalency diploma examination offered by the government to new immigrants in situations similar to mine. She and Zitta thought I should try it in the coming few months. That meant cramming five missed school years into three months—and in Hebrew no less. It was going to be almost impossible.

The required subjects were physics, chemistry, science, algebra, geometry, and Hebrew composition, all at the eleventh-grade level. How in God's name was I going to do that? And I still had to work my eight hours and fulfill my other obligations in the commune! I lacked money, knew little Hebrew, and had nobody to tutor me. Again, Zitta came through for me, by suggesting that a university student might be willing to help me. No sooner said than done—she found a student who, for a fee, was ready to work with me daily. We were introduced, I showed him the requirements, and we agreed on both the time and the fee. He was from Poland, and his residence was a closed gazebo in the middle of a public park.

Where would I get the money? I had to overcome my pride and, for the first time in my life, was forced to ask for a loan from my family. Aunt Toni and Uncle Simon themselves had little money, but nonetheless they lent me an amount probably equal to $15.00 (U.S.), almost two weeks' salary. I promised to pay them back as soon as I earned my first paycheck.

Now I needed the commune to assign me to special working hours so that I would be free to go to Jerusalem during the day. As an excuse I told them that I was preparing myself for a high-school diploma exam, without talking about the next step, namely nursing school. They were accommodating in assigning me to two new jobs: taking the cows out to pasture at 5 A.M., which allowed me to leave early for Jerusalem, and night shift on guard duty, which allowed me to study.

My new schedule was strenuous. I herded the cows back to their sheds at 7 A.M., slept a few hours, after which I started my daily journey to my tutor. There was no public transportation, and our only truck left very early for town, so I had to walk every day from the kibbutz to the main road, a distance of approximately four miles. Once I reached the main road, the wait for an accommodating driver began.

Hitchhiking was a way of life in Israel, as most of the population had neither cars nor money. Army trucks, vans, Jeeps, oil tankers, and a few private sedans were my means of commuting. There were, of course, public buses and trains, in addition to taxis that several people would share on a route, but they all cost money, which I did not have. Since hitchhiking was unreliable, my tutor never expected me at an established hour; instead we agreed to either the morning or the afternoon of the following day. If lucky, a car would stop within a few minutes, but other times I stood on the road in simmering heat for hours. After my lesson, I had to walk back to the main road, wait for a "tramp" vehicle to give me a ride, and then climb the two kilometers of mountainside to L'hagshamah. To make it less boring, I would sing songs along the way. When I reached my infirmary bed, I threw myself onto it, exhausted, for a few hours of sleep before resuming my studies and the nightly vigil.

I shared the night-guard shift with male partners who allowed me to study in the dining room for an hour or longer while they stood outside alone. I kept myself awake through those nights with mugs full of black coffee. This was my life-style for several months.

Like a sponge, my brain absorbed huge amounts of information in a limited time. In retrospect, I think that it was possible only because of a surge of enthusiasm and perseverance.

When my tutor asked for his first fee, I started a philosophical discussion with him as to how unfair it was to have to pay for tutoring. "It seems so unjust," I protested, "to have to pay for helping one to study when in the Soviet Union education is free, and in our commune those who taught others never got paid."

He tried to explain: "I understand what you mean. I come from the same system, but I am slightly older and have learned how capitalism works. If I didn't charge you, I could not feed myself." After a lengthy discussion, I reluctantly paid him and this topic never came up again. I soon learned to cope with the system.

Sometime in August 1949, the Ministry of Health advised me to present myself in the following month for the exam. In early September, twenty of us sat in a trailer on the outskirts of Tel-Aviv and took the test.

When I was handed the question sheets, I got my first shock. Naive as I was, I did not anticipate the difficulty in understanding the questions which, of course, were in Hebrew. It took an effort to read and an even greater one to understand each sentence. My anxiety rose to the roof. The first questions were on algebra and science, subjects which I thought I had mastered, but with the rest I had a hard time.

Just when I thought that the worst was over, we were asked to write a short essay in Hebrew on any topic. For a few seconds my heart stopped, then started racing out of control. How on earth could I do this with my limited vocabulary?

I looked at the blank sheet of paper with a desperation that threatened to paralyze me. I felt like walking out and abandoning the whole ordeal. Instead I plunged into the essay, describing my life in Cyprus. It must have looked like the creation of a first grader, considering that I relied solely on phonetics. I imagined the reaction of the people who graded it; it must have provided them with many moments of laughter. When the day was over, I returned to L'hagshamah.

As the nursing school year was about to begin, my anxiety about getting the test results in time increased. I feared the worst.

To find out if anything at all had transpired in the meantime, I traveled once more to visit Zitta. As soon as I opened the door, Zitta handed me an invitation from the school to attend the graduation exercises of the nursing class of 1949. I knew it was customary for the ceremony to serve also as an initiation for the incoming first-year nursing students, but not having heard from the examiners or having yet been accepted to the program, I couldn't understand the meaning of all this. If anything, it sounded cruel to have me witnessing the joy of all the new and graduating students whom I wouldn't be allowed to join.

Instead of just accepting the invitation at face value, I became suspicious of Mrs. Margalith's intentions. I decided, out of pride, not to go. Zitta threatened not to talk to me if I did that. She added that Mrs. Margalith wanted to see me before the ceremony. In the end, I agreed to go in spite of my doubts. Mrs. Margalith met me with a friendly, yet mischievous smile. "Sit down, Glasberg, I want to talk to you about your equivalency exams. How did it go?" she asked calmly.

"I am afraid not very well," I said. I tried to explain to her the many obstacles I had to overcome, particularly in Hebrew composition.

"I have a surprise for you. I got the results yesterday. You passed them all except for geometry." I was perplexed and overwhelmed by the good news. " By law," she said, "I am not supposed to admit you to the school, but I am willing to gamble on you. I believe a highly motivated person like yourself will surely become an excellent nurse. Therefore I accept you into the program, and I hope you will not disappoint me." Mrs. Margalith beamed.

The bonus she saved for the last. "I convinced the Ministry of Health to let you retake the failed test sometime later in the year, provided you pass the six months probation."

As she delivered the good news, my heart was touched again by this human kindness, and secretly I put her on the same pedestal with all my other mentors and benefactors, those unsung heroes, those caring human beings whose positive influence can change a person's entire life. Mrs. Margalith certainly changed mine. I had to control the urge to hug and kiss her in gratitude, but she knew from my expression and strong handshake how I felt. Returning to the kibbutz, I realized that to abandon my ideals, my friends and comrades, was like dying a little, but then there was the indescribable jubilation of my recent achievements and future plans. I was riding a roller coaster of emotion.

As soon as I told the commune's chairman of my intentions, he called for a general meeting, during which I made the dramatic announcement. While my friends shared my happiness at new opportunities, they also expressed their regrets.

The commune's bookkeepers calculated the total collective assets in order to pay me my share. This procedure would have been excellent material for a satire, but to us it was serious business. We kept an inventory of the common and personal possessions, the total value of which we divided by the number of members. The sum determined the share each member would receive upon leaving. Including my cheap wristwatch, a few clothes, and a pair of shoes, my share came to $IL 13.00 (Israeli lira) in cash—about U.S. $10.00.

Conflicts

CHAPTER 14   With thirteen Israeli *lira* to my name and a single bundle of clothes, I entered nursing school and a competitive society that I did not fully understand.

Our class consisted of 70 percent *sabras* (natives) and 30 percent new immigrants for whom intensive daily Hebrew classes were offered. Since no nursing textbooks existed then, we had to rely solely on the lectures presented by the professors of the Hebrew University Medical School. Having not yet mastered Hebrew writing, I took my notes in the Latin alphabet. The struggle to decipher them was at times more difficult than the studies. To pass the probation period was an important milestone to all, but in my case my whole future depended on it.

Six months later, on the day of judgment, each student met individually with the dean for an evaluation. It was my turn now.

"Congratulations, Glasberg," Mrs. Margalith said. "You've done well in both the academic and practical areas. I'm very proud of your performance. Thank you for not disappointing me. Given your excellent work, you'll be excused from having to repeat the government test in geometry. Good luck!"

I could not believe my ears. After thanking Mrs. Margalith for her support and for belief in me, I practically danced out of her office, hugging the girls still awaiting their turn.

We now became full-fledged student nurses, working eight-hour shifts—without pay, only pocket money amounting to $IL 1.00 per month. Even though I had very little time for socializing and I missed my friends at L'hagshamah, I was happy in my nursing role. Not even cleaning an incontinent patient bothered me. I did it all with enthusiasm, telling myself that, directly or indirectly, I was helping the helpless.

In the interim, I enjoyed my second year in school, particularly in the dorms, where we were now divided into smaller rooms with only seven girls instead of twenty-eight. My room was a miniature United Nations: three Bulgarians, two Romanians, one Swiss, and one sabra. The spirit of camaraderie and friendship that prevailed among us could have served as a classic example of how the nations of this world could and should get along. Our room was also the center for group studies and entertainment. Five of us from the Eastern Bloc even formed a little choir, with a predominantly Russian repertoire.

My colleagues never made me feel as though I was different, but I could not always overcome my self-consciousness at being an orphan. I felt especially lonely when my roommates left to join their families on holidays or weekends. Except for sporadic visits to my aunt or Zitta, I had no one to go to.

Giving the valedictory speech at graduation (at right, Mrs. Margalith in nursing uniform).

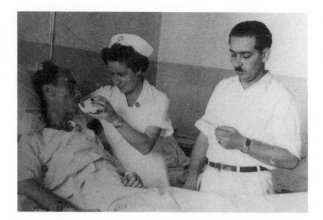

Tending to a patient at Hadassah Hospital in Jerusalem.

Sensitive to my situation, my Bulgarian friends, Becky and Chemdah, often invited me to sleep over in their homes. Their parents, like most new immigrants, occupied a single room of an apartment they shared with other families. Nevertheless, they welcomed me to share their only bed in the winter or to sleep on the floor in the summer. I will never forget their warm hospitality.

Luckily, in my second year, Aunt Anna arrived by boat from Romania. Since she had always been like a mother to me, seeing her after four years was a soul-stirring event. All at once I was provided with love and care and a place I could call "home" again. Lucie and Willy soon joined her in Haifa. From then on I spent all my vacations with them, even though I had to sleep on the floor.

Aunt Anna's brother, Uncle David, who lived with his family in Boston, kept in touch with her, and soon he sent us a series of CARE packages. Later I personally received a small but much-appreciated amount of money which I used to get rid of my gold-framed incisors, replacing them with more flattering porcelain ones. The result was so spectacular that it changed my attitude and added another dimension of contentment to the positive parts of my life.

Needing to nurture my socialist philosophy, I joined my Bulgarian friends for meetings of the Communist party. Although I never became a member, my belief in that ideology was rock-solid until March 5, 1953, the day Stalin died. I remember walking down Jaffa Road in a state of shock, feeling as if the whole world had collapsed, as if I had suffered an enormous personal loss. I refused to believe that my omnipotent father-figure, my role model, and the "world's only redeemer" was gone forever. If that was not bad enough, soon after came the disclosures of his atrocities. Deeply disillusioned, I became apolitical.

Still, equality and justice remained important issues to me, and whenever I encountered a lack of either I would try to change things in my small way. One such injustice was the exploitation of the nursing students by the Hadassah Hospital. Working full time we received IL $1.00 a month. Outraged, we called an assembly of the student body. Amid heated discussions, I made a motion in favor of a strike, should our demands for an increased monthly allowance not be met. Everybody seconded it; they elected me to the Student Committee and to the National Nursing Student Association.

To represent my school, I was invited to a meeting of the Board of Nursing in Tel Aviv. The meeting dealt with a variety of student problems on a national level. As time passed and none of the other delegates seemed to touch the sensitive topic of money, I gathered my courage and spoke up. Explaining our situation, I asked for an immediate increase in our allowance from IL $1.00 a month to $5.00. The board's immediate reaction was to reject the idea with much rhetoric about our noble profession, humanitarian concerns, and sacrifices. Sensing that their position was not going to change without pressure, I threatened a general strike of all Hadassah student nurses. The faces of the elderly board members reflected shock. They verbally assaulted me for daring to say such an "unethical" thing as "strike." To strike was unprecedented in the entire medical profession. I felt uneasy but remained firm.

Upon my return, I called a meeting of all three nursing classes to explain what had happened. Although we did not know what the outcome would be, the girls applauded my efforts—but not the dean. A few days later, Mrs. Margalith called me in.

I could predict the bad news. She wanted to know what happened at the meeting, as the Nursing Board complained about my unethical approach. I related to her the episode verbatim. She empathized with our plight but thought that threatening with a strike was too radical.

In spite of all, the victory was ours. Just a month later, our request was granted, thus winning a breakthrough not only for our school but for all nursing students in Israel. The second-year students received $IL 10.00 and the third-year $IL 15.00.

All was not sheer bliss for me, though. I did have to deal with two major problems: one had to do with night shifts, the other with the dead.

The night shifts took their toll on me, as my body categorically re-fused to switch its natural clock and make believe that day was night. Consequently, I could not sleep during the day, even in the dark, quiet room set aside for students on night shift. I tossed and turned, living on only two or three hours sleep.

The other problem had to do with handling the dead. One would think that after all the horrors I had witnessed as a child, I would have been completely immune to such exposure. Yet I continued to have a hideous fear of corpses.

According to Jewish ritual, preparation of the deceased called for wash-ing them, filling every orifice with cotton, wrapping them in a white sheet, and tying the shroud at the neck, waist, and ankles. Eventually, I had to find another nurse to prepare the deceased in exchange for some other service I would do for her. That worked sometimes but not always. When I had no choice and had to do the job myself, I tried everything, includ-ing autosuggestion techniques, so as not to collapse. Why humans chose the night to die and to be born was an enigma to me, but it was a fact that caused me to fear night shifts even more. The only exception was the maternity ward, where the joy of a newborn baby made night duty a pleasurable experience.

As much as I would have liked my romantic life to mirror the success of my academic and civic one, that was not to be. Except for one pla-tonic relationship with a young captain that lasted a short time, I did not get involved with men for the next three years. I did accept some sporadic dates to go to the movies, a party, or a concert, but nothing serious. In fact, it was not until after my graduation that I got involved with anyone romantically.

Thinking later about the reasons for not having found a soulmate to my liking, I am almost convinced that the stigma attached to a Holocaust survivor—and in my case being a homeless orphan—may have been one of them. For the young Israelis who at that time fought heroically in the War for Independence, it was particularly hard to understand why we had not resisted the Nazis.

That was especially true of some Israelis who looked down on us. They called the extermination camp survivors "soaps" because of the soap made from humans in the those places and said that we were cowards who, like sheep, let the Nazis drive us quietly to be slaughtered. It was even implied that one might be mentally or emotionally disturbed as a result of experiencing the inhumane conditions of the camps. The latter was partially true. So who would want to be involved with a homeless orphan with such problems? I seemed unable to escape even the indirect influences of the Holocaust.

And then I had to deal with another misconception: that by not having a tattooed number on the arm, one was not believed to have been in a camp. The notoriety of camps like Auschwitz and Treblinka overshadowed the existence of camps like Transnistria, which were never mentioned even at official commemorations, as if survivors of one camp were more important than the others. This practice had almost discriminatory implications that encouraged some of us to remain silent for the next thirty years.

In my case, internalizing the experience caused many psychosomatic afflictions and weary nightmares. Strange dreams plagued me and do to this day; they vary from natural disasters to being chased, always experiencing that agonizing, last moment before imminent death but always waking up before expiring. Another repetitive dream was one of having found out that my family was alive and we would be reunited. But my joy at these reunions would always be marked by deep pain, when Mama seemingly gone mad, wouldn't recognize me, and wouldn't accept me as her daughter. These nightmares must have stemmed from my memories of her last days when, after my brother died, she didn't want to continue living.

To fit in with the rest of the youngsters, I continued to present a cheerful, healthy appearance, pretending I was as normal as they, but I was screaming within. Apparently, I did a good job hiding my true feelings, because most of the people never suspected that I was a survivor. Those who occasionally got to know about my past seemed surprised, and would always remark, "You don't look like someone who has been in a camp." Although I always felt different, I was proud to hear these words.

But life went on, as did the daily struggles. It was almost graduation, and in desperate need of money I grabbed at an offer to donate blood in exchange for $IL 5.00. Walking toward the hospital's blood bank, I ran into Amos, a gynecology intern. He had often flirted with me, but I never took him seriously because of his reputation as a womanizer. This time, though, he greeted me in a particularly warm way and voiced his concern about my paleness. When he suggested I go for a blood count, I couldn't help but laugh at the irony. Seemingly shocked to learn that I was on my way to donate a pint of blood, he tried unsuccessfully to dissuade me. Although I did not listen to his advice, his genuine concern touched me and ignited a spark in my heart.

From that day on our friendship developed. Strangely, he did not ask me out on a date for some time, but then I knew that he was not the serious dating type and I was not ready for anything more than a friendship either. By now, we had discovered our mutual interests: classical music, literature, dancing, and the sea. To my great astonishment, he finally broke the ice and invited me to a piano recital. My joy was two-fold—first because he actually asked me out, and second because it was going to be my first live concert.

In 1952 there were no concert halls in Jerusalem. Performances were held in movie houses with a stage. These theaters were relatively small, but they had balconies and loges. The pianist that night was Claudio Arrau. We enjoyed every piece he performed, in particular, the Sonata No. 23, the "Appassionata," by Beethoven, which he played with such feeling and sensitivity that I was moved to tears.

Arrau had just started the final movement, when, suddenly, all the lights went out in the theater. Arrau continued to play without missing a note. Instead of panicking and dashing out into the street, the audience remained seated in complete silence, probably inspired and mesmerized by that great artist. The lights came back just in time for the thunderous applause and screams of appreciation for both his virtuosity and his courage. Blackouts were a frequent occurrence in Jerusalem, but never before had they turned a concert into such an extraordinary adventure.

The fact that the last movement of the "Appassionata" implies the destruction of the world during which Lucifer, the carrier of light, crashes from heaven into eternal darkness made this an unforgettable, almost spiritual experience for me, as it must have been for many.

Amos and I also went to movies and dances, and, contrary to his reputation, he behaved like a gentleman. I grew fond of him, and suddenly I was in love. But I still feared intimacy and probably projected a nonverbal message which he obviously picked up and therefore did not pursue the matter.

Besides dating Amos, I kept busy studying, reading, and often visiting Aunt Anna and family. I loved Haifa for its wonderful beaches and the woods of Mount Carmel, for the breathtaking day view of the bay and the golden cupola of the Baha'i temple. I especially loved the sparkling lights at night that gave the city an aspect of an immense jewel box. And I planned to move to this city as soon as possible.

I also found time to visit my friends at L'hagshamah, which at some point had changed from a kibbutz to a collective settlement, Moshav Shoresh, in which everybody was paid a salary and lived an individual life. They had even built a resort hotel with all the amenities, the realization of one of our original ideas. By then the seedlings we had planted had grown into a young forest. In a pompous ceremony to which government officials and guests had been invited, Prime Minister David Ben-Gurion delivered the inaugural speech and named it Yaar Hagiborim or "The Heroes' Forest." I was touched and proud to have contributed to the forestation of Israel.

Time flew rapidly during these last months. Before we knew it, the date of the finals had arrived. After completing the written essay exams, it was time for the oral tests before a panel of Health Department officials and the dean.

Afterward Mrs. Margalith called me to her office. This time I did not anticipate bad news, but neither was I prepared for what I was about to hear. She asked *me* to deliver the valedictorian speech! I felt terribly honored and proud. What a reward for my perseverance and hard work! Of course I accepted. In an atmosphere charged with excitement and joy, an avalanche of preparations for graduation day started. Our new white uniforms had to be fitted, and we sent invitations to families and friends. Our daily routine was spiced with anticipation.

Sometime before graduation, Miss Helen Keller visited the Hadassah Nursing School. She sat on the sofa in our lounge with her secretary, Miss Thomson, at her right and with me on her left. Sitting next to that extraordinary human being, touching her, and listening to her messages was almost like meeting a deity. In spite of her being blind, deaf, and mute, she had achieved goals many normal people never would. Miss Keller spelled out words with her fingers into the inner palm of her secretary, Miss Thomson, her translator and her "voice," who in turn would speak the words to us, and vice versa.

That unforgettable afternoon left me deeply impressed and reinforced my philosophy as she urged us to maintain hope, never take things for granted, and fight for success against all odds. Her personality and outstanding courage certainly inspired us all, and though my struggles were of a different nature I closely identified with her. She certainly was a role model for many, but to me she was the living proof that indeed "where there is a will, there is a way."

September 9, 1952. Graduation. For me, this was a day of happiness and great pride, one I could hardly believe was really occurring. Yet it was not without a tinge of sorrow, as it again made me aware that I was an orphan.

I imagined my parents and brother sitting in the audience sharing my victory over adversity, patting me on the shoulder and cheering me on. I held that vision until I was able to bring myself back to the here-and-now, contenting myself with the presence of a few cousins, aunts, and friends.

The end of my long endeavor was about to be celebrated with the capping ceremony. We assembled in the monastery patio, dressed in the new white uniforms of graduating nurses. Our class sat at the left, the incoming students at the right, with families and guests behind both groups. Facing us were all the dignitaries, who sat at a long table on an improvised podium. One by one they approached the microphone to deliver their speeches, until finally my turn came.

Although I knew mine by heart, I felt very nervous as I was being called to the podium. I started to speak into the microphone with noticeable emotion. "Mrs. Margalith, Dr. Mann, esteemed guests and friends: In the name of the seniors who are today concluding their cycle of studies, the pleasant duty was bestowed upon me to bring before you a few words of summary and gratitude. I remember decades ago. . . ."

There was giggling in the audience.

It took me a second or so to realize why there was laughter. Of course I couldn't remember "decades ago". I had made a slip of the tongue. Blood rushed to my face. I cleared my throat in order to continue, but before I could do so Mrs. Margalith got up from her seat, took my place in front of the microphone, and started speaking. Not knowing what she was about to say, I shrank in humiliation.

"Ladies and gentlemen, I remember this girl, Ruth Glasberg entering my office for the first time three years ago, hardly able to speak any Hebrew, so we had to speak Romanian. Today, she is graduating as an outstanding student, delivering a speech in Hebrew. Therefore, I ask you all to give her a big round of applause."

Both her gesture and the applause touched me profoundly. In humbleness and gratitude, I accepted the recognition. When the applause subsided, I continued my speech as if nothing had happened.

After the ceremony, we went upstairs to have photos taken of the entire class with the dignitaries. In the evening a dance party was given for us. Whoever had a boyfriend brought him along; we also invited unattached medical students and doctors to help us celebrate. Naturally, I invited Amos, delighted to spend this special time in his company. That he was an excellent dancer was an additional bonus: I was on cloud nine.

After the celebration was over, I suddenly felt a void and a fear of having to fend for myself. Because the country was on a war footing, registered nurses were automatically assigned a corporal's rank. Through a lottery, only a few graduates had been drafted into the Israeli Army. The rest of us had to fulfill one year of work for the Hadassah Hospital as compensation for our nursing education, but we had to provide our own living quarters. Amos helped me find a servant's room, and six months later I moved to a regular apartment shared with three other nurses.

My first job was in the recently established surgical recovery room. I was one of the three nurses who shared the shifts. The total responsibility for up to eight patients at a time was a challenging yet gratifying experience for me. I worked feverishly to monitor intravenous feedings, gastric tubes, and dressings and to keeping the still-groggy postoperative patients comfortable. After a few months, I was transferred to the men's ward of the surgical floor, where I worked either as the head nurse's assistant during the day or as the nurse in charge of the ward on evening or night shifts.

As soon as I had accumulated a few lira, I bought myself a new dress and my first pair of high-heeled shoes. These small luxuries added to my overall happiness and satisfaction at work. Still, a gnawing, negative thought persisted—doubt about my "normalcy" as a woman. Although our relationship failed to go anywhere, I continued seeing Amos. We were good friends and trusted each other, but in spite of his seeming fondness for me the relationship was devoid of love. I, on the other hand, continued to be madly in love with him. He did attract me, and secretly I thought that if anyone it probably would be Amos to whom I would one day confess the reason for my fear of intimacy.

Destiny tipped its hand when both of us were invited to the wedding of mutual friends in Haifa. As usual, I stayed with my family, while he stayed with his friends. We spent time together swimming, dancing, and strolling in the park. At one point, when he attempted a romantic overture, the issue of my resistance to his advances finally came up. He wanted to know the reason, and for the first time ever I talked about my experience with Marius. My secret was out, and his reaction was comforting. Embracing and caressing me tenderly, he assured me that I was normal and that such things are not unusual. He spoke from his experience both as a man and as a practicing gynecologist.

The moment was ripe to let myself be seduced, and I decided to let events take their course. In the next few days, he became more romantic and I less resisting, both of which led to what was natural. I was totally surprised to feel that surge of pleasure I once thought was just a myth. And so with my doubts dispelled once and forever and my confidence in my womanhood restored, I felt invigorated and reborn. At the same time, I hoped that intimacy would enhance our relationship, but I was wrong.

Despite my suspicion that he was not the right partner for me, intimacy intensified my infatuation with him to the point of obsession. He was no fool; he understood how I felt. The very next day at the beach, he greeted me with a Hebrew aphorism: "Not to become enthusiastic, not to fall in love, and not to be disappointed."

This indirect but clear statement of not wanting a commitment felt like a slap in the face. My ego was deeply wounded, but at the same time I could not let go and accepted this condition out of gratitude to him for having helped me rid myself of a heavy burden.

In the next few months our relationship went nowhere. Our meetings became less frequent until we almost did not date anymore. A few young doctors did ask me out, but I could see after the very first date that it was not worthwhile continuing. Once I accidentally met Marius. He begged me to go back to him, but it was out of the question. A few months later, I heard he had gotten married—to my great relief.

As my obligatory year at Hadassah neared its end, I started searching for a job and a place to stay in Haifa. Luck was with me. My cousin Lucie, who worked as a laboratory technician at a private hospital, heard about an opening for a head nurse on the medical-surgical floor. She made an appointment for me to be interviewed by the director of nursing, who hired me right away.

I became head nurse on a thirty-bed floor, working only day shifts, and as a bonus I was given an inexpensive room on the hospital's basement floor. Professionally I was gratified.

Having made a sort-of peace with my reality, I enjoyed life to the fullest. Only from time to time, my chronic intestinal pains flared up and disrupted my happiness. At one point, they got so bad that I had to be hospitalized. For the first time, a thorough check-up revealed the problem as spastic colitis. This inflammation of the large intestine was apparently a result of my internment in Bershad and was exacerbated by amoebic superinfections that did not respond to treatment. The amoeba was indigenous to tropical and subtropical areas like the Mediterranean. For some reason, an unscientific theory circulated that a change of climate might cure the disease.

I talked about it with Aunt Cilli, who had recently moved to Israel, and she made me an offer I could hardly refuse. Since she was going to join her husband in Vienna anyway, she suggested I go with her and stay with them for two months. She would even pay for the treatment, so I would only have to pay for the trip. The offer was tempting. The mere thought of being so near to my homeland rekindled my eternal dream of returning to my beloved Bukovina and also to Transnistria, the place of pain.

After being granted a two-month leave of absence for medical reasons, I began feverishly preparing for my first-ever luxury boat trip. The excitement was almost unbearable. We embarked for Italy on the small Italian cruise ship, S.S. *Messapia,* on which I had the time of my life. Most passengers disembarked in Venice, while we continued to Trieste, the last port of call. My younger cousin Guido was waiting there for us.

In his Volkswagen, he drove us through northern Italy. We stopped overnight in a hotel and continued the next morning, finally crossing the border into Austria. Driving through the wooded Austrian Alps alongside wide rivers and lakes and breathing in the crisp familiar air, I was overcome with pleasant childhood memories of my native Bukovina. Simultaneous with those pleasant memories, flashbacks to scenes of the camps forced their way into my consciousness.

Such conflicting feelings prevent me from experiencing extreme joy with complete abandon. A tiny pilot light eternally burns in my unconscious mind and ignites a large fire in the most enjoyable moments—a scorching reminder of my past. It does not allow me to forget the fate of my loved ones and my own part in the tragedy; that it is *I* who is really alive and here; that it is *I* who has really been in that surrealistic, Hadean world.

With these repressed thoughts and feelings, I faced Vienna, the city of my dreams. Only this time it was neither a dream nor a vision; it was reality. I had come a long way indeed.

Ah, Vienna! It seemed so cozy and familiar, a feeling of déjà vu. Just as in Czernowitz, there were the same architecture, streetcars, boulevards, atmosphere, and language. Later I realized that the déjà vu was but a recall of the vivid descriptions of my father's bedside stories. I felt at home and instantly in love with this romantic and exciting city. Conflicting with this euphoria was the awareness that Austria had bloodied its hands in the same way, or even worse, as the Germans. It was hard to overcome the uneasiness.

Despite its reputed splendor, parts of Vienna bore witness to heavy bombing sustained during the war. Many buildings were still in ruins, including the famous Vienna State Opera.

In ruins also was the once-large Jewish population of more than two hundred thousand. Most of them had been exterminated in the Nazi death camps, my father's sisters, Dr. Pepi Drimmer and Maryem Schaerf, and Maryem's husband, Gedalia, included. The few Jews inhabiting Vienna after the war were mostly refugees from other countries, with just a few native Viennese here and there. With my scarce savings, I started visiting the least expensive of all cultural sites, the museums. For operas and concerts, I would stand in line for hours until I succeeded in purchasing a cheap student ticket in the last rows of the gallery or on the stairs. Almost every day and every night I went to another event, which bemused my aunt. Too soon it was time for my admission to the *Wiener Poliklinik*, a teaching hospital, for treatment. Luckily, I was to be treated by Professor Grueneis, who proved to be a most outstanding physician and human being. Two days later I was discharged and started preparations for the return home. With my last Austrian schillings, I purchased a train ticket to Trieste, where I boarded the S.S. *Messapia* to return to Haifa and resume my position as head nurse.

But my first visit to Austria whetted my appetite for more of the marvels of Europe, and after two years I started to search for a new travel opportunity. The problem, as usual, was money. As a result, for my second trip, I accepted a job as a nurse-secretary to a seventy-two-year-old Israeli engineer, residing in Cyprus. He turned out to be a highly eccentric and unbearable person. After having traveled with him through six European countries for two months, I felt completely drained and in no shape to resume my strenuous job at Elisha.

We returned to Zurich where we met his business associates. Knowing him as they did, they advised me to get somebody else to take him back to Cyprus. The Marxes then invited me to stay with them in Kreuzlingen, Switzerland, to recover from my ordeal. They picked me up and drove me to their splendorous villa overlooking Lake Konstanz. They were astonished at how I could have endured that long with the old man, whom they knew to be a tyrant. But, as the saying goes, "Nothing ventured, nothing gained." I had seen the highlights of five countries, and the impressions and adventures I had gained provided a valuable learning experience.

I was ready to go back to Israel, but since I was so near to Vienna, Aunt Cilli asked me to come and visit them. While I debated whether to go to see them, destiny helped me make a decision. Israel was once more drawn into a conflict with the Arabs, namely the 1956 Sinai War. In my state of mind, I couldn't bear the thought of being exposed to yet another war, so I gladly accepted their invitation. My relatives met me at the Vienna train station and took me to their new residence near the center of the city.

Unfortunately my relationship with Uncle Max did not improve. In fact we could barely tolerate one another. But Aunt Cilli genuinely wanted me to lead an easier life. She decided that nursing was too strenuous a profession for me, and the pay too low. She also thought that life in Israel was much too harsh and suggested that I change both profession and domicile. In her opinion, the quickest and least expensive way to acquire a new profession was through a secretarial course.

Another endeavor, another challenge. While I spoke and read German, I had never formally studied the language. To my great surprise, I did pass the admission exam and started the two-month course at the Wiener Handelsschule (Vienna Business School).

Little did I know that my aunt's intentions were more far-reaching. She also wanted to help me get married—and soon. In a very adroit way, she managed to introduce me to Karl Meth, a lawyer from Czernowitz, claiming that he could be helpful in obtaining restitution money from Germany and also for his many connections, which might help me find a job.

Soon enough Karl called and suggested a business meeting over dinner, which I accepted. He was a bachelor, twenty years older than I, a charming and interesting character. But, as a man, he did not attract me at all. Eventually he got the message, and once the issue of romance was eliminated Karl and I became good friends.

He tried to persuade me to let him be my lawyer and help me obtain monetary restitution from Germany. I had been approached before, in Israel, about that matter, and flatly refused even to listen to details. It seemed a monstrous concept to suggest that money could repair the damage that had been done to me. Besides, I did not want to have to deal with the Germans for any reason. However, Karl was persuasive and eventually convinced me that I was wrong and very naive.

From the day I entrusted my case to Karl until its conclusion, it was a full twenty-five years before I saw any money. A small suitcase full of letters and documents attest to my struggle for justice. Aside from stirring up the tragic past, it caused me many anxious days and sleepless nights. I also had to deal with the additional difficulty of proving my prewar status and identity. Since I had no bona fide documents to show, my case was interpreted by the German authorities as a false claim. They required witnesses to state details about my parents and my father's occupation and yet other witnesses to declare that they had been with me in Bershad during the Nazi persecution.

While many adult survivors were able to hide a few documents or leave some behind with relatives or friends, orphans like myself had none. This problem was common to most child survivors, and as a result few were compensated. Unfortunately, these facts were not taken into consideration by the German bureaucrats. But following Karl's instructions, I started gathering evidence, first of my physical ailments.

The only doctor I knew in Vienna was Professor Grueneis, who treated me in 1954, so I asked him for a certificate. This Austrian doctor listened to a short résumé of my life and said, "Miss Glasberg, after all that has happened to you, you should be wrapped in cotton and put in a crystal villa on the French Riviera for the rest of your life. Such happiness should be yours and no harm should ever come to you."

I shall never forget his eyes brimming with tears as he spoke these compassionate words. His reaction substantiated my conviction that not all Austrians or all Germans were Nazis and therefore I should never ever generalize. His affidavit proved to be more than a document; it was a medical evaluation, with a humane emphasis on the emotional and physical repercussions.

The need to be wrapped in cotton and have "Fragile: Handle with Care" written all over me was an ironic statement when in real life I was being buffeted as if I had been made of steel.

I never broke, though I surely suffered a lot of cracks.

The hope of getting money from the Germans sometime in the future did not help my urgent need in the present. While studying to become a secretary, my scant savings began to dwindle, and my relatives offered not even a cigarette.

I was finding out that Vienna without my friends and without money was not such a cheerful place after all. I could have gone back to Israel where I had been happy, but I never liked to leave unfinished business. Having started the secretarial course, I wanted to bring it to completion and see what benefits I might derive from it.

After I graduated, Karl recommended me to a friend of his for a job. This businessman, also from Czernowitz, had a chain of offices in many cities, with Vienna to be added imminently. I was to be his secretary and trusted agent. The interview went well; he seemed to like me and hired me right away. All I needed was a work permit.

Karl escorted me to the permits office. However, as soon as I showed them my Israeli passport, my request was denied: Foreigners were not permitted to work in Austria. What a letdown! I looked at my friend; he looked at me. We could not believe this was happening. But instead of resentment, I perceived the event to be an omen that said, "Go home to Israel where you belong," so my six-month stay in Vienna ended. I readied myself for my return to Israel.

Upon my arrival in Haifa, I found that my position at Elisha hospital had been filled. That was a shock, although I had expected it might happen after such a long absence. The critical part was that I had no place to stay, and that meant imposing on Aunt Anna, Willy, and Lucie. With the birth of Lucie's second son, there were now five in her tiny apartment. I had to sleep on the living room floor. But no matter; this was my home for better or for worse.

After some job hunting, I landed a position in the surgical outpatient division of the Kupat-Cholim clinic in midtown. An elderly couple rented me a room in their apartment without access to the kitchen. This made it impossible to eat at home, but at least I did not have to impose on my family anymore.

During that year of living in a sublet room, I harbored dreams of having my own simple studio apartment; meanwhile I had to be content with what I had. And I had plenty of nonmaterial things: a good profession, many good friends, and my family. I lived amidst honest and hardworking people in my very own country, far from the persecution and discrimination of the Europe of yesteryear.

Six months later I found a better and more interesting job, at Rambam Hospital in Haifa. It was more in line with my administrative capabilities. I worked mostly evening and night shifts at the five-hundred-bed hospital and liked the challenge of the big responsibility.

My romantic life, though, left a lot to be desired. I had met and dated several men, but none seemed to meet my expectations. I was not worried, but my relatives and friends kept nudging me to lower my standards and get married before I reached the fatal age of thirty.

I had almost given up the hope of meeting the right person until just before my twenty-eighth birthday. I took a week's vacation to celebrate it with the Laufer relatives in Jerusalem. After the party, my cousins Isiu, Max, his wife, Ika, and I traveled to Tel Aviv to visit Aunt Cilli, who came from Vienna alone to sell her apartment.

That same evening, Isiu picked me up to meet some of his friends at the Café Noga. He led me to a table where Max, Ika, and two strangers sat waiting for us. One was a short, stocky, rather unattractive man, who introduced himself as Ludwig. The other—younger, handsome, slim, and tanned—introduced himself as Salomon Gold, Ludwig's friend.

We ordered coffee with ice cream, and an animated, conversation followed in various languages. Salomon told us that he was a tourist from Colombia, South America. I was immediately impressed by his impeccable, literary Hebrew, aside from the fact that we had six languages in common: German, Yiddish, Romanian, Russian, Hebrew, and English. There was an instant familiar feeling between us that was enhanced because he had lived in Czernowitz for a few years. Just as I was drawn by his intellect and good looks, it seemed that he was equally taken with me.

Besides languages, we had much in common. Not only did we share the same background and culture, but we were both survivors of the war. His entire family perished in the Holocaust, except for one sister who lived in Israel, and she was the one he had come to visit when we met.

"Salo," short for Salomon, did not hesitate to show his fondness for me. The next morning he sent a huge bouquet of roses to my aunt's apartment, along with an invitation for dinner. It was the beginning of an intense two-month courtship. After my return to Haifa, he called me frequently and commuted to Haifa several times, even staying a week to be near me. Luckily, he found a hotel on my street so we could have more time together, since I was working the evening shift.

After several weeks, Salo awkwardly proposed marriage, making it sound almost as if he were inviting me on a trip to Europe. I pretended not to understand, but I knew exactly what he was hinting at. A few days later, he suggested we get engaged. I asked him for time to think it over.

My decision was based neither on love nor on chemistry. This time I made a logical evaluation of the odds in favor of such a commitment. He was older than I by eleven years, and I needed someone more mature. He was also someone I could look up to and learn from. His demeanor evoked respect, and it was true that his intellect was what I most admired. I thought we would have a solid foundation for trust and friendship and hoped that from there the love would grow.

But before giving him my answer, I had quite a debate with myself over two more troubling drawbacks—the prospect of having to leave Israel and of what would happen to my profession. Israel was now my

(Above) *Marriage to Salomon Gold, Tel-Aviv, 1958.* (Left) *Dancing barefoot at the wedding reception.*

home, and it was where I had finally replanted my roots. Here I had my only relatives and friends, and here I felt free and confident and happy. I could not envision living among non-Jews again, especially in South America, which was so far away.

Several times I tried to convince Salo to move to Israel by using the argument that it was the place every Jew should live—and he in particular, as his only sister and her family lived there. But he had a self-created, one-man electronic import business in Bogota which he could not easily abandon. To help me make up my mind, he promised that in a few years we would come back to live in Israel. Still, I was unable to decide.

But as often happens in life, a course of events which I call "fate" plays a major role in any decision making, and a single factor can be the proverbial straw that breaks the camel's back. One such factor was a crisis during one of my night shifts. As usual, I had received the nightly report and was about to start my rounds. It was July, and the atmosphere was hot and silent. Suddenly there were wild, shrieking sirens of ambulances. The howling multiplied, indicating a major disaster. I instinctively diagnosed it as an outbreak of yet another war.

Within a few minutes, the hospital grounds became frenzied. From ambulances and from trucks, dozens of dead and wounded Arabs were being unloaded, casualties not of war but of a prison revolt. They were inmates of the neighboring town of Akko, where they had staged a major uprising. As supervisor, it was my responsibility to organize, to direct the entire operation. Seeing even one cadaver was more than I could bear, but seeing dozens of them during one night was a hideous nightmare, one I never want to relive. That was *my* breaking point. This incident tilted the balance in favor of my decision to marry.

When Salo met me the next morning, I was still shaking from the horror of that night. After I told him about what had happened, he was shocked. Salo then and there counseled me to quit the job immediately. That I did not do. But I did hand in my resignation.

August 23, 1958. Salo and I got married in Tel Aviv, and a week later we left for Bogota, Colombia.

Culture Shock

Fourteen years in Bogota were not exactly Shangri-La. I had comforts beyond anything I had before, but I missed Israel and the emotional bonds with family and friends there. The adaptation to a yet another language, Spanish, which I learned by phonetics only, to another country and its culture, called for reinventing another self. Feeling completely uprooted again increased my yearning to return to Israel, but Salo wouldn't hear of it. And nostalgia took over.

My marriage was not what I had expected, mainly because of the crass differences in our personalities. Salo, albeit an honest, hard-working person, lacked warmth, and compassion and was possessive and unemotional. I, on the other hand, tended to be oversensitive and to crave attention, particularly in that new, alien environment. Over and above that, I missed nursing and the social and financial independence it gave me.

The abrupt transition from a highly socialized Israel to an undeveloped capitalistic Colombia was difficult, as was the blatant contrast between social classes. Opulent villas in the north of Bogota clashed grotesquely with the corrugated tin or cardboard huts in the south.

Worst of all was seeing begging, homeless children, sleeping in doorways, covered with newspapers to protect themselves from the extremely cold Bogota nights. It was especially jarring to stumble upon them when coming out of a movie theater or a restaurant.

Scenes such as these incited a rebelliousness in me that I soon found difficult to control. No matter how much Salo would try to rationalize the situation by telling me that those children were runaways who chose this life-style, I could not make peace with the injustice I saw.

In this new and strange environment, I found myself imprisoned in an unfurnished apartment with a maid I didn't know what to do with and days I didn't know how to occupy. A radio and a few books provided me with some entertainment until Salo would return from work, only to give me a detailed report about his electronics business, of which I understood nothing.

Besieged by melancholy and solitude, I didn't get excited about a missed menstrual cycle. I simply ascribed it to the change of climate and life-style. The likelihood of pregnancy never even crossed my mind, for I had never completely overcome the feeling of not being a "normal" woman.

At the recommendation of a new acquaintance, I consulted a gynecologist, a recent emigrant from Hungary, who diagnosed a pregnancy. Oddly enough I was not ecstatic. In fact I didn't believe his diagnosis. But as the pregnancy advanced, I slowly accepted the truth, and both Salo's and my happiness knew no limits. However, about three months later, I began spotting and recognized it as a danger signal. But the young doctor was unimpressed, assuring me that it was nothing significant and recommending I lead a normal life. Instinctively and professionally I knew he was wrong, yet I chose to believe him for reasons I still cannot explain to this day. Why didn't I ask for a second opinion? And why did I fail to recognize my doctor's incompetence? Perhaps I harbored an unconscious fear of giving birth to a child whose fate might be similar to my own. But I adored children and was eager to have them for all the reasons any woman desires to have a child, only I had one more important reason: it symbolized giving life and defying and undoing the genocide of the Holocaust, if only in a most modest way.

Then one morning at the beginning of my seventh month, the amniotic sac ruptured. I frantically called the doctor, who finally admitted that it looked bad and told me to go to the hospital where he would join me shortly. When we arrived at the hospital, I was immediately taken to the delivery room.

Panicky and confused, I did not know what to expect. The problem was that I did not have labor pains, and the doctor did nothing to induce labor. Instead, he just held my hand. And so we sat, patient and doctor, holding hands, helplessly hoping for a miracle.

I was not dilating, the fluid was gone, the baby was probably dead inside me. I drifted in and out of consciousness, and every time I opened my eyes, I would ask, "Is it out?" His answer was always the same: "Not yet."

For twenty-four hours, I agonized in the labor room, almost dying. In one of my few lucid moments, I begged Salo to call his Aunt Dora or anyone to save me before I died on the delivery table. That simple idea would not have crossed my husband's mind, as he abhorred asking people for assistance or favors. But now that I pleaded for help, he went to get his aunt. Upon her recommendation, Salo summoned another obstetrician/gynecologist Dr. Juan Rodriguez, to confer with mine. Together they decided to induce labor, and under anesthesia I delivered the baby.

Back in the hospital room and still groggy, I felt someone holding my hand. Opening my eyes, I recognized Dr. Rodriguez, and heard him say: "I'm sorry, Doña Ruth, but the baby didn't survive." Then he added quickly. "It's better this way, because it would have had lots of problems."

"What was it, Doctor?" I managed to ask, choking back tears.

"A girl, but she was very weak," he said, trying to console me. I cried silently, and for the first time I saw my otherwise unemotional husband cry as well. He sat by my bedside and we cried together. From that moment on, I was convinced that I would never be able to have a child.

I was still groggy when some time later, one of the nuns approached my bed and said, "Señora Gold, congratulations! You have a beautiful daughter who looks just like you."

"Thank you very much," I replied politely, convinced that she had gotten me mixed up with another woman—or else, under the influence of anesthesia, I had imagined hearing it. I did not want to embarrass her. Besides, I had no energy to explain the contrary.

The conflicting messages, the talk and preparations for the burial done while I was half-asleep, were all painful and confusing, to say the least. I must have denied some of the occurrences, thinking they were just dreams. But I knew better when Salo went home to bring a piece of his pajamas to serve as a shroud for the baby, something required by Jewish law. I was not allowed to see the body, and, in fact the next day it was buried without my knowledge.

A week later, I was home. I felt like an empty bag, ashamed and defeated, painfully aware of being deprived of the most basic and natural function of a woman. The guilt of having disappointed my husband almost consumed me. Often enough he had insinuated that his main objective in getting married was to have children—not a very flattering thing to hear, but it was the truth.

That new loss, the baby I had carried in my womb but was unable to bring into the world, haunted me constantly. I never saw her in real life, but in my dreams I saw a clear image of my tiny girl stretching out her small arms from beyond some deep abyss. She seemed to be asking me to save her, forming the word "Help" with her tiny lips without uttering a sound. But in this dream I am unable to help her, as if I am paralyzed (my mother's real situation). Every time I woke up from such a nightmare I was drenched in sweat and cried mournfully.

The few people who came to visit me while I was convalescing did me no good with the soothing clichés; "You are young and will have plenty of children" or "These things happen quite often." Nobody could understand what that loss meant to me, because nobody knew anything about my past. I was again convinced that the Holocaust had, after all, marked me for life.

That conviction, in addition to the nightmares, and the mourning, brought on a depression. All I did was sleep and cry, feeling very lonely and sad.

Although of little moral support, Salo at least offered a charitable gesture: to pay for my Aunt Anna to come from Boston to Bogota. It so happened that she had been there, visiting her only brother, my Uncle David, whom she had not seen for the past fifty years. That opportunity was my lifesaver. She came to stay with us for two months. Together with Julia, the maid, we prepared the now-furnished apartment for her arrival. Her presence and her maternal love lifted my spirits considerably, and by the end of Aunt Anna's visit I was almost my old self again.

Some time after she left, I started cleaning and organizing closets and drawers when I accidentally stumbled upon some hospital bills. Thinking that Salo had forgotten to pay them, I carefully read all the charges. There was, among others, one that absolutely stunned me: it listed the cost of five hours of incubator oxygen. *What incubator?* There must have been a mistake. Then it hit me! I suddenly remembered incidents at the hospital that slowly merged into a clear picture, solving the puzzle. I almost fainted when I realized that my baby had been born alive after all, and the nun who congratulated me was right—it was not my imagination, nor was it a mix-up. Those who told me that the baby was born dead had lied atrociously.

As soon as Salo came home, I hysterically confronted him with the bill. With great effort, he managed to tell me the truth. The baby was indeed born alive, prematurely, and kept in an incubator, but it died a few hours later. I felt betrayed. My nightmares made more sense to me now, and again I became mournful and inconsolably dejected but even more determined to have another child.

Dr. Rodriguez assured me of a complete recovery but prohibited another pregnancy for the next six months. I asked if he could suggest a contraceptive method, but he indignantly replied, "I am sorry, but as a Catholic, it is against my religion to prescribe such things."

His words hit me like cold water. I had never heard such absurdity. We were young and recently married, so what were we supposed to do? Practice abstinence?

Sure enough, in spite of precautions, three months later I was pregnant again. As much as I celebrated the fact of being able to conceive after all I had gone through, I was also fearful of what might happen with an untimely pregnancy. I was sure the doctor would recommend an abortion, or the baby would be born either prematurely or with some abnormality.

My fears led to a state of extreme nervousness that could only be controlled with tranquilizers. Not surprisingly, bloodstains, the first signs of a miscarriage, appeared again in the third month. I was devastated. Dr. Rodriguez put me on hormone treatment and recommended complete bed rest.

For one month Salo hired a nurse to take care of me during the day, and at night he took over. The bleeding stopped after a few weeks, and I was allowed to sit up for short periods and even go by myself to the toilet. But I had to stay in bed during most of the pregnancy.

Those circumstances of complete isolation and solitude were trying for me. Except for the new maid and a neighbor, I had few visitors and nothing to keep me busy during the day. By then Salo had rejected most of the few friends I had made and even refused to let some of them into the house. I read and slept and read and slept, hoping for a happy ending.

One morning, I woke up and noticed an unusual hoarseness and a deepening of my voice. At first I blamed it on a cold, though I found out later I did not have one. My deep voice did not go away, so I consulted several specialists. They found the vocal chords swollen but did not know the cause of such a phenomenon. They speculated that it might be a side effect of the hormonal treatment. This particularly distressed me, because singing had always been my spiritual outlet and it pained me not to be able to sing as I could before. My voice now sounded ugly to me, masculine and unflattering, especially when people would call me "señor" over the telephone. The voice remains deep till this day.

July 21, 1960. The sun shone brightly, obliterating whatever suffering I had endured up to that day. With his first cry, my newborn son brought tears of unspeakable happiness to my eyes. Holding this blond, blue-eyed, seven-pound bundle of health to my breast was a mystical experience. It was too good to be true. I had given life to another human being! With his birth, a new cycle began: a reincarnation from the ashes of the Holocaust, a replacement of the perished families. Salo and I were ecstatic. We named him Michael in memory of my father, Mendel.

The family in Colombia.

Like all mothers, I was apprehensive about the health of my first-born, only my anxiety was carried to the extreme. A lurking fear of loss kept me overalert during the day and awake at night. My hovering over Michael seemed to create a vicious circle: he became a colicky baby and I a neurotic, overprotective mother.

My neurotic mother's pattern of trying to protect my child from some invisible evil continued. It was probably an emotional disturbance stemming from the days of persecution. Now that I was a mother, I couldn't help but recall the agony of my own mother at the loss of her son, my brother, Bubi. I was morbidly worried about Michael's destiny. I felt the new responsibility for another human being, my own child, to be a difficult and scary task. My joy and happiness were overshadowed by this anxiety.

About that time, Salo and I discussed having another baby, mainly to provide a sibling for Michael. We definitely did not want our son to be an only child, something that was important to Holocaust survivors. In 1963, three years after Michael's birth—and after a normal pregnancy— our daughter Liana was born. We named her after my mother, Leah. It was my birthday, June 21, and she was the most valuable birthday gift a mother could receive—a living doll.

Before Liana's second birthday, we moved to a larger apartment. But even this improvement and a busier life did not diminish my yearning for Israel. Salo knew I was not happy in Colombia, and that knowledge created continual tensions in our marriage.

As if that was not enough, in 1965 Salo suffered a sudden heart attack. The scare of almost losing him made me realize that in spite of our strained relationship, I was, in a paradoxical way, very much attached to him. As always I appreciated his good qualities, and my loyalty to him as family superseded everything else—even my constant nagging about moving to Israel. Fortunately, Salo recovered and resumed his routine, but from then on I lived in constant fear for his life.

Though I kept busy learning to play bridge, to do flower arrangements, to sew, and to entertain, and my children were a source of great joy, I continued to be terribly unhappy in Colombia. Deep down I knew that even if I resigned myself to staying, my children, in spite of being native Colombians, would never be accepted as such because of their fair complexion and their names. I didn't feel that Colombians were either anti-Semitic or xenophobic, but to them we were simply *different*.

It happened time and time again that my children's statement "I am Colombian" would be met with an ironic remark like "With the name Gold, with fair skin and blue eyes, you can't possibly be a Colombian— you're a *gringo*." That feeling of uprootedness and of not belonging was something I was not going to permit to happen to my children. I gradually became more and more determined to take them out sooner or later.

In the interim, Salo's behavior had become totally irrational, culminating in threats to cut me off from my precious relatives. It got so bad that I asked him for a divorce numerous times, but he would only respond with a threat: "You can leave with only your underwear anytime, but the children stay with me." Without a place to go, without a penny to my name, and in danger of losing my children, I was trapped.

One of my friends who knew about my problem suggested that I go for counseling to a Dr. Jaime Villareal. At my request—and contrary to orthodox psychoanalytical procedures—he allowed me to tape my Holocaust experiences. At the conclusion, he said: "Did you notice that you related the events as if talking about another person?" This was the first time I had told my story in detail, and I had done it in a detached way. Apparently moved, Dr. Villareal suggested that I write a book. I owe him a debt of gratitude for reinforcing the idea that many, including Salo, had suggested. At the end of the treatment, my shattered self-confidence was restored.

The doctor also suggested marital counseling with his wife, an expert in that field. I succeeded in convincing Salo to come with me. After only two sessions, however, he denounced her as a "bitch" and refused to return. Left with few options, and well aware that I had no chance for a divorce in Colombia, leaving the country became imperative.

Aside from my personal problems, I also foresaw impending political ones, even before the era of Colombian narcotics trafficking and terrorism. And since Israel was unacceptable to Salo, the only solution was to go to America. At least the law would protect me there.

I presented my emigration plan to Salo as an ultimatum. This time, due to my firm position, he did not belittle me but listened carefully. After all my arguments were laid out in the open, he agreed to the idea of trying life in the United States. Normally, Colombian citizens, which we were, had to wait for years to get a visa. I didn't expect anything different, but the chance for a new life gave me hope and strength.

In planning this move, I was cognizant of one big problem—my phobia of driving, which stemmed from an incident during my early experiences: I had accidentally hit a sidewalk. "You need another three hundred lessons before you'll be able to drive!" Salo said and meant it. His exaggerated yelling and uncontrolled anger so immobilized me that I gave up driving for the next twelve years. Faced with the possibility of moving to the United States, the necessity of being able to drive became paramount. The motivation was strong enough to undertake about anything to get back my initial confidence. It took a year of continuous, patient, and calm coaching by a Colombian driver I hired before I was able to overcome this phobia and drive in the crazy traffic of Bogota.

With Salo's approval, I started to put all gears into motion. One of them was facing the issue of Salo's business. Assuming he would come with us, the question was how we would run it during his periodic absences. I searched and eventually found a Swiss gentleman—the owner of a Colombian handicraft store—whom I thought Salo would trust. The man called Salo and introduced himself as being interested in a partnership. Sure enough, that meeting led to a lengthy and mutually cooperative business relationship, and Salo felt confident enough to leave Colombia for short periods of time.

Next, I made an appointment with the vice-consul of the U.S. Embassy. During the routine interview, this friendly young woman, upon learning something about my life, seemed eager to help. She was explaining that the procedure might take a while, when suddenly, in mid-sentence, she stopped. "Where did you say both of you were born?" she asked.

"In Romania," I responded, slightly apprehensive because of its communist regime. "Let me make a call to Washington, because I think there's no quota for Romania at the moment," she said, holding up her right palm, meaning "Wait."

The call took less than a minute—a minute that sealed our fate. When she hung up the receiver she beamed: "Mrs. Gold, you are very lucky. There is, indeed, no quota for Romanian-born subjects, which means that you and your husband can get a visa in a few weeks. Once you have received the resident [green] card, you must leave for the U.S. within six months."

"I don't believe it!" was all I could say at first. Was it a miracle or just good luck? Who knows?

August 1, 1972. We arrived in Miami, U.S.A., as new immigrants. Once more I had a dream come true. This was my fifth country, my fourth continent, and even at age forty-two I was still full of expectations for a new life. We had chosen Miami because of its proximity to Colombia and because we knew it from earlier visits. I loved the American democracy and its freedom, but I particularly loved Miami with its ocean, warm climate, and casual life. The children and I were happy in our new homeland but not Salo. He commuted every two months, and each time he came to Miami he tried to persuade us to return. We rented a furnished home and registered the children in public schools. After we settled, Salo returned to Bogota, and the children and I started our new life.

The sudden switch from the sheltered environment of a private school to the large, impersonal classrooms of the American public school system was difficult for the children. However, Michael, twelve, and Liana, nine, adapted quickly and did well. Both made it into the gifted student program.

Then, without any previous experience in business, and with the limited budget Salo allotted me, I set out to establish a business of Colombian handicrafts. I managed to get a second-floor walk-up on a commercial street. I tore myself to pieces working eight hours a day in the store, doing the household chores myself, and taking care of the children. I became an importer, buyer, and salesperson, spurred by a single driving force: enthusiasm. The pressure was intense.

Two years later, Salo finally realized that I was here to stay and agreed to buy a house in Bay Harbor Islands, Florida. He even helped me in the store on his periodic visits. After years of working long hours without seeing any profit, I came to the conclusion that I was not cut out for commerce. What especially disturbed me were the many accepted but unethical practices used in the world of business. Overlooking them was not in my character, and I wanted out. But by now Salo had grown fond of our little boutique because he had a place to go every morning. Even if it was wasted time and energy, he would not hear of selling it. Then fate played another little trick: one day Salo was held hostage during a holdup at the store. That scary event made him change his mind, and he agreed to sell it.

Now I began seriously entertaining the idea of returning to nursing after a twenty-two-year hiatus. With the encouragement of my son and a cousin, I embarked upon the difficult road of preparing for the Florida Nursing Licensure. The bureaucratic part was almost as difficult as the studies, since to enter a college or university the issue of a high-school diploma surfaced again. With much effort I was able to get my equivalency grades from Israel, and at age fifty I was back in the classroom, this time with young nursing students. Having to absorb the vast amount of new information that had accumulated over three decades, as well as to refresh the nursing knowledge I had by now forgotten, was awesome. To understand the English academic language was no small effort either. For several months, my only dedication was to these studies. Sprawled on the floor with many books around me, I studied for eight to ten hours a day. Finally, presenting myself at the exam, I passed it the very first time. To say that I was euphoric would be an understatement.

My first position was at St. Francis Hospital on Miami Beach. I worked there as a part-time staff nurse on a medical floor. Being back in my profession and earning a salary of my own was enormously gratifying. The success of obtaining my license coincided with another achievement: that of monetary restitution from Germany. It took twenty-five years to obtain an obscenely small sum of money, compared with my sufferings, but it helped in giving me that long-desired feeling of *some* financial independence and a boost in self-esteem.

In a short time I developed new friendships and a new social life. We became part of a stimulating circle of friends, some of whom were involved in the world of music. In 1979, Salo and I were invited to a musical soirée held at the home of one of our friends. We were entertained by a chamber orchestra of the University of Miami, after which a lively discussion ensued. The main topic was music students and how influential a teacher can be to their careers. Naturally, I brought up the story about my late brother and his teacher, Professor Samuel Flor. As soon as I pronounced the name, a lady from New York turned to me and asked, "What did you say the professor's name was?"

"Samuel Flor," I repeated.

"I know him well," she stated with satisfaction.

"You mean you *knew* him well," I corrected her.

"Why do you put it in past tense?" she asked. I explained to her that Flor was a man whom I as a child perceived to be already in his middle age, and therefore I assumed that he was no longer alive.

"What you are telling me is very confusing," the lady said shaking her head. She then introduced herself as Dr. Stella Saslow, a pediatrician from Czernowitz and a friend of the Flors. She told me that Professor Flor was now in his late seventies and lived in Pennsylvania with his wife, Gerti, herself a pianist. He was also the director of the Vermont Music and Arts Center. "I can't believe this is true," I said to the apparently amused woman.

She promised to send me his address and telephone number, and in a few days I received the information. Excited as a schoolgirl, I called him. "Hello! is this Herr Professor Samuel Flor from Czernowitz?" "Yes," came his slightly surprised answer.

"Does the name Bubi Glasberg mean anything to you?" I asked, my voice quivering.

"Of course, he was my best student. He played the Bach Violin Concerto on Radio Kishinev. Who are you and where is he?"

"I am his sister Ruthi," I said as tears of emotion threatened to choke me. "Bubi perished in Transnistria."

"I remember you, the little blond girl with long braids, who hid under the table during the lessons." Suddenly I felt as if I had established contact with my beloved brother's spirit.

We kept in touch and planned to meet either in Florida or New York, but each time our plans fell through. Only two years later we had finally arranged a meeting in New York. Before my departure, I dared to ask if he had some pictures of his students, as I had hoped to see Bubi with his violin once again. His answer was negative, but he promised to give me something else of genuine interest instead. Although I was extremely curious, I did not pressure him to reveal what it was. I just took the next plane to New York.

On that fateful day the weather was not friendly. From a dark menacing sky, a roaring downpour inundated the busy Manhattan streets. By sheer luck I was able to get a cab in front of my hotel. I arrived at the designated restaurant before the Flors, who had been driving all the way from Abbington, Pennsylvania in this adverse weather. I recognized him instantly, even though he was now an older version of the tall, blond, handsome man I remembered. His face was brightened by the same warm and kind smile as then, and the mischievous twinkle in his eyes remained unchanged by the years.

To ease the first tense minutes, he started teasing me as he did when I was a child. Although he still amused me, deep down I really wanted to cry. After lunch I asked him to tell me anything he remembered about Bubi, and he kindly complied. I stood in awe of his astounding memory as he recounted many vignettes about my brother. I later told them of the horrible experiences in Transnistria and about the loss of my entire family.

Professor Flor then got up and handed me a folder. "Here is something for you," he said. "Before the deportation to Transnistria, I hid important papers in a neighbor's garden in Czernowitz. I was lucky to find them after liberation." With trembling hands I opened it. There were several sheets with newspaper clippings of invitations to Flor's student concerts and short reviews of their performances.

In a state of great agitation, I returned to my hotel and looked carefully at the reviews dating from 1937 to 1940. They were not pictures, but in a way they brought back images. Scanning the last page, I froze with emotion. Here was a review of Bubi's debut on Radio Kishinev in Bessarabia!! It was like an echo from a distant past. And that is how I got possession of the clipping from the *Morgenblatt* newspaper, which appeared in an earlier chapter.

Just as I had wondered about the fate of Professor Flor, I also often wondered about what happened to other people I used to be close to in my childhood.

I mainly wondered about the fate of Ilse, my childhood friend from Czernowitz, the German girl whose family had left at the start of the Soviet regime. In the decades that followed, such a search seemed impossible, so I never pursued it. But middle age makes one do things that might not take priority in youth. And so early in 1979, I decided to embark on that mission to find Ilse and her parents.

I did not even know where to start, so I decided to call the German Consulate. Someone there told me to write to the German Red Cross and the *Aufbau* newspaper in New York, which I did. Fortunately, I remembered the first names of Ilse's parents as well as the name of their Edison lamp store in Czernowitz. Two months later, the Red Cross replied, asking for more details and advising me to be patient.

Then, nine months later, they informed me they had located an Ilse Ulrich, now Ilse Kaese, living in Sontra, Germany. In addition, I was sent a letter written by her confirming the data I had provided.

The next day, I received a telephone call from a perplexed woman who wondered who Ruth Gold was and why she was looking for her. When I told her that I was Ruth Glasberg, she screamed, "You are little Ruthi, the girl I used to play with next door?"

I thought I was going to faint from excitement. My shrieks of joy and incredulity summoned my family to the kitchen phone, all happy to hear about the outcome. She was as excited as I was but sorry to tell me that her parents had recently died. Soon afterward she sent a letter and pictures of herself as the little girl I remembered. It was Ilse, all right.

I promised to visit her and made good on my promise the following year. I was in Duesseldorf for yet another restitution hearing, and from there I made a five-hour trip by train to meet Ilse. Our reunion at a small station was charged beyond belief. Normally, we would not have recognized each other on the street, but here on this lonely platform, she was the only one waiting. We were both so excited that we could not find the first words to say, so we just cried in each other's arms.

But later I realized that Ilse had only a very vague recollection of me. She was two years younger and did not remember much about anything to do with her childhood. That made the visit trying if not downright disappointing. We exchanged information about our past and present lives, during which I learned that she was about to be divorced, and, except for her two children, she had no relatives.

Ilse told me how they were forced to leave Czernowitz in 1940 after the Soviet annexation of that part of Romania. Her father had been drafted into the German army as a reserve officer, while her mother continued working in the German consulate. She was left with some acquaintances in Prague. Later her father found her, and they both ended up in a Silesian transit camp in Poland.

Her mother left Czernowitz as one of the last German nationals and later joined the two of them. Her father was able to take over a lamp store in Upper Silesia until the advancing Soviet troops marched into the area. At that point he had to stay on to help defend the Reich, while Ilse and her mother fled to Berlin. Her uncle found them and brought them to the town of Sontra. Before the war ended, her father rejoined the family.

Among other things she told me about one particular problem she

The sunshine in my life: my daughter, Liana, a trauma nurse, and my son, Michael, an M.D. and professor in behavioral neurology.

was faced with, that of discrimination by those of the same nationality—a lesson in yet another ugly aspect of the human character. Because the Ulrichs were refugees from Romania, *Volksdeutsche* and not *Reichsdeutsche* (Germans who lived in Germany), the townspeople nicknamed them "Gypsies." As nobody believed her about her family's previous privileged status, she invited her best friend to listen to my stories about her life before the war. I was the first and only person who was a witness to her childhood. I was happy to have contributed in a small way to her rehabilitation.

I returned to Miami slightly disillusioned, but I was able to validate a stage of my childhood and to get it out of my system. Ilse and I continued to correspond a few times, but eventually we lost contact.

Over the years, I continued to travel to Israel and nourish my relationships with family and friends there. At the same time, Salo and I maintained a tenuous friendship. The children were both grown now and attending the University of Miami, Michael in a pre-med program, Liana in nursing school.

I had not gone to Israel for five years, and now that I had some money of my own I decided to visit again, especially since Aunt Anna was getting old and frail. I even invited Salo to come with me as my guest. Reluctantly he agreed.

After one month, Salo returned to Miami, while I stayed on for another few weeks to visit additional relatives and friends. I also wanted to spend more time with Aunt Anna, whom I felt I was probably seeing for the last time. (Indeed she died a few months later.)

I returned home and busied myself with cofounding the Women's International Zionist Organization in Miami in 1982. I no longer worked at the hospital, because it had become too strenuous for someone my age.

On the evening of June 3, 1982, we were all watching a specially televised concert of the combined New York and Israeli Philharmonic Orchestras under the direction of Zubin Mehta. When it ended, we all went to bed.

About 2 A.M., Salo woke me up, complaining of a tight feeling in his chest and shooting pains in his left arm. He had suffered another heart attack. We rushed him to the emergency room, but all efforts to save him failed. At the news of his death, I broke down and cried. He was the first person with whom my life had been intertwined for twenty-five years, and in spite of our difficulties we were attached to one another. He was also the first person in my immediate family—aside from aunts and uncles—that I had lost since the death of my parents and my brother.

My children could not understand my prolonged depression. My grief was deeper than I had expected and lasted many years. The shock of Salo's death probably triggered the long-repressed need for mourning, a process I had been unable to experience during the Holocaust because of numbed emotions. My mourning was not only for Salo but also for my family that was never buried.

As if that loss was not enough, a few months after Salo's death my daughter emigrated to Israel to finish her nursing studies and my son returned to medical school. To overcome that difficult period of widowhood and an empty nest, I returned to work at the outpatient clinic of Mount Sinai Hospital in Miami Beach. There, alongside my nursing duties, I also interpreted in several languages for patients and doctors. Feeling needed and able to help so many was not only rewarding; it also gave me renewed motivation to carry on.

It was also during that period that I began to play with the idea of writing my memoirs. I even promised my son to do it as a New Year's resolution. But the moment I began writing about my family, I could not continue. Tears came in rivers; I would get depressed and put off the project. Periodically I attempted to put my experiences on paper, but the pattern repeated itself until 1991, when I finally gathered all my courage and persevered with my resolution, in spite of the excruciating pain and crying the writing caused me.

Back to My Roots

"When, from a long distant past nothing subsists, after the people are dead, after the things are broken and scattered, still alone, more fragile, but with more vitality, more unsubstantial, more persistent, more faithful, the smell and taste of things remain poised a long time, like souls, ready to remind us, waiting and hoping for their moment, amid the ruins of all the rest; and be unfaltering, in the tiny and almost impalpable drop of their essence, the vast structure of recollection."

MARCEL PROUST

After Salo's death and the children's departure from the house, the constant leitmotif *all alone in the world* reappeared in my life. In spite of my work, and other responsibilities, I couldn't help but feel as if I were an orphan again.

This feeling was intensified by reliving my past as I was struggling with the writing of the first chapters of this book. That in turn triggered a renewed and more intense yearning to connect with my roots. I longed to return, if only temporarily, to the place from whence I came. I felt a strong need to validate my previous existence as an ordinary child with love, family, and a home and also to validate the tragedy that followed, in order to stop the cycle of pain.

I have since forgotten many important things that had happened, but strangely enough I *do* remember the smallest flower, the smells, tastes, and sounds of things gone for almost half a century. Like some secret force, these remembrances from my lost paradise seemed to be continuously calling me back. Throughout the years of joys and sorrows, I had many repetitive dreams with the same theme: the search for people and places that provided me with a happy childhood.

Sometimes I would see myself going back to my grandfather's farm, finding that a busy, unfamiliar resort had replaced it. In spite of all these changes, I would still look for a familiar landmark or piece of furniture. And often I would indeed find a faint reminder of things that once were. Oddly enough, amidst all the distorted sights, the little Teplitza Creek kept on flowing undisturbed in the same serene pastoral setting. And the venerable, ancient double-log bridge was still the only means to cross it.

The most uncanny dream was one in which I heard the lovely, melodic chime of the tall pendulum clock that used to stand in my grandfather's room. I would follow the sound, but nowhere could I find the clock, the only reminder of time in the otherwise leisurely world of my paradise.

How badly I wished to see it all again! But during the period of the Cold War, even if I had had the money to travel, it would have been impossible because of the restrictions placed on foreigners within the Soviet Union. Every time I tried to obtain a permit, the Soviet Intourist agency would give me the same answer: "These towns and villages have no hotel accommodations." In other words, Intourist, which was sort of an arm of the KGB, could not keep an eye on foreigners in such small settlements. Later, the communists opened the big cities to a few select tourists but still prohibited access to smaller places. So even if I had the means, I still could not have visited Bershad or Milie.

It was only after the advent of *perestroika* that I dared to call the Soviet Embassy in Washington directly, explaining my request. It worked. I spoke in Russian to an intelligent and empathetic female employee. She listened to my plight and offered some valuable recommendations. She suggested I write to the regional Intourist directors and ask for one-day permits to visit Milie and Bershad. Following her suggestion, I immediately wrote emotional letters to two such directors, and six months later I was finally granted permits.

On June 2, 1988, accompanied by my American cousins, Rita Farrell and Al Katz, I embarked on a journey to my past. It was my first visit behind the Iron Curtain in more than forty years.

Our first stop was Bucharest, Romania. There I hoped to find the newspaper edition of the *Romania Libera* in which an abbreviated version of my ordeal in Bershad had been published during the war. (The only copy I possessed was lost in the shipwreck of 1946.) I wanted to have documented proof that children *do* remember their experiences and that their stories are not a product of imagination or fantasies.

Bucharest was dispirited and gloomy; everywhere one could sense the oppressive Ceaușescu regime. The shops had little merchandise, all of poor quality; grocery stores displayed only a few cans of beets, cabbage, and sardines. Radically changed, the city no longer had the elegant boulevards bustling with well-dressed people. The gaiety and spirit were gone, there was only a pervading whisper, "Dollars to change?"

Around the hotels a bristling black market thrived, in spite of the risks posed by the ever present secret police. Inside our hotel we suspected that even our room had been bugged. But that didn't discourage Rita from loudly voicing her criticisms. She would cast a glance at the ceiling and call out loudly, "Do you hear me up there?"

The next day we ventured out to the *Romania Libera* newspaper building to begin the search for my article. Upon entering the lobby, we were stopped by an old, toothless guard. No matter how I tried to explain to him who we were and what we wanted, he would not let us through. Rita, a reporter, used all the tricks of the trade to get him to change his mind but to no avail. Finally, he succumbed to our pleas and made a couple of phone calls. The only person available on that late afternoon was a lone reporter who vaguely promised to look into the matter. Frustrated, we left.

Surprisingly, a day later I got a call from the newspaper explaining that the only way I could obtain a copy of the article was to search through the newspaper's archives. After numerous telephone calls, my request was finally granted.

Upon entering the archival building, I was led to the supervisor's office. He insisted on interrogating me, asking what I specifically came to search for and why. After telling him my story, I showed him a carbon copy of the original manuscript. He looked at it but seemed to have some doubts as to my real objectives, probably thinking I was an American agent.

To convince him that I wasn't one, I decided to read him the last paragraph of my manuscript in which I described my loathing of the Romanian fascists and my joy at returning to Russia. Instantly, his friendly disposition turned to anger. "No, I changed my mind," he said. "I'm not going to let you into the archives."

I was stunned. Regardless, I was not going to give up. I threatened to appeal to a higher authority, saying that, as a U.S. citizen, I would appeal to the embassy. That did it. Within half an hour, a young man brought about sixty newspapers dating from December 1944 and January 1945 into the reading room. I had requested that many because I couldn't remember the exact date. This was a new experience for me, and with great excitement I started leafing slowly and carefully through the yellowed papers. It took me three hours to go through the whole batch. To my bitter disappointment, I did not find the article. First objective—first failure. I was so depressed that the only thing I could do to raise my spirits was to go sightseeing. So, joined by my cousins, I did just that.

Wherever I was exposed to the sounds and sights of Romanian culture, I was overcome with nostalgia. Nevertheless, the depressive environment of Bucharest dampened our enthusiasm. So after a few days, we were happy to leave.

We began a twelve-hour journey from Bucharest to Czernowitz. The train, which originated in Sofia, was filled with Bulgarians, Romanians, and Russians, mostly peasants loaded with bundles and baskets. The cars were stinking, dirty, and not at all what one would expect by Western standards. Upon entering our compartment, we noticed four soiled bare mattresses on the bunk beds. The thought of sleeping on these nauseated us, and we wondered how we would ever spend the night. Half an hour later, a grim-looking woman in charge of hospitality appeared with a stack of bedding. She gave each of us a set of clean sheets and pillowcases, and only then could we settle down for a good night's sleep.

About 2 A.M., we were awakened by uniformed inspectors wanting to check our passports. What should have been a fairly simple procedure turned into a two-hour ordeal. We were subject to a lengthy and rigorous search. They looked through every paper and garment, said nothing, and left.

In the predawn hours, the train slowed down and came to a standstill. We looked out of the window to discover we were at a small station named Seret. Coincidentally, it was the same border town on the Romanian side in which we, the Czernowitzian Jews, had arrived in 1946. My stomach began to tighten. I was near my hometown.

A new crew of inspectors in civilian clothes—this time Ukrainians—boarded the train. They were even more meticulous than the Romanians. All jewelry, watches, cameras, and currency had to be registered to prevent us from selling them in the Soviet Union. Every travelers' check and paper currency had to be declared. In addition, an English-speaking woman from Intourist took us individually into an empty compartment for an interview. When my turn came, I spoke in Russian, telling her the reasons for my return to the places of my childhood, as well as the former concentration camp of Bershad. She showed genuine sympathy and wished me luck.

In the interim the train stood in the station for hours without any indication as to when we would proceed. We later learned that, as a security precaution, it was necessary to change the wheels to a different gauge in order to adapt to the wider rails in the Soviet Union. After what seemed an infinity, the train slowly rolled out of the station, and soon we were on the other side: North Bukovina—now Ukraine.

The early morning aura, the monotonous, drum-like rhythm of the wheels, and the smell of the cool, crisp mountain air stirred in me a turmoil of emotions, reminding me of my trips to Milie. Now as then, peasants came to offer pickled apples, candies, and other goods at each small station. The same stretch of land, the same unspoiled rural scenery filled my heart with yearning. Almost fifty years had passed, but the associations became more and more vivid the closer we got.

The outskirts of my hometown crept slowly into view. With a few shrill whistles the train rolled into Czernowitz, now called Chernovtsy.

Immediately I recognized the station. My emotions ran so high I could hardly contain them. How would I feel when I found myself face to face with my past?

An Intourist driver found us and told us how lucky we were to have him pick us up at the last moment, because none of our vouchers had arrived at the hotel. It was only after the Seret Intourist office called to alert the hotel of our arrival that he was called at home and asked to meet us.

As I looked around at the masses of people circulating through the railroad station, I noticed the radical change in the ethnic population, particularly the predominance of Ukrainians. This was no longer the Czernowitz of my childhood; I felt like a stranger in my own home.

Driving through downtown, I recognized many streets and buildings, but as we drove farther from the center I grew more and more disoriented. A completely new town had mushroomed in the outskirts. Even our hotel, the Cheremosh, was a modern high-rise, the only one of its kind in Czernowitz.

We soon found out that because of the missing vouchers, our rooms were not ready, nor were our reservations valid for the rest of our trip. I asked to speak to Mr. Chorney, the director of Intourist, the person I had corresponded with regarding my requests to visit Milie. He was as warm and amicable in person as he had been in his correspondence. Aware of the mistake, he tried everything in his power to solve the problem. "Don't worry," he said. "Go get something to eat and take a walk while I call Moscow and straighten everything out." He apparently did, and we were later taken to our rooms, which were small but cozily decorated with local handwoven motifs.

With every moment that passed, I was getting more and more anxious to revisit familiar places, so despite exhaustion I decided to venture out, dragging Al with me. Without the slightest idea of how to get around the city, we boarded a bus and asked the driver to let us out in the vicinity of the main street, the name of which, remarkably, I still remembered. He dropped us off at a huge square surrounded by a park with a "Victory" monument dedicated to Soviet heroes. I was totally lost. Where was I? What had this square been called before?

Luckily I had instincts to follow, and they led me straight to the famous Herrengasse, now unrecognizable as a shopping mall called Kobilianskaya. It was closed to traffic, lined with a few dismal shops, mostly bookstores. There was a dingy supermarket, a bakery, and a few shabby restaurants. A heavy gloom overcame me. With resignation I took in the new appearance of this elegant, once-bustling street. The beautiful buildings on the town's main square and those of the old town still reflected the skill of the architects who built them during a glorious time. But now they looked dilapidated, with broken, twisted gates and overgrown, abandoned gardens.

Here and there I came upon stores or cafés I used to visit with my parents; they still bore a resemblance to what they had originally looked like, but the spirit was gone. Looking back with nostalgia on my vanished childhood, I recalled the small pleasures that this city used to offer. One image remembered brought out another, and another, and all contained the charm of happier times.

This was my beloved town, and I still felt strongly for it in spite of the changes. Is it wrong to love my birthplace, my native land, even though I was cruelly deported from it? By now I had lived in a multitude of places, but Milie and Czernowitz are where my heart is and my roots run deepest.

As I walked down the same sidewalks that I had tread as a child, every house and landmark I recognized triggered a vivid memory. It all seemed phantasmal to me. Only my cousin's remark that he was hungry brought me back from my reveries. We found a restaurant to eat lunch, after which we planned to go to a museum and buy tickets for a performance of an Indian ballet. But what I really yearned to see most was my former apartment.

"Al, do we have to go to the museum?" I asked. "I would much rather visit my old apartment."

"I'll go with you," my cousin offered, and we left.

It was raining when we stepped out onto the wet sidewalk. To my surprise, I discovered that I was near the street that led to my old neighborhood. Right there stood the same large kiosk that was once full of fruits and groceries, now just a vacant shack.

Under the protective cover of Al's umbrella, I confidently led the way. I tried to take a picture, but the camera wouldn't work, as if bewitched by all the excitement. My emotions swelled with every new house I recognized. I would have thought that time had stood still were it not for the renamed streets. Ours was now named Zhdanova.

At last we stood in front of my old building, once the glory of the neighborhood, now a run-down old dwelling with missing glass panes boarded up by broken plywood, its sidewalk in shambles. I looked at Al and asked him, "Should I go in?"

"Go for it!" he said encouragingly. And so with Al close behind me, I climbed up the familiar stairway until I reached our floor. There, as if by coincidence, three teenaged girls stood chatting in front of the open door of what once was "our" apartment. I was all choked up and had difficulty uttering a word. How could I explain to them the purpose of my visit? With great effort I asked who the occupant of this apartment was.

One of the girls said, "I am, and my name is Ida." She was seventeen, and lived there with her family of four—just as I had. With tears flowing, I tried to tell her how almost fifty years ago I used to live in the same apartment with *my* family and how much I would appreciate her letting me take a look at it once more. Ida was very pleasant and invited us in, at which point her girlfriends left.

I wanted to take pictures, but again my camera wouldn't work. That upset me terribly. Ida promised to let me come back in three days when she would be finished with her exams. Fortunately, I had a Polaroid camera at the hotel which I could use then.

With Al and Ida following behind me, I pointed out where the furniture used to be and tried to paint for them a picture of our home. My emotions peaked when I approached the tile stove, next to which my divan once stood. It was a kind of upright floor-to-ceiling ceramic tile stove, the same one where Papa used to warm the eiderdown to cover me on cold winter nights.

I opened the creaky iron door. To my astonishment inside was a gas burner instead of the coal or wooden logs we used in my time. Still caressing the cold tile stove, as if by merely touching it I could reproduce

After forty-seven years, touching again the unforgettable tile stove of our old apartment in Czernowitz.

the feelings of a pampered and sheltered infancy, I collapsed into a nearby chair. The river of tears would not stop flowing for several minutes, overwhelmed as I was by this physical contact with my past.

I stared lovingly at the French crystal-paned doors and the parquet floors we used to walk on. I could almost see Mama meticulously polishing it with the two brushes mounted on her shoes. As I walked toward the kitchen balcony, I looked out, hoping to see the once-manicured flower garden. But all that was left was an overgrown, abandoned yard.

Suddenly something unreal caught my eye. The startling discovery sent me running down to the garden. There it was! The horizontal iron bar on which everybody used to beat the dust out of rugs and on which we children exercised our acrobatic prowess. It was unchanged for over fifty years. I got goose bumps as I touched it. There were no other reminders of the previous inhabitants, their language or their culture, only lifeless, stationary objects like this iron high-bar remained behind. Leaving the building, I looked across the street to where Reli and Friedl's building used to stand; staring back at me was a row of new houses.

My next important goal was to visit Milie as soon as possible, but Mr. Chorney suggested waiting a few days because of the heavy rains. Two days later he arranged for our trip, putting a Volga sedan and an Intourist driver at our disposal. In anticipation, I became extremely excited. My cousins were also anxious to see their father's birthplace. We started our trip through small villages unchanged by time. Horse-drawn carts and buggies and old women herding cows by the side of the road were just as it used to be. The sky turned gray, and it started raining hard again. We hoped it would soon stop, but it only got worse.

We wanted first to stop in Banila, a village that bordered on Milie. Its cemetery used to serve both villages and was the one where our grandparents were buried. After receiving directions from a peasant woman, we quickly found our way.

The monuments were still there, even though some had fallen or were lopsided. The vegetation was so tall that it hid the ancient markers, and in the rain it was difficult to flatten the grass in order to read each name. We were anxiously searching for our grandparents' markers. But as was customary in those days, Jewish tombstones were identical in shape and size and bore only Hebrew inscriptions, which made the search even more difficult. Luckily, my Hebrew came in handy, to decipher the names. After a lengthy search, I happily discovered our grandfather's tombstone with "Littman" printed in large letters. His family name, "Katz," is derived from the Hebrew acronym of "**K**ohen **TZ**edek," a reference to the "Righteous Priests" who are the descendants of Aaron, the first high priest of the Israelites. I photographed my grandfather's stone and the whole cemetery before we continued toward Milie. Nowhere could we find our grandmother Reisel's marker. Soaked to the bone after an hour of futile search, we gave up.

Soon we read a road sign that said "Milievo," the Russian name for Milie. My excitement was now boundless. I was happy, anxious, sad, and scared all at the same time. What did I really expect to find? How would it be to enter that lost paradise of mine, now totally devoid of its Jewish inhabitants?

I was sure that on seeing the old railroad station I would know my way to Grandfather's place. But just as in my recurring dreams the layout looked different, and once again I was disoriented. Luckily, it occurred to me that Milie must have a Town Hall, and I asked the driver to help us find it. It was my hope that someone there would know how to get to our grandfather's farm. We found it in a small house on main street.

I approached a young secretary sitting at a desk. "Could we please speak to the Mayor?" I inquired.

"He is out on lunch break. How can we help you?" she asked. For a moment I stood there almost tempted to ask the secretary—too young to know—for directions to Grandfather's house, which probably did not exist anymore. Instead, I decided to ask for a villager, who was my grandfather's mill partner, the only name I could think of. "Does anyone here know Ostashek?"

"Which one of them?" she wanted to know. "We have a Vasily, a Gregory, etc., etc." How would I know his first name? After fifty years, that was too much to remember. Besides, I thought, what good would it do anyway, since the old man must be dead by now if he was my grandfather's partner.

"There's a Ghiorghe Ostashek a few houses away," she happily informed and offered to accompany us there. She climbed into our car and guided the driver to the Ostashek house, although it was only a few yards away.

We entered a muddy courtyard with a communal water pump in the center. Opposite the house were several barns with pigs and rabbits and a shack full of wooden logs. A foreboding apprehension seized me in anticipation of meeting a living link to my past. Led by the secretary, we entered the house. An elderly, stocky woman, wearing a blue, flowered babushka on her head, greeted us with obvious but friendly perplexity. At the foot of a neatly covered wooden bed, adorned with two large lace-covered pillows, an old man sat smoking a cigarette. Typical of that region, the walls of the humble but comfortable home were decorated with local motifs of colorful, handwoven *kilim* tapestries.

Contrasting with the rather primitive setting was a twenty-one-inch television set on which the historic meeting between Presidents Reagan and Gorbachev was being transmitted live. As we entered, two teenaged boys sat watching the program with great interest. Startled, to hear an American speaking Ukrainian, they looked quizzically at me as I told

I talk with Ghiorge Ostashek (center), one of the surviving witnesses of the Milie massacre.

the old man that I was Littman's granddaughter and was looking for the Ostashek who had been Grandfather's partner. "Which Ostashek are you?" I asked.

"He was my uncle, but he is dead. I am Ghiorghe Ostashek," he answered. Seemingly moved by my sudden appearance, he added, "I remember Littman, his children Leah and Anna, Moishe and David." His wife, Katherina, added proudly that she too remembered them. That was too much! I couldn't believe there was still someone around who remembered our family. "You are such precious guests. We must drink to this occasion," Katherina said with genuine excitement, offering a round of vodka.

Originally, we only wanted to get directions to Littman's place, but now things took a completely different turn. Rita, ever the reporter, with tape recorder in hand, took the opportunity to ask Ghiorghe if he could tell us anything about the massacre of the Milie Jews.

Reluctantly, he answered. I interpreted Rita's questions into Ruthenian and translated back into English in a choking voice. The old man gave us *his* version. While he spoke, the name "Ostashek" suddenly rang a bell: I had heard from the Milie survivors that one of the Ostasheks had been a leader in those murders. I needed to hear first-hand, verbal testimony about the massacre directly from the mouth of a non-Jewish villager. I had to control myself to keep from breaking down.

"Ay, that Friday," he exclaimed, "I will never forget that Friday evening. The Jews were sitting in their homes praying over the Sabbath dinner, when suddenly we heard a big 'Hurray!' The *Benderovtzes* [a gang of mountain bandits named after their leader Bendera] broke into the Jewish homes. They killed everybody in sight. I ran to my father's house to hide, because we were all in danger. The local people didn't harm anybody; it was the *Benderovtzes* who did all the killing."

"How many people were killed?" I asked.

"Somewhere between 140 and 150, including children."

"Were all of them Jews?"

"All of them, except the wife and children of one communist villager. He escaped, but they were killed."

"What happened next?"

"Oh, that was terrible. When we went out the next day, the *Benderovtzes* had disappeared, but there were dead bodies everywhere. We then collected the corpses and buried them in a mass grave."

"Is there a monument there?"

"No. There's only one monument at the Christian cemetery, the Soviet authorities erected for the wife and children of the communist villager."

The different treatment of the dead infuriated me. "Where is the mass grave for the Jews?"

"At the foot of the mountain near the Christian cemetery."

His version of the massacre, so different from others I had heard from survivors, stunned and bewildered me. But I swallowed the bitter pill and then asked him about my grandfather's house. "The old house doesn't exist anymore, there's a new one. The Fratzovir family lives there."

My heart sank. Although I had expected the house not to be there—just as in my recurring dreams—or to be occupied by others, I did not like to hear it.

"Do any of the houses that once belonged to the Jews, still exist?" I asked.

"Oh, yes," he replied, and he enumerated several names I well remembered.

While we interviewed Ghiorghe, his wife and grandchildren busied themselves preparing a lavish lunch, consisting of goulash, dumplings, coleslaw, and pickles from a barrel like those we used to make at

Dziadziu's farm. I hadn't tasted them again until that day. They invited not only us but also the driver and the secretary. The Ostasheks seemed overwhelmed by our visit.

"This is a great honor to be hosts to such dear guests," they repeated over and over again. The vodka made several rounds. I needed it to help soothe my inner storm.

It was getting late, and we were anxious to see Grandfather's place as well as other sites. As we got up to leave, in came two young men who introduced themselves as the mayor of Milie and a reporter from the town of Vizhnitsa that we would be visiting next. Polite as they were, I got an uneasy feeling that the news about our visit had spread rapidly in that small village and that some suspicion as to our motives might have arisen.

They proceeded to ask some questions, and, apparently convinced of the innocence of our visit, the mayor began to treat us as regular tourists, suggesting that we visit the Bread Museum housed in the new schoolhouse. Still feeling uneasy, I told my cousins "Let's get out of here." Before leaving, we asked Ghiorghe to show us the way to both the new school and my grandfather's place.

The museum consisted of a room full of a variety of cereals grown on the Milie collective farm. Besides typical handicrafts, the rest of the exhibits told the story of how the different grains were ground locally. But nowhere was there a single mention of the first mill that Littman Katz had built there, and there certainly was no mention of the massacred Jews who had inhabited this village only forty-five years earlier.

This omission of such a historic truth prompted me to react. My first impulse was to take the matter up with the principal. He listened to my story as if he were hearing it for the first time. "The children need to be told the truth so that such atrocities will never happen to any ethnic minority," I said. He agreed and promised to do something about it.

With Ostashek's guidance, we finally headed toward what used to be Grandfather's farm. I could not recognize any landmarks because of the new homes and all the other changes. But as soon as we turned into a narrow, dirt road, everything became familiar. When the car stopped, just as in my dreams, I stared at a distorted view of the farm. This differ-

The old double-log bridge behind Grandfather's farm was still there in 1988.

ent picture made me realize that it was now also a different time and a different Ruth that had returned to her lost paradise. At this moment, my highly charged emotions became almost uncontrollable. The first change I noticed was a green wrought-iron gate replacing the long, old horizontal logs that used to mark our entrance to the farm. Still sitting in the car, seeing the Teplitza Creek continuing its perpetual, peaceful flowing, I wept, repeating the same words, "I don't believe it; I don't believe I'm really here."

"Take a few minutes to calm down," Rita said sympathetically.

I finally stepped out of the car, and impulsively ran toward the water to touch it with both hands, as if to assure myself that this time it was not a dream. In doing so I noticed the same old double-log bridge over the creek preserved for over fifty years. Except for the scenery, it was the only unchanged, stationary feature.

We walked into the yard through sticky mud as the heavy rain continued to pelt down. Slowly, peasants from the vicinity came out of their homes to see what the commotion was about. On the same huge foundation stones on which Grandfather's home used to stand was a newly built house. Instead of a white facade, it was now painted sky-blue with bottle-green siding, and the top of each window was adorned with a yellow trim.

A rather heavy-set older woman came out of the house, followed by a short, unattractive man in his sixties. Ghiorghe made the introductions. "These are guests from America," he said.

The short man stepped forward and said, "My name is Yuri Fratzovir, and this is my house. And who are you?" he asked me.

"Before I tell you who I am, would the name 'Littman Katz' mean anything to you?"

"Sure," he said, and his face lit up. In Ruthenian, he enumerated all the people he remembered. "There was Leah . . . there was Anna, Lucie, Bubi and . . . little Ruthi." I felt as if I were hearing names resounding from another planet. I started shaking. Did he mean he remembered all the family, myself included? "Ruthi, that's me," I said.

The whole unnerving conversation took place outside in the pouring rain. Wading in the mud, I managed to take Polaroid pictures, which astonished our hosts who had never seen an instant photograph. My eyes scrutinized the once-splendorous garden, the yard, and the orchard. The changes I had seen in my nightmares had astonishingly became reality! The farm was now subdivided by several wooden fences and dotted with plain little cottages and storage sheds. The only imposing house in this perimeter was the Fratzowirs'.

They invited us into the house which now had a slightly different lay-out. Replacing our five rooms were now only three. It was eerie to stand in their drawing room, decorated in the traditional Ruthenian style, and reminisce about what used to be decades ago. Everybody was very emotional, our hosts included.

I was trying hard to balance my warm sentiments toward the hospitable and compassionate villagers with my absolute abhorrence of the murderers who came from the same community. With my whole being I wanted to believe their version of the story—that it was all the fault of crude marauders from the hills. I would have preferred to think that they were innocent.

Before the last good-bye, I asked Yuri to bring me some water from our well. He brought a filled bottle from which I took slow sips, savoring its heavenly taste, as if drinking a holy elixir. For a furtive moment I believed that this water would indeed numb my emotional pain.

Our time was limited since we had to travel to the neighboring town of Vizhnitza and return to Czernowitz by late afternoon. Rita and Al went ahead to the car while I continued chatting with Yuri in the yard.

A new house where Grandfather's used to be; inside with the new owners.

He was completely mesmerized by our surprise visit and still could not believe that it was I.

"You used to have freckles on your nose, and now you don't have any," he said, as his eyes scanned my face intently. At that remark, I laughed through my tears. By that time more and more peasants, relatives of our previous neighbors, were coming out of their homes to see the Americans.

We drove on to Vizhnitza, my birthplace, and that of my cousins' mother. As soon as we left Milie, I realized that I had forgotten the Polaroid pictures I left to dry on the porch of the Fratzovirs' house. There was no time to return. It seemed like a conspiracy against my having pictures of all these memorable places. To have come all this way after forty-five years and have to return without a single picture was absolutely devastating.

We entered Vizhnitza, met with a few Jewish residents, and asked directions to the City Hall, where my cousins wanted to search the local archives in order to find out more about their families.

When we arrived at City Hall, the only clerk present would not let us look into the archives without special permission. Rita tried to argue with her, but the woman was adamant. Frustrated, we left. All this time our guide went out of his way to help me retrieve the pictures from the Fratzovirs' porch. He even called the secretary of the Town Hall and asked her to send a messenger to bring the photos to the mayor so that he could mail them to the hotel.

Strolling in the town's square, we accidentally ran into the same reporter who had appeared with the mayor at Ostashek's house. He was so impressed by our visit that he offered to write a story about it, even calling it "historic." After a quick consultation with my cousins, I decided to hand him the testimony about the Milie Massacre. I had carried it in my pocket, waiting for the opportunity to leave it in the right hands. We hoped that he could influence the authorities to at least erect a monument to the Jewish victims.

I handed him the document and said, "I want to place this responsibility in your hands: After you have read about what took place here in 1941, I hope the facts will be disclosed to the authorities and taught in the schools. I want you to direct the whole issue into the right channels so that a monument will be built to remember the martyrs. Do you promise me?"

"Yes, I promise," he said, and put the testimony into his pocket. We exchanged business cards and he promised to send us a copy of his article. We never heard from him again.

We returned to Czernowitz feeling dissatisfied, frustrated, and angry. For me it was more than that. I knew that I wouldn't be able to find peace of mind unless I returned once more to Milie on a dry, sunny day in order to get around. That seemed unlikely because we were granted permission for only a one-day visit. But the optimist in me hoped that Mr. Chorney would make an exception.

When we entered the hotel lobby, there he was. I approached him, complaining about our misadventures, the bad weather, and how sad I felt at not having seen more of the village. He seemed genuinely moved. "Could you possibly allow me to go back again?" I asked. He promised to look into the matter and advised me to wait another day in the hope that the rain would subside.

The next day my cousins went sightseeing while I visited places of personal interest by myself. The first stop was my old school. Later that afternoon, I managed to gain access to Aunt Anna's apartment and to the Zloczowers' house. How strange to feel at home there and out of place at the same time!

The following morning, I repeated the excursion to Milie with only a Moldavian driver. This time I had purchased a pair of high rubber boots and was prepared for the muddy fields. Fortunately the rain had subsided somewhat when we arrived in Milie.

Unlike the first trip, this time, I felt confident in directing the driver to the Fratzovirs' house. But somehow I sent him down the wrong road, only to end up in an unfamiliar area. A young man came toward us, asking whom we were looking for. I explained that I wanted to go to Littman Katz's place, where the Fratzovirs now lived. "By the way," I asked, "Are there any older villagers here who would remember my grandfather Littman?"

"Yes," he said, "as a matter of fact my mother-in-law is inside, and she might." At the man's invitation, I entered the house, and followed him into a room where a sick old woman sat on the only bed, flanked by two lovely granddaughters. "Who are you?" she asked.

"I am the granddaughter of Littman. Do you remember him?" She nodded her head knowingly. "And what is your name?" I asked her. "I am Maria Ostashek, the sister-in-law of Ghiorghe Ostashek."

"Glad to meet you," I said, shaking her hand. She started to tell me about my grandfather and all the family. "Where is your husband?" I wanted to know.

"Ivan is not here. We were both exiled to the Urals because he was convicted of having helped to kill the Milie Jews. But it was all a lie. He only gave the Benderovtzes some food, and some people confused him with one of them. Then, while we were in exile, my husband left me for a younger woman. But I wanted to come back to Milie because our children were here."

By now, I had made the connection. It was *her* husband, Ivan Ostashek, whose name was repeatedly mentioned by the surviving witnesses as the peasant leader in the massacre. A chill ran through my body. I quickly took a picture of her—to show it to the few Milien emigrants now living in Israel—and left.

With the directions given us by her son-in-law, we drove straight to the Fratzovirs' house. As soon as we stepped into the house, Yuri came in with another villager, Reshka Alexei Tanassovich, who claimed he once worked at Littman's mill and remembered the entire Katz family. Together with Reshka and Yuri, I started to walk toward the place where the mill once stood.

We crossed the familiar double-log bridge and walked through the fields along the creek, on the same path I had walked numerous times as a child. Once again ducks with their chicks swam peacefully downstream, and once again the smell from the fields and the sight of the tall haystacks reminded me in a pleasurable way of a distant past. Impulsively, I picked a few flowers typical of that area and pressed them into papers to take home.

Then from the distance, I noticed a dilapidated, abandoned building instead of the old mill. Yuri explained that this used to be a power station for many years but was closed now, as a new one had been built elsewhere. It was a pathetic sight. There was nothing more to see.

We returned and walked along the path that still led to the church and to our neighbors' house. Both remained unaltered by time. Bordering our neighbor's fence at the far end of our orchard stood the old Czetiner apple tree—once my favorite place for reading. To my surprise, not only was it still there but it was in full bloom with large white flowers, as if wanting to show off to a returning lover. Because it was behind the neighbor's fence I could neither touch it nor pick the flowers, but I photographed it, grateful to have seen it still alive and well, probably for the last time in my life.

Walking along those memory lanes, I took the opportunity to ask Reshka, "Tell me, what happened here in 1941?"

"It was terrible. All we heard that day was '*Gwalt, gwalt,*' [a cry for help in Yiddish] as the Benderovtzes came and killed the Jews," he said, apparently upset.

"Do you mean to tell me that *nobody* from this village participated in the killings?"

"Look, if there were some, they are here no longer," he said, with a tone that kind of implied resignation.

It seemed useless to press the issue any further, so I went back to the house. Yuri gave me the pictures I had forgotten and beamed with pride as he showed me one of them displayed on the mantel in their living room.

The driver and I proceeded to Ghiorghe Ostashek's house. His wife Katharina seemed glad to see me but did not invite me in. "Where is your husband?" I asked.

"He is asleep."

"Well, I need him. Maybe you could wake him up," I asked her.

She hesitated but finally asked me in. Old Ghiorghe sat on the bed's edge slumped forward, smoking one of the Kent cigarettes I had given him on my first visit. Unlike two days ago, this time, he did not appear very thrilled to see me.

"You wonder why I'm back? When I was here last time, you said you would show us where the mass grave was. But it rained so hard we couldn't get to see it. Could you take me there now?"

"Oh, it's very far, and with all the mud it is difficult to get there," he said. "Anyway, you wouldn't be able to see anything; there is nothing to be seen."

I detected a total change from his previously friendly attitude. I began to wonder why and kept begging him to take me there. He agreed under one condition—that a neighbor accompany us. While he went to fetch him, I returned to the car and sat waiting with the driver. I figured it would only take a few minutes, considering the short distances between houses. As the minutes ticked away and he did not return, I began to feel uneasy.

Half an hour later, I got impatient and went to ask his wife about the delay. "He is getting dressed. He is going to get the old mayor to go with him, since he was a witness, too, and knows about the grave."

After forty-five minutes Ostashek returned, not with the old mayor but with the new, young one who had met us on the first visit. I was totally confused but asked no questions about the switch. Without a word, we drove to a field at the foot of a mountain. Ostashek made the driver stop at the side of the muddy road. We stepped out of the car, and I looked around. Except for a telegraph pole, there was nothing else in sight, and there was no sign of a grave. "Where is it?" I asked Ostashek.

"Here." He pointed to the green fields.

"What do you mean *here?* This is a field of vegetables!" I snapped in indignation. There was no marker, just as I had feared. It hurt me so much that I started to cry. There was nothing I could do at that moment but take a picture of the field and pick up as many little stones as I could to give to the scant group of Miliens living in Israel. Saddened, I went back to the car. I looked at the mayor, and he looked at me. I believe that he, like many other young people, had no idea of the past. Suddenly he asked Ghiorghe, "How many people were killed here?"

"With children and babies, about one hundred and forty," came his laconic response.

The mayor turned to me and asked, "Mrs. Gold, do you think there still might be some people alive in Milie who participated in the massacre?"

"I don't know, but I wouldn't be surprised," I said. "But I do know from the survivors that there were a few courageous, righteous peasants who dared to warn their Jewish neighbors of imminent danger, to hide them and to personally abstain from participating in the mob hysteria, sometimes at the cost of their own lives."

The mayor promised me solemnly to do something about erecting a monument to the massacre victims, and on that note we parted. I had the feeling that our unexpected visit, in addition to my talks with the principal and the document I had given to the reporter, caused the whole issue to resurface. I now understood Ghiorghe's reluctance to go alone with me to the grave and why he went to call the mayor. He was probably deathly afraid of what the Soviet regime might do to him for having given us his testimony.

Before leaving Milie, I asked the driver to stop at the railroad station. To my great amazement, it remained unchanged. Standing outside the building, I spied an eerie sight: the same two old, wooden benches, ravaged by time. I sat down on one of them. With closed eyes I could see myself surrounded by my loved ones, waiting for the train to take us back home at the end of our vacation. Embracing Dziadziu, waving to friends and neighbors, I could almost hear the train's whistle. I was completely lost in thought when the compassionate driver called gingerly, reminding me it was time to leave.

"Goodbye, Milie, for the last time," I said aloud. If I were to return, I knew it would never be to my childhood paradise. It was truly gone.

On my last day in Czernowitz, I took advantage of the kindness and hospitality of Ida, who now lived in our former apartment, and returned to take pictures. I photographed many things of sentimental value to me, particularly the immortal tile stove, the hearth of the Glasberg family, whose light went out in November 1941.

Bershad Revisited

EPILOGUE

On the road again by train, we headed in the direction of Vinnitsa, the largest town near Bershad. The train stopped at Oknitsa, Verzhanka, Moghilev, Bar, and Zhmerinka. Traveling the same route as I did in 1941, I came to the astonishing realization that this train ride was going to take about six hours, whereas back then we were forced to trudge on foot toward Bershad for nearly two weeks to cover the same distance. With considerable difficulty, I chased away the bitter memories of that trip to face the here and now.

An Intourist official met us at the station on Sunday afternoon and drove us to the only hotel in town. We were supposed to leave Monday morning at 8 o'clock for Bershad, but we still had not gotten permission. That same morning the Intourist director apologized, saying that our vouchers had reached him only a few days earlier, so he had not been sure of our arrival. As a result, he did not have an Intourist car at our disposal. He began to search for a regular taxi, something that took him half a day. Meanwhile that shortened our allotted time by half. At midday, both the driver and a guide finally arrived. The trip would take three hours each way, leaving us only one hour to explore Bershad. Rita did not feel well, so only Al accompanied me.

We traveled along green pastures and beautiful hills sprinkled with colorful flowers. The fields as far as the horizon brimmed with cereals. Winding its course among those fields was the wide and serene Bug River. "Look how beautiful it is here," I would repeat to Al.

Usually he would share my enthusiasm, but not this time."What's so special about this part of the world?" he finally asked. "Surely you've seen more beautiful places."

Indeed, what was it that made it so beautiful to me? Suddenly I understood: It was the contrast. Here were the same fields and collective farms we had been driven through on foot and by cart, in mud and snow, during the winter of 1941. Back then, all I could see were desolate, snow-covered fields and corpses beside the roads. During my three-year confinement at Bershad, I could not have imagined such beauty existing outside the camps. In fact, I hardly remember ever seeing a flower or a butterfly. But now I was a free person, allowed and able to enjoy the beauty of this Ukrainian region, no longer the infamous Transnistria of yesteryear.

The driver showed me a map on which I found the names of the villages and collective farms we had stayed in overnight during the deportation march. They were all along a route on the west side of the river, ending with Bershad at a distance of a few miles from its bank. In fact, we had never actually seen the river then, because the Bug was the border east of which the Germans executed most of the Jews. In those times the Bug was synonymous with execution by the SS. At present, we were coming from the opposite direction, traveling on its west side.

June 5, 1988. At 3.00 P.M. we crossed the bridge and finally entered notorious Bershad. I felt as if I were dreaming, but there we were. Sitting in front of an isolated house was an old man, whom I approached and asked, "Do you remember where the concentration camp was?"

"Ho, ho. What was, was!" he said, with a shrug. In other words, it was so long ago it was not worth stirring things up. Nonetheless, he pointed into the distance.

"And where is the Jewish cemetery?" I wanted to know. "Far, far from here," he answered curtly.

We realized that it was getting late, and we had only about one hour left before we would have to return. That barely gave us enough time to visit the cemetery. Following his directions we drove off toward the outskirts of Bershad.

There was no watchman, nor were there any visitors at the cemetery. As we stepped out of the car, an overpowering odor of human waste hit me—the very same stench I had lived with for so many years in Bershad. For an instant I was confused and appalled. I thought that as a result of my intense anxiety, I was having some kind of olfactory hallucination.

However, as my cousin and the driver seemed equally repulsed, I knew I was not hallucinating. The odor was so strong that I had to cover my nose with a handkerchief so as not to faint. Handkerchiefs to noses, Al and I walked into the cemetery.

Beautiful, black marble tombstones with intaglio portraits of the deceased—the typical Russian-Jewish commemoration of the dead—filled the cemetery. Reading the dates, I realized that all those markers had been put up for local Jews who had died *after* the war. We searched for the large monument with the names of my family and all those who had died in Bershad during the Nazi occupation. But it was nowhere to be seen.

Utterly frustrated, and with a sunken heart, I gave up my search. But Al continued to search all over; he even walked into the nearby forest, but finally he too had to give up.

I badly needed a moment of meditation, some spiritual contact with my loved ones to let them know that I had come back to pay tribute after all these years. But where could I do that? Accidentally, I located a small, weathered monument, still bearing a few names of people from towns near Czernowitz. Its sight was pitiful, yet it bore the only testimony to that time of infamy. I leaned on it and poured out tears of sadness I had accumulated over the last forty-five years. Then it was time to leave.

Aided by my cousin, I walked shakily toward the exit. There we met a Jew, who had come by bicycle to see what was going on. We asked him about the monument built in memory of the martyred Jews, and he offered an explanation that made sense.

Because of a lack of materials during the war, the monument had been poorly built. It could not withstand decades of harsh weather and had crumbled. The marble plaques fell to the ground, and with the years grass and trees grew over them; therefore, we could not find a trace. This reality did not appease my deep disappointment.

"What is the terrible stench here?" we wanted to know.

"That is human waste from the town's outhouses dumped near the cemetery."

This profanation, added to the one in Milie, escalated my ire beyond limits. Who had the audacity to dump human waste near a sacred resting place for approximately twenty thousand victims who perished here during the Holocaust, unburied and without a marker? Was there no dignity at all, no respect for the dead?

I decided to do anything within my power to see to it that a new monument would be built by the Soviet government. Only the day before, we had seen in Vinnitsa, in the middle of a grove of trees, an impressive sculpture honoring the Soviet victims of fascism. The same was true throughout the entire USSR. Wherever we went, young brides dedicated their wedding bouquets to the soldiers who had died a generation earlier. Everywhere, huge monuments with sentimental inscriptions reminded the citizens of the martyrs—but no mention of the Jews.

On the trip back to Vinnitsa I could not shake off a heavy depressive feeling. About two hours later I noticed the familiar white acacia trees in full bloom lining the highway. "Please stop the car for a moment!" I cried. "I want to smell the acacias once more. They remind me of my hometown."

The kind driver stopped and picked several branches from a nearby tree and handed them to me. I buried my face in the flowers, drowning my sorrow, and seeking solace in their sweet, balmy aroma. And so, inhaling the pleasant fragrance to diffuse the horrible stench, to soothe my stormy sorrow, and to calm my emotions, we returned to Vinnitsa.

Emotionally drained from the day's ordeal, I said good night to Al and Rita and went immediately to my room. But sleep eluded me. That night, I saw before my eyes a kaleidoscope of events that happened in the camp of Bershad. It seemed almost unreal to have stepped anew onto this death-permeated soil. As much as I had wanted to come here, now I could hardly wait to leave. It was too sad.

And so a new vision emerged—one that deals with my own quest for justice, whereby I want to rectify the silence that shrouds the Holocaust in Romania. I want the world to know about the Transnistria atrocities, and the massacres of Jews in hundreds of villages like Milie throughout the entire area of Bukovina and Bessarabia. I strive to commemorate the death of the tens of thousands of forgotten victims and champion those who fell under brutal persecution.

Since then I have written to American senators and even former Soviet Prime Minister Gorbachev, as well as several Soviet ministries that were in charge at the time, in an effort to bring to light the need for public recognition of these deaths. I received little response, and the political changes in the former Soviet Union have not been helpful either. Still I pursue my goal.

Until I see the erection of those monuments, let this book be their perpetual, indestructible memorial written from the heart of one who has been at the bottom of human misery and survived to speak about the unspeakable.

Sources

Ancel, Jean, ed. *Documents concerning the Fate of Romanian Jewry during the Holocaust.* 12 vols. New York: The Beate Klarsfeld Foundation. 1986. (Reproduced documents in Romanian and German.)

———. *The Romanian Way of Solving the 'Jewish Problem' in Bessarabia and Bukovina, June–July 1941.* Jerusalem: Yad Vashem Studies, 1988.

Ben-Zion, Shmuel. "Jewish Children in Transnistria during the Holocaust." Doctoral dissertation, Institute for Holocaust Research, Haifa University, 1989.

Butnaru, I.C. *The Forgotten Holocaust.* New York: Greenwood Press, 1992.

———. *Waiting for Jerusalem.* New York: Greenwood Press, 1993.

Fisher, Julius S. *Transnistria: The Forgotten Cemetery.* New York: Thomas Yoseloff, 1969.

Gilbert, Martin. *Atlas of the Holocaust.* London: The Rainbird Publishing Group Limited, 1982.

Gold, Hugo. *Geschichte der Juden in der Bukovina* (History of the Jews in Bukovina). Tel Aviv: Olamenu, 1962. (In German.)

Litani, Dora. *Transnistria.* Tel Aviv, 1981. (In Romanian.) (Printed with the support of the Tel-Aviv Fund for Art and Literature.)

Romania Libera. Periodical, Bucharest, 1944–45.

The Martyrdom of the Jews in Romania, 1940–1944: Documents and Testimonies. Bucharest: Editura Hasefer, 1991. (This anthology includes my article of February 19, 1945.)

Schaari, David. *The Cyprus Detention Camps for Jewish "Illegal" Immigrants to Palestine, 1946–1949.* Jerusalem: Hassifriya Hazionit, 1981.

Geographic Index

Adriatic Sea, 168, 212
Aegean Sea, 170
Akko, 240
America. *See* United States
Ataki, 49
Athlith, 198
Auschwitz, 225
Austria, 154, 162, 232, 233, 236

Balanovka, 61
Balta, 91, 92, 93, 116, 176
Banila, 268
Bar, 283
Beit Machsir, 202
Beit Meir, 202
Belgrade, 163
Berlin, 255
Bershad, 61, 62, 63, 71, 88, 91, 92, 93, 102,
    107, 108, 110, 111, 114, 115, 116, 122,
    129, 140, 144, 160, 260, 261, 263, 283,
    284, 285, 286, 287
Bessarabia, 14, 18, 30, 37, 42, 49, 95, 127,
    152, 254, 287
Black Sea, 125, 133
Bogota, 239, 240, 241, 242, 244, 249, 250
Boston, 222, 224
Briczene, 107
Bucharest, 30, 36, 116, 122, 126, 130, 134,
    157, 160, 176, 261, 262
Bug River, 62, 110, 284
Bukovina, 16, 17, 37, 42, 43, 66, 95, 107,
    127, 232, 287
Buzau, 122, 123, 124, 125, 155, 156, 209

Carpathian Mountains, 18
Cheremosh River, 4, 39, 40
Chernovtsy, 139, 263
Colentina, 157

Colombia, 238, 240, 241, 247, 248, 249,
    250
Constantza, 125
Cosautzi, 53
Cyprus, 175, 176, 177, 185, 188, 218, 233,
    234
Czernowitz, 2, 18, 19, 24, 30, 37, 38, 40,
    42, 43, 47, 49, 61, 67, 68, 79, 87, 88, 99,
    123, 136, 137, 138, 139, 143, 149, 157,
    166, 167, 177, 185, 188, 212, 213, 233,
    234, 236, 238, 252, 253, 254, 255, 262,
    263, 264, 265, 274, 276, 281, 286. *See
    also* Chernovtsy

Dniester River, 49, 52, 54, 55, 117, 118,
    138
Donbass, 130, 131, 149

Europe, 28, 149, 162, 233, 237, 238

Famagusta, 196
Florida, 251, 253
France, 162
Galautzash, 158, 161
Galicia (province), 17
Germany, 43, 154, 235, 252, 254, 256
Greater Romania, 16, 18

Haifa, 164, 174, 196, 197, 199, 200, 222,
    227, 230, 231, 233, 236, 237, 238
Heroes' Forest, the, 227
Hungary, 154

Iassi, 118, 120, 122, 126, 131
Israel, 155, 164, 184, 193, 196, 200, 202,
    206, 211, 212, 213, 216, 224, 227, 232,
    234, 235, 236, 238, 239, 241, 247, 248,
    249, 251, 256, 257, 278

Italy, 154, 158, 162, 232

Jaffa, 213
Jerusalem, 200, 201, 203, 204, 205, 208,
    210, 211, 216, 226, 227, 237
Jordan, 211,
Judean Hills, 200, 201

Kachikovka, 60, 61
Kishinev, 14, 16, 30, 253, 254
Kreuzlingen, 234
Krizhopol, 61
Kuty, 17
Lake Konstanz, 234
Latrun, 201
L'hagshamah, (commune, kibbutz), 157,
    160, 162, 163, 169, 174, 177, 179, 185,
    186, 189, 196, 198, 200, 201, 202, 203,
    205, 206, 209, 215, 217, 218, 221, 227
Lithuania, 63
Lobodovka, 61

Marculeshti, 49, 50
Miami, 250, 256, 257
Milie, 2, 3, 4, 10, 13, 16, 21, 24, 26, 29, 38,
    40, 74, 76, 77, 79, 85, 100, 143, 155, 200,
    260, 263, 264, 265, 267, 268, 270, 272,
    275, 276, 277, 278, 280, 281, 286, 287.
    See also Milievo
Moghilev, 49, 116, 283
Moldova, 14, 119
Moscow, 264
Moshav Shoresh, 227
Mount Carmel, 197, 227
Mount Scopus, 211

New York, 252, 253, 254, 256, 257
North Bukovina, 18, 30, 263

Obodovka, 61
Odessa, 130, 131, 133, 138, 149, 176
Oknitsa, 283
Olashanka, 61
Old Romania, 30, 158

Palestine, 29, 30, 37, 91, 92, 115, 117, 120,
    122, 123, 124, 125, 126, 127, 129, 135,
    152, 154, 157, 158, 160, 161, 162, 163,
    164, 173, 174, 175, 178, 180, 182, 183,
    184, 187, 188, 194, 195, 197, 199, 200

Poland, 4, 29, 40,
Prague, 255
Prut River, 18, 37

Rhodes, 170
Roman, 155
Romania, 2, 4, 16, 18, 27, 30, 33, 35, 55,
    91, 105, 108, 115, 116, 117, 118, 119,
    122, 127, 136, 138, 152, 154, 160, 162,
    209, 211, 222, 250, 255, 256, 261, 287.
    See also Greater Romania; Old
    Romania
Romanovka, 61
Russia, 127, 129, 130, 212
Saris, 201
Seret (town), 263, 264
Seret River, 153
Shoeva, 202
Siberia, 30, 36
Sirina, 170, 172, 176
Sontra, 254, 255
South America, 238, 239
Soviet Union, 18, 37, 152, 154, 217, 260,
    263, 288. See also Russia; USSR
Switzerland, 234

Targu-Neamtz, 155
Tel Aviv, 200, 217, 223, 237, 240
Teplitza Creek, 5, 10, 26, 260, 273
Tighina, 118
Tiraspol, 118
Transnistria, 40, 47, 50, 63, 64, 88, 92,
    102, 105, 117, 118, 125, 129, 131, 133,
    136, 137, 138, 141, 148, 153, 225, 232,
    253, 254, 284, 287
Treblinka, 225
Trieste, 232, 233
Tsibulovka, 61

Ukraine, 18, 37, 40, 42, 55, 56, 102, 110,
    131, 138, 263
United States, 35, 41, 198, 249, 250
Usha (kibbutz), 188, 198
Urals, 277
USSR, 287

Valegotilovo, 102
Vashkautz, 13
Venice, 232
Verzhanka, 283